Positive Discrimination, Social Justice, and Social Policy

Positive Discrimination, Social Justice, and Social Policy

Moral Scrutiny of a Policy Practice

JOHN EDWARDS

Foreword by Lord Scarman

Tavistock Publications
London and New York

First published in 1987
by Tavistock Publications Ltd
11 New Fetter Lane, London EC4P 4EE

Published in the USA by
Tavistock Publications
in association with Methuen, Inc.
29 West 35th Street, New York NY 10001

Set in 10/12 pt Bembo Linotron 202
by Graphicraft Typesetting Ltd., Hong Kong
Printed in Great Britain by Richard Clay Ltd, Bungay, Suffolk

British Library Cataloguing in Publication Data
Edwards, John, *1943–*
Positive discrimination, Social
justice and social policy: moral
scrutiny of a policy practice. —
(Social science paperback; 350)
1. Social policy
I. Title
361.6′1 HN17.5

ISBN 0-422-61400-9
ISBN 0-422-78990-9 Pbk

Library of Congress Cataloging in Publication Data
Edwards, John, B. Sci.
Positive discrimination, Social justice,
and social policy.
(Social science paperbacks; 350)
Bibliography: p.
Includes indexes.
1. Great Britain—Social policy.
2. Discrimination—Great Britain.
3. Social justice.
I. Title. II. Series.
HN387.E48 1987 361.6′1′0941 86–22976

ISBN 0-422-61400-9
ISBN 0-422-78990-9 (pbk.)

To Bridget

Contents

Acknowledgements

Many people (most, unwittingly) helped in the writing of this book. My thanks go to all of them. I wish also to thank the Publications Committee of Royal Holloway and Bedford New College for a grant in aid of the preparation of the manuscript for publication. The manuscript was typed with unfaltering accuracy and great speed by Kathryn Kerr, to whom I owe a special debt of gratitude. Anne King tidied up the final version and fought for time on the photocopier. My thanks also go to her.

The greatest debt of gratitude is owed to my wife.

Foreword

This is an ambitious work. John Edwards describes it, correctly, as a 'moral scrutiny of a policy practice'. The morality is that of western civilization, the roots of which lie in Graeco-Roman philosophy and in the religions of the Jews and the Christians. By criteria developed from these origins he concludes that the policy practice known as 'positive discrimination' is a morally flawed, unjust, and in the ultimate resort, a socially unacceptable mechanism or process for determining who shall benefit from certain advantages and opportunities which the State can require to be made available to certain persons or classes.

Our author has to define his terms. First and foremost, what does he mean by 'positive discrimination'? It is the necessity of defining his terms that explains why the early chapters of the book appear to be concerned more with the meaning of words than with the substance of his argument. The meaning he gives to 'positive discrimination' is critically important to an understanding of the argument. I hope that I can indicate it briefly and not too inaccurately. It is the process of discriminating by laws and policies in a society's distribution of benefits, advantages, and opportunities, not by reference to individual needs, or a person's entitlement, or his deserts or merit but by reference to 'irrelevant criteria', e.g. race or sex. There is, he maintains (rightly) no necessary relationship between the colour of one's skin or one's sex and need, entitlement, or one's deserts. Therefore distribution on the basis of race or sex, will in some cases, probably in many cases, be wrong and unjust. Not all black men, for example, will have the need which justifies the conferment of the advantage or the opportunity; some white men will have a greater need, but will lose out in competition with black men.

John Edwards develops his thesis with a wealth of scholarship and learning. In illuminating and challenging chapters he compares and contrasts the differing American and British approaches; and he emphasizes that Britain has much to learn from American experience. It is his deep analysis of these two contrasting approaches which marks out his book as a truly important study of a very difficult problem.

John Edwards does not, I am sure, expect all of us to agree with him; not even, I hope, the writer of the *Foreword*. Whether one agrees with him or not, all who are concerned with the problem of race relations in our society will be grateful to him for his profound study of the morality of the practice of positive discrimination.

He establishes, I think, that the practice is a social process or mechanism which can result in injustice. Having got that far, he has no difficulty in showing that it is a practice which when scrutinized will be seen in some instances to offend moral principle. But, for me, this is not the end of the argument – I am a practical lawyer, a constitutionalist, and a judge. I ask myself: can we hope to unite the peoples inhabiting the United Kingdom into one civilized society without policies designed to advance minorities who we can see by and large are disadvantaged? Whether one goes for 'tougher' positive discrimination or 'soft' affirmative action programmes in specific fields (e.g. education, housing, or job-training), there will be individual injustices; but without such programmes the objective of a united society within the United Kingdom is likely to prove unattainable.

Policy, principle, justice, morality – these are big words. Social policy and legal principle should be formulated and directed towards the attainment of justice and morality. But perfect justice and a perfect fulfilment of moral obligations may have to wait upon the success of policies and principles which move towards each without immediately achieving either of them. The price of success will be a continuing vigilance in the formulation and practice of policy and principle: but to reject policies and principles because of their dangers will, I believe, result in total defeat and endless discontent.

When John Edwards counsels prudence and caution – I accept his advice. But he does not persuade me that we should abandon such social mechanisms as positive discrimination or affirmative action. I believe that their value is such that we must accept the risk of their defects. I may be wrong. Read, therefore, this fascinating book, and make up your own mind.

LESLIE SCARMAN
8 May 1986

Chapter 1
Introduction

There is a wide gap in British academic and non-academic thinking between the substance of social policies on the one hand (the study of which until relatively recently was very descriptive), and moral thought on the other. All too rarely are social policies and the ideas behind them subjected to critical moral thought. And all too often the substance of policy has been the 'football' between one unthinking politicial reaction and another.

What follows is an attempt to bridge the gap between social policy and morality in respect on one particular policy practice. Positive discrimination is a relatively minor component of social policy in Britain but because it is a controversial topic and one that is much misunderstood, and because the ranks of those for and against it are so often drawn up on party-political lines, it provides an excellent example of a policy practice that ought to be subjected to critical moral thought. Since much of the criticism of it is couched in terms of its 'unfairness', then again there is good reason to analyse it from a moral point of view.

Much of the political controversy about positive discrimination (some of which is described and analysed in Chapter 2) is unnecessary because it is misconceived, confused, and premissed on a misunderstanding of what the practice and the idea behind it consist of. Indeed, there is probably no more misconceived and misunderstood (sometimes wilfully) social policy practice in Britain. Positive discrimination has been seen as the way forward out of the arid debate about universalism and selectivity (which it is not); it has been applied to practices and policies that are not positively discriminatory; and it has joined (along with 'Marxist') the lexicon of abuse of the present government. Precision of usage is also compromised because in the race relations industry 'positive' tends to be used as a punctuation mark (listen to any spokesman or -woman from the CRE), and 'positive discrimination' itself has become the sort of catch-phrase that trips lightly from the lips of effervescent inner-city clergymen.

All this is in marked contrast with the United States debate on what is called there affirmative action and reverse discrimination. True, that debate has had its bombasters and bumblers but on the whole it has been conducted, both in and out of the court room, in a rigorous and informed manner.

The main concern of this book is with positive discrimination in Britain, although, for the reasons mentioned above, we shall frequently make use of arguments that have developed in the United States (though we shall deal only briefly with the history of events there). The first task will be to analyse and make sense of the idea and practice of positive discrimination in Britain and to examine how much of the argument and rhetoric has been about something that can distinctively be called positive discrimination. We shall also analyse how and why positive discrimination first found and then lost favour between the mid-1960s and the late 1970s.

Our concern is not only or even mainly with the past and present debate about, and practice of, positive discrimination. It is rather with the case (if any) for the further and more widespread use of the practice in Britain. This case must rest upon a prior discussion of whether positive discrimination is or can be a just practice. It turns out that the characteristics of positive discrimination that distinguish it from other policy practices with which it has often been confused are the very ones that render it unjust when tested against basic canons of social justice. Whether, then, it can ever be a just practice will turn on whether, in any given set of (empirical) circumstances, it would prove to be the only or the best way of fulfilling the requirements of justice. The two requirements of justice in fulfilment of which it might theoretically most often be called into service are the needs principle and the principle of rights to compensation for harm. The former has most often been adduced in Britain; the latter has been the main motive force behind affirmative action and reverse discrimination in the USA. But because our primary concern is with Britain, we need to examine whether the particular circumstances here are such as to make of positive discrimination a just practice in pursuit of both need and compensation. In short, is positive discrimination 'justified'[1] in Britain, and under what circumstances? This debate takes up Chapters 3 to 7.

Justice is not the whole of morality. Practices that are not strictly just may nevertheless be 'justified' on grounds of utility or broad consequence. So it is with positive discrimination. We shall find that calls for positive discrimination in Britain have often in practice been made on grounds of general utility – or at least to avert worse consequences than the reaction of outraged whites at preferential treatment for ethnic minorities. Such calls were made in the aftermath of the urban riots in 1981 and 1985. Chapter 8 therefore looks at consequentialist and utilitarian arguments for positive discrimination. The discussion is largely theoretical but sets out to formalize the requirements for estimating a balance of utilities. It also distinguishes between arguments that could claim to be about utility maximization and those that, although they assert this, are in fact only prudential (such as those referred to above).

Positive discrimination provides, perhaps more than any other practice in social policy, an excellent vehicle for testing the relative force and conviction of utility and justice. Chapter 8 concludes with two comparisons: firstly, when positive discrimination as an unjust practice might none the less be implemented on grounds of general utility (and might at the same time override justice in the form of the merit principle). Secondly, there is the case in which positive discrimination, being 'justified' as the only way of fulfilling the requirements of justice in the circumstances, is not implemented on grounds of general utility. When utility jousts with justice where positive discrimination is concerned, the outcome can sometimes be bizarre.

The discussion throughout the book is conducted in terms of positive discrimination for ethnic minorities and, except where the theoretical arguments do not apply, for women. Most of the arguments will apply, for example, to racial and nationality groups. The empirical discussion as it relates to Britain is conducted only in respect of ethnic minorities.

Although the particular subject-matter of the book is positive discrimination and morality, at a more general level it is an exercise in bringing together the study of social policy on the one hand, and moral thought on the other. No particular methodology has been used except to explain and establish certain moral principles as 'test criteria' and then to subject the policy practice to them. The study is not intended to be only an academic exercise. Positive discrimination, for all its ambiguities, is important and contentious. It is hoped at least that what follows clarifies in some measure what positive discrimination is, and perhaps settles some arguments.

Chapter 2

Positive discrimination in Britain: the idea and its practice

A good deal of the debate about positive discrimination in both policy and academic circles in Britain has been misconceived; it has not been about a practice to which the name positive discrimination can rightly be applied. And much of the social policy practice to which the label has been applied is not positive discrimination either. One of our first tasks therefore must be to clarify some of the conceptual and terminological clutter that surrounds the idea of positive discrimination. This chapter will try to chart a course through the confusions, ambiguities, and misconceptions about positive discrimination that litter policy orthodoxy and academic social policy literature; it will identify the particular policies, social practices, and programmes to which the term has been applied in Britain; it will trace the development of the idea of positive discrimination since the Second World War and its incorporation into the lexicon of social policy; it will examine current practice and assess how much of this practice really is something to which the term positive discrimination can be applied; and it will demonstrate how an idea that was welcomed in the immediate post-Plowden era turned sour by the beginning of the present decade.

Sources of information for an analysis of this kind fall into two broadly identifiable but overlapping categories. The less problematic of the two is the 'academic' social policy literature. This provides us with ideas and arguments useful for an understanding of positive discrimination and also acts as a guide to the 'state of the art' in the debate about it. In this sense, the academic literature must be treated not only as a part of the debate but also in some measure as a data source. The second source of information is more problematical. It consists of what we may call 'policy orthodoxy'; that is, material that is not in itself commentative or analytical, but which constitutes the material and substance of policy thinking. It is not easy (nor probably very useful) to specify precisely what constitutes policy-relevant documents, but they would clearly include internal government department memoranda, papers, and guidelines, as well as the more accessible Bills, Acts, and codes of guidance that form the substance of policy legislation. These are not the only, nor necessarily the most useful, source of information about current orthodoxy on social policy matters however. The policy process is informed by a wide variety of sources outside the Civil Service, including politicians, interest and pressure groups, researchers and academics, practising professionals, élites, and the media (see Hall *et al.* 1975, Smith 1976, Edwards and Batley 1978, Ham and Hill 1984). If we want to know what current thinking is about any particular policy issue, therefore, we need to know what politicians, pressure groups, professionals, and other policy influencers are thinking. We need to cast our net wide to catch all the material that will enable us to construct a picture of what policy orthodoxy is. No claim is made that the material trawled for this analysis is anything like comprehensive – the net has many holes in it and further trawling often produces rapidly diminishing returns – but it should be sufficient to provide an adequate picture. The bulk of the analysis relies upon records of parliamentary debates, evidence (both oral and written) to two Home Affairs Committees and one Environment Committee, enquiries (particularly useful and often overlooked sources), reports and annual reports of the Community Relations Commission and the Commission for Racial Equality (as the main interest group in respect of positive discrimination), a variety of reports from Newsom to Scarman, and a miscellaneous selection of other (mainly local government) documentation and newspaper sources.

The distinction between the two types of information source is not a neat one (apart, that is, from the problem of identifying any given piece – like a CRE research report – as an 'academic' or a 'policy' document). Academic policy literature and research findings contribute to policy thinking, just as do the output of interest groups, the thinking of professionals, and the fancies of politicians; but there is a useful difference between what academic commentators say about positive discrimination and what party politicians, trade unionists, or local councillors and officials take it to mean. The first is largely commentative (it also produces its own academic orthodoxy), while the latter constitutes what for present purposes will be called the conventional wisdom or policy orthodoxy.

1 The confusion of terms and concepts

Even Plowden got it wrong, and that is where it is all supposed to have started. So did Titmuss, and Pinker, and many of the Fabians, and Scarman (partly), and many politicians and professionals in between. We shall return to the academic literature later in the chapter; here our concern is the confusion that has abounded in policy orthodoxy. Although practices that in the 1960s and 1970s came to be labelled as positively discriminatory can be traced back to the immediate post-war era and beyond (see Batley 1978), the terminology of positive discrimination can be said to have begun with the Plowden Report on *Children and their Primary Schools* (Plowden 1967). It was from this source that the phrase entered the social policy literature and the language of policy orthodoxy. It was also from Plowden that the concept of positive discrimination and all its attendant confusions derived.

In part 3 of the report Plowden notes the redistributive effect of the Rate Support Grant formulas on resources as between local authorities. She then goes on to note that the same redistribution is not so marked *within* authorities and argues:

> '"Equality" has an appealing ring, "discrimination" has not. It is simpler and easier, for example, to defend staff–pupil ratios that are roughly the same in each school than to explain why they should be better in some and to decide which are to be the favoured. Even so, more and more local authorities do discriminate. They look with a more generous eye on schools whose "social need" is greatest.'
>
> (Plowden 1967: 56)

The report continues:

> 'The formulae for allocating grants (RSG) are designed to equalise the financial resources of poorer and wealthier authorities. But equality is not enough. The formulae do not distinguish between the districts within authorities' areas in which children and schools are most severely handicapped. These districts need more spending on them.'
>
> (Plowden 1967: 56)

This simple and uncontentious point is then elaborated in the succeeding pages, where the idea of Educational Priority Areas is introduced. And here we come to the oft-quoted passage about positive discrimination.

> 'The principle, already accepted, that special need calls for special help, should be given a new cutting edge. We ask for "positive discrimination" in favour of such schools and the children in them, going well beyond an attempt to equalise resources. Schools in deprived areas should be given priority in many respects. The first step must be to raise the schools with low standards to the national average; the second, quite deliberately to make them better. The justification is that the homes and neighbourhoods from which many of their children come provide little support and stimulus for learning. The schools must supply a compensating environment.'
>
> (Plowden 1967: 57)

These passages provide the context into which the notion of positive discrimination is introduced. What they are arguing for is a move away from equality of resources towards equality of welfare (see Weale 1978: 69–70) and, in so doing, an extension of the principle of selectivity (but not on an individual basis). The call to make the worst schools better than the average is not a call for positive discrimination but a call for the more rigorous pursuit of the needs principle whereby resources are differentially distributed according to different needs. If needs are greater than the average in some schools, then the needs principle will require them to get more resources than the average. Thus far the argument is straightforward. However, the element of positive discrimination in Plowden has often been taken to reside in the notion of compensatoriness; the schools should supply 'a compensating environment'. This is misleading. When Plowden talked about compensatory education what she meant (and this is clear from the context) was not compensation for past harm or injury, which has been the essence of positive discrimination policies in the United States, but compensation as making up for a deficiency – which is again nothing more than the operation of the needs principle. The deficiency of home and neighbourhood constitutes a need that requires to be met.

So far, then, there is nothing new in Plowden. What she was calling for was not positive discrimination if the term is to mean something different from straightforward selectivity and the operation of the needs principle. Had the dominant ideology within the academic and practice policy fields at the time not been one of universalism, there would not have appeared to be any novelty in all this, and the new doctrine of positive discrimination within a universalistic infrastructure that Titmuss was soon to champion (Titmuss 1968: 135) might never have got off the ground. Certainly, it all seemed familiar enough to convinced selectivists. In the debate in the House of Commons on the Plowden Report on 16 March 1967, Sir Edward Boyle, as he then was, was able to say: 'In principle, we on this side of the House accept this concept of positive discrimination. Indeed, we stated in our 1966 manifesto that "We shall give special help to areas where there is most need"' (Hansard, 16 March 1967: cols. 737–38). Another Conservative MP, Mr Hill, welcomed the notion of Educational Priority Areas, saying, 'It is a classic Conservative principle to concentrate help where it is most needed' (Hansard, 16 March 1967: col. 789).

There are none the less two separate elements in the passages cited from Plowden that have not been, but ought to be, separately identified. The first is the issue of the amount of resources or social good to be distributed, and in this, as we have seen, there is no novelty and nothing that can be described as positive discrimination. The amounts of resource to be distributed should be in proportion to the needs they are to meet. This is selectivity, nothing more or less. The second element is the issue of *who* should be the beneficiaries of the resource distribution. A seemingly[1] new idea was introduced here – that of Educational Priority Areas – and this again has sometimes been taken to constitute the essence of positive discrimination in Plowden. This is a more difficult issue, and its fuller consideration must wait until the concept of positive discrimination in the context of social justice is elaborated in the next chapter. However, we may comment here on the apparent novelty of the idea. The recipients of resources were not to be individuals identified on the basis of a means test, but groups of children identified by the school they attended or the area they lived in. Thus individuals might benefit from greater resources but *not on a direct individual basis*,[2] not because *they* had passed a test of means but because their school or neighbourhood had. This gave rise to the view of positive discrimination as a form of selectivity without stigma (Pinker 1971: 188), which must have seemed like a brilliant new specific, able to complement the blanket remedy of universalism by getting to the seat of the malady without harming the psyche of the recipient. What then constitutes the element of positive discrimination in this? It must be that the beneficiaries were to be identified as a group rather than as individuals. But if this is the case, then positive discrimination had been with us a long time before Plowden (see note 1). The question therefore remains: is the group identification of resource beneficiaries positive discrimination in a way that their identification as individuals is not? We must consider this question at greater length in the next chapter.

Despite the fact that Plowden was not proposing anything new (and that, if there was an element of positive discrimination, it was a practice that had been around, in the form of area policies, for a long time), the notion of positive discrimination was launched. No one seemed to notice that even if the emperor did have some bits of clothes on, they didn't leave much to the imagination (though, as we have noted, selectivists thought they recognized something familiar). And so began the muddle.

The subsequent debates in the House of Lords and the House of Commons show that whilst the new terminology had been taken on board, and whilst a few saw the proposals as controversial, what was being talked about was really a set of old ideas under a new name. Plowden had proposed more selectivity; selectivists were happy to accept this, albeit under the new name; non-selectivists (almost all on the Labour benches) thought they saw something new and were also happy to accept it. Lord Newton argued: 'I am sure that this recommendation [positive discrimination] should be welcomed in principle. It is fully in keeping with the policy we pursued when in office of favouring deliberately school building in the North East and favouring the replacement of primary schools in Inner London' (Hansard, 14 March 1967: col. 177). He recognized it as the operation of the needs principle through more selectivity. Lord Plowden was able to say: 'I urge the Government to discriminate in this way. . . . But to do this will require courage because the electorate continues to identify discrimination with a means test and the mass unemployment of the 'thirties' (Hansard, 14 March 1967: col. 208); and again: 'a different approach to this problem of need by discrimination within the Welfare State as a whole in favour of those least privileged would, I believe, give much more positive results for the money we spend' (Hansard, 14 March 1967: col. 209).

What is this, other than simple selectivity and distribution according to needs? For Viscount Eccles, positive discrimination was 'really an extension of slum clearance . . . and . . . a wholly admirable principle' (Hansard, 14 March 1967: col. 214). We have already noted that in the lower House Sir Edward Boyle MP and Mr Hill MP saw no difficulty in reconciling Plowden's notion of positive discrimination with their own predilection for selectivity; and Charles Morrison MP perhaps spelt it out most clearly when he said that positive discrimination 'emphasises once again that in yet another sphere the day of the blanket benefit is over, that flat rate government aid for whatever purpose is outdated.... If, in education, we are to endeavour to provide more equal opportunity for all children, we should have to discriminate positively in favour of the less fortunate areas' (Hansard, 16 March 1967: col. 824). Positive discrimination was straightforward selectivity for areas (or, in practice, schools). There was no new radical principle involved, but all seemed happy either to believe there was or to accept a new name for a familiar practice.

Twelve years later, confusion still reigned in the lower House, although by this time, as we shall see, more MPs disliked positive discrimination – whatever it was. The concept got an airing during the debate on the Local Government Grants (Ethnic Groups) Bill,[3] which, had it been enacted, would have replaced the Section 11 provisions of the 1966 Local Government Act.[4] There is again ample evidence in this debate that MPs had little clear idea of what positive discrimination involved, and of whether the proposals they were discussing involved positive discrimination or not. Thus Alex Lyon MP, whilst arguing that most Conservative MPs saw the proposals as positively discriminatory, claimed they were not; Joan Lester MP agreed with him. Their colleague Arthur Latham thought they *were* talking about positive discrimination, as did Anthony Steen and several other Conservative members. But in summing up, Brynmor John, Minister of State at the Home Office, claimed that the Bill was not about positive discrimination: 'it [the Bill] gives the lie to those who have alleged that it involves a form of positive discrimination – if by that they mean giving advantage to people who are already on equal terms' (Hansard, 12 March 1979: col. 166).

The most common confusion in policy orthodoxy has been to equate positive discrimination simply with the needs principle and to claim that to allocate according to need is to discriminate positively in favour of the beneficiaries. We have already witnessed this in the Plowden Report and the subsequent debates in both Houses of Parliament. The same confusion crops up regularly in the evidence to the Home Affairs Committee investigation of racial disadvantage. Both the Association of Metropolitan Authorities and the Association of District Councils in their evidence to the committee demonstrated that they did not know what positive discrimination was. Thus they cited in their written evidence such examples of positive discrimination as 'ensuring that meals are provided which do not offend religious beliefs', 'respecting cultural requirements relating to dress or jewellery', and 'making arrangements for physical education which take into account religious beliefs' (Home Affairs Sub-Committee on Race Relations and Immigration, Session 1979–80, Minutes of Evidence; 392) – none of which are positive discrimination. They claimed that positive discrimination is enshrined in the 1976 Race Relations Act (Minutes of Evidence, Association of District Councils: 406) – which it is not. Their oral evidence moreover included references to positive discrimination such as 'my authority positively discriminates on educational and social need' (Minutes: 414) and, in reference to positive discrimination, 'we . . . put in more teachers. We give more books. We put in community workers, and we put in youth leaders, and we just give what we believe are that actual school's needs' (Minutes: 419). Another examinee however argued that allocating more resources to schools with greater needs did not constitute positive discrimination, and Mr Lyon – one of the committee members – was at pains to explain that he did not think that meeting the special needs of ethnic minority groups constituted positive discrimination.

The Community Relations Commission, a body that ought to have set the record straight, also claimed in its Annual Report for 1973–74 that 'It is these difficulties [the special needs of minority groups] that the Commission has in mind when policies of "positive discrimination" are recommended: this has nothing to do with special privileges' (Community Relations Commission 1974).

A variety of reports in the field of social policy have also confused positive discrimination with the needs principle. The Seebohm Report echoed Plowden's recommendations in calling for more discrimination in favour of areas with the greatest needs (Seebohm 1968: 150). So did Cullingworth's report on council housing allocation (Cullingworth 1969: paras. 392–96). So did the Black Report on health inequalities (Townsend and Davidson 1982: 164 ff.). Scarman in the closing paragraphs of his report also slips into the terminology of positive discrimination in respect of action to meet the special needs of minority groups

(Scarman 1981: para. 9.4). There is, however, a further complication in Lord Scarman's report when earlier he argues that 'given the special problems of the ethnic minorities ... justice requires that special programmes should be adopted in areas of acute deprivation. In this respect, the ethnic minorities can be compared with any other group with special needs, such as the elderly or one-parent families' (Scarman 1981: para. 6.32). It is to this argument that Scarman refers in his subsequent claim for positive discrimination (para. 9.4). Now if ethnic minorities are to be the beneficiaries of 'special programmes' *because* they have special needs, then this is not positive discrimination. And the equation of ethnic minority groups with other 'special need' groups avoids what is a central issue in positive discrimination: whether the definition of the group is itself constitutive of need. We shall return to this issue later.

What these various reports have in common, and what has been a characterizing feature of positive discrimination in Britain, is an emphasis on *priority areas*. It is fair to say that, in policy orthodoxy, positive discrimination has in large measure been *equated* with special or priority area designations. This has been a common theme from Milner Holland to Plowden, Seebohm, Cullingworth, Black, and Scarman. But the area allocation of resources on the basis of differential area needs (even when the emphasis is on giving *extra* resources to areas of *special* need) is not positive discrimination.

The confusion about the meaning of positive discrimination has been reflected in, and exacerbated by, an indiscriminate use of terminology. I want later to question the moral distinction between positive discrimination and positive action which seems at present to be generally acknowledged (with the latter being a more acceptable practice than the former). This distinction was not until recently reflected in general usage of the two terms. The evidence to the Home Affairs Sub-Committee on Racial Disadvantage is replete with references to positive discrimination when in fact what is being referred to would more properly today be considered positive action. Thus the Manpower Services Commission in Manchester in evidence refers to the provision of training courses through the (then) Youth Opportunities Programme for ethnic minority youth as positive discrimination. The Association of Metropolitan Authorities refers to local authority policies to counter racial disadvantage as positive discrimination. The Association of District Councils calls equal opportunities policies positive discrimination. The Banking, Insurance, and Finance Union refers to the positive action allowed under the 1976 Race Relations Act as positive discrimination. And the Department of Employment in supplementary information printed in the appendices to the committee's final report refers to 'Research and Initiatives by Industrial Training Boards towards "Positive Discrimination"', the substance of which would all more properly be called positive action (Home Affairs Committee, Session 1980–81, Fifth Report, Vol. IV: 15).

The debate that followed on Lord Scarman's recommendations about increasing ethnic minority representation in police forces also provided ample opportunity for misunderstandings (or misrepresentations). At the Police Federation's annual conference in 1982 a letter from the then Home Secretary, urging that minority applicants to the police not be turned away simply for want of vacancies, was attacked as positive discrimination, as were Lord Scarman's proposals on training for under-qualified applicants. Both sets of proposals were more akin to positive action in its current usage. *The Times*'s leader on the Scarman Report attempted to draw a distinction between 'acceptable positive action and unacceptable reverse discrimination' (*The Times*, 30 March 1983) but then proceeded to use the terms (and 'positive discrimination') fairly indiscriminately.

Confusion with 'positive action' is but one part of the terminological quagmire. As if the home ground were not treacherous enough, we have also on occasions imported more confusion from the United States. To put beside 'positive discrimination' and 'positive action', we find the chairman of the Home Affairs Sub-Committee on Racial Disadvantage introducing and using synonymously the terms 'reverse discrimination' and 'affirmative action', both borrowed from the USA and both meaning different things. In evidence to the committee we find a Home Office examinee referring to 'positive discrimination' and 'reverse discrimination', again synonymously, but with more justification, as do a couple of MPs in the debate on the Local Government Grants (Ethnic Minorities) Bill and also Lord Scarman in his report, but this time with an implied difference between the two – 'reverse discrimination' being applied to the use of quotas for ethnic minority entry to the police force (Scarman 1981: para. 5.7) and 'positive discrimination' to practices that in other parts of his report he calls 'positive action'. To complicate matters, the Commission for Racial Equality in its report on *Urban Deprivation, Racial Inequality and Social Policy* mistakenly, uses 'affirmative action' and 'positive discrimination' synonymously (CRE 1977). The same conjunction (but this time between 'affirmative action' and 'group-based positive discrimination') crops up again in another CRE report on transmitted deprivation, ethnic minorities, and affirmative action (Little and Robbins 1982). Perhaps the representative of the Association of Metropolitan Authorities giving evidence to the Home Affairs Sub-Committee can be forgiven for wondering if the disadvantaged position of ethnic minorities in public housing might be due to positive discrimination by local authorities against them!

It has to be admitted that, when compared with the richness of the United States lexicon in this field, our own range of expressions is positively parsimonious. Thus the US literature offers us 'reverse discrimination', 'affirmative action', 'preferential treatment', 'affirmative discrimination', 'compensatory opportunity', 'compensatory reverse discrimination', 'inverse discrimination', 'preferential consideration', and 'compensatory justice'. We need not at this stage attempt to make sense of this variety of terminology (and given the indiscriminate use of terms in the literature, it may be a pointless task) other than to say that 'affirmative action' is the term most used in legislative and administrative contexts (such as Executive Orders) and that 'reverse discrimination' is sometimes, although by no means always, used in a pejorative sense (see, for example, Nickel 1972, Thalberg 1973–74). 'Affirmative action', as first used in Executive Orders Nos. 10925 (under the Kennedy administration) and 11246 (under the Johnson administration in 1965), meant that employers were 'to act affirmatively to recruit workers on a non-discriminatory basis' (Glazer 1975: 46) and was more akin to the practices that in Britain today are called 'positive action'. However, the meaning of 'affirmative action' changed during the 1970s as further guidelines imposed more rigorous requirements and gradually introduced the idea of targets and quotas for minority-group representation in workforces, colleges, and universities. Affirmative action came to take on the attributes more commonly referred to as 'reverse discrimination', and the two terms increasingly became synonymous.

For the present I shall retain the distinction in the British context between positive discrimination and positive action. In the longer term, the distinction will prove to be less useful; but since in the present climate the term 'positive discrimination' is in general negatively valued and 'positive action' (more) positively valued, it is worth maintaining the distinction. United States terminology will be avoided except when addressing the US experience, and then I shall confine usage as far as possible to 'affirmative action' to refer to policies, practices, and programmes, and to 'reverse discrimination' to refer when necessary to the nature of what is being done. Separate usage for the British and US situations is necessary to avoid any danger of equating 'positive discrimination' with 'reverse discrimination'. In moral terms, as we shall see, there is no difference between them, but in common currency and usage their meanings are not synonymous – what is commonly meant by 'positive discrimination' in Britain is not the same (indeed, is broader and more inclusive) as what is meant by 'reverse discrimination' in the USA.

2 The scope of positive discrimination in common usage

We need now to survey the range and variety of practices and policies to which the label 'positive discrimination' has been applied in Britain. We shall then be able to show with the aid of a rigorous definition of the term that much of the practice to which it has been applied is not in fact positively discriminatory in any sense that distinguishes it as a separate and peculiar practice. With our path thus cleared of much unnecessary undergrowth we can proceed to our investigation proper.

Foremost among the policies and practices that have been called positively discriminatory in Britain are those programmes collectively constituting inner-city policy. These include (in chronological order) Section 11 grants (under the Local Government Act 1966), the Educational Priority Areas, the Urban Programme, the Community Development Projects, the Comprehensive Community Programmes, the Six City Initiatives, the Partnership authorities, Programme Authorities, Designated authorities (under the Inner Urban Areas Act 1978), and perhaps more questionably the Urban Development Corporations, Enterprise Zones, and Freeports (see for discussion of these as positive discrimination programmes Glennerster and Hatch 1974a, Townsend 1976, Coates, Johnston, and Knox 1977, Edwards and Batley 1978, Higgins 1978, Higgins *et al.* 1983, Edwards 1984). What all these programmes have in common is their selectivity between areas – mostly at the sub-local authority level. All involve in some degree the allocation of resources (whether these are 'extra' resources is a moot point) to particular areas on the grounds that those areas have concentrations of urban or social deprivation.[5] They have thus been represented as 'priority area' or 'area-based positive discrimination' programmes.

There is a sense in which inner-city policies can be called 'special' policies in that they are additional to main-line social policies, relatively small in scale (although current expenditure is in excess of £3.5 million per annum), self-contained, and finite. In this sense they lend themselves to a separate appellation like 'positive discrimination'. The term has not been confined to this set of specific and self-contained policies, however. Its use has become much more generalized to the extent that many long-standing and main-line practices and policies have, at one time or another, been cited as examples of positive discrimination. Among those most frequently mentioned are Rate Support Grant (Reddin 1970, Hatch and Sherrott 1973, Robson 1976, Townsend 1976, Aldridge 1979), Housing Action Areas (Barnes 1974, Holtermann 1975, M. Brown 1977, McLeay 1982), slum clearance (Pinker 1971, Glennerster and Hatch 1974a, Hatch, Fox, and Legg 1977), General Improvement Areas, improvement grants, and priority areas for housing improvement (Donnison 1974, Coates, Johnston, and Knox 1977, McLeay 1982), and regional policies, especially regional employment policies (Hatch and Sherrott 1973, Coates, Johnston, and Knox 1977, Hatch, Fox, and Legg 1977). As with the inner-city policies, all these have an area component; but Rate Support Grant stands out from the rest as being a blanket provision, whereas the others involve some form of designation of *some* areas as warranting 'special' treatment. The *area* focus of positive discrimination therefore remains strong in these commonly cited examples.

There are a wide range of other policies and practices that at one time or another have been called positively discriminatory. In the general field of housing, Cullingworth in his report on the functions of council housing (Cullingworth 1969) considered the case for positive discrimination in favour of ethnic minority members. For Cullingworth, this would have included such measures as granting additional housing points to all minority members (the criterion *being* ethnicity), so accelerating their progress up the waiting-list, and special subsidies for housing ethnic minority families.[6] In fact, although this report was published in 1969, when the term 'positive discrimination' was only just beginning to gain common usage, Cullingworth came nearer to the real essence of the concept than many who followed. Still in the field of housing. McLeay cites local authority housing subsidies and tax relief on mortgage interest repayments as examples of positive discrimination (McLeay 1982), and Pinker would include differential rent schemes in public housing for richer and poorer households (Pinker 1971).

In the wider area of income maintenance and income support, Holtermann (1975) cites supplementary benefit, rate rebates, and free school meals as examples of positive discrimination *at the individual level*. Robson (1976) would include tax credit schemes within the pantheon of positive discrimination. Scarman (1981) considered quotas for minority group entry to police forces to be positive discrimination. The Manpower Services Commission in evidence to the Home Affairs Sub-Committee on Racial Disadvantage said that running more short training courses in areas of high ethnic minority concentration was positive discrimination (Home Affairs Committee, Session 1979–80, Minutes of Evidence: 646). Donnison (1974) thought that priority areas for personal social services would be positive discrimination; and Coates, Johnston, and Knox considered that almost all urban planning was positive discrimination of a sort and that 'one of the most commonly used forms of positive discrimination is the transfer of financial resources from prosperous to disadvantaged regions' (Coates, Johnston, and Knox 1977: 232). Titmuss believed he saw the dimension of positive discrimination 'in income maintenance, in education, in housing, in medical care and mental health, in child welfare' (Titmuss 1968: 135)

With such an abundance of practices as this, all laying some claim to be positively discriminatory, the only question that might seem to remain is, what is *not* positive discrimination?

3 The essence of positive discrimination

If the practice of positive discrimination is to be identified as peculiarly distinct from other practices common in social policy such as those of selectivity and the allocation of social goods and benefits according to an assessment of need, it must mean this: *that the criteria used to identify beneficiaries and potential beneficiaries are different from those for which the benefit is being given.* If the reasons for giving a benefit or social good are need or merit or restitution or rights, and the recipients are identified solely according to their needs, merits, deserts, or rights, that is *not* positive discrimination. If, in fulfilment of the same objectives, recipients are chosen according to other criteria, such as ethnicity, sex, race, and – more arguably – age and residential location, that *is* positive discrimination. In more general terms, we may say that if in pursuit of morally relevant ends by the distribution of goods, services, benefits, positions, and rewards, we distribute according to morally arbitrary criteria, we are positively discriminating. This is not what is meant (when anything specific is meant) in common policy parlance by 'positive discrimination'. But, as we have seen, it is difficult to identify just what *is* meant by 'positive discrimination' in its common usage. What I hope to show in subsequent chapters is that, both morally speaking and in practical terms, if 'positive discrimination' does not mean what is described above, then it means nothing particular or peculiar; the term is functionless.

What makes the practices described above interesting and contentious from a moral point of view is that they are designed to *benefit* the selected groups (hence *positive* discrimination). Where policies or practices are designed to, or in effect do, *disadvantage* certain people selected on morally arbitrary criteria, then the moral considerations are much easier to deal with. We would, and do, simply consider such practices morally wrong and unjust, and we enact anti-discrimination legislation in that conviction. Whether, to what degree, and in what circumstances positive discrimination is just or unjust it will be the task of subsequent chapters to investigate. However, the formulation outlined above *necessarily* depends on a conception of social justice and is therefore only a partial consideration of what is moral. It leaves unresolved such issues as whether the separate but equal treatment of individuals selected on morally arbitrary criteria under conditions of fair equality of opportunity is right or wrong. Such questions are probably better dealt with by moral considerations other than those of justice.

We shall leave further discussion of the morality of positive discrimination until the next chapter and return now, armed with a strict idea of what positive discrimination is and is not, to its concept and practice in Britain.

4 The development of a notion of positive discrimination in Britain

We have seen how the term 'positive discrimination' came in with the Plowden Report and subsequently gained widespread if indiscriminate use. But the practice, if not the words, was not new – at least if some of the examples cited really do constitute positive discrimination. Thus the notion of priority areas designated for special treatment (area-based positive discrimination) can be traced back to the Special Areas Act of 1934; and in his report on the distribution of the industrial population, Barlow (1940) called for the decentralization of planning policies and machinery the better to be able to direct assistance to the depressed areas (Cullingworth 1976: 22), (Cherry 1982: chs. 2, 3). The Milner Holland Report of 1965 called, as we have seen, for the designation of 'areas of special control' (Milner Holland 1965: 122). And if we are able to include slum clearance and improvement, local authority dwelling subsidies, mortgage tax relief, and income maintenance and support provisions, as some commentators would, all these pre-date the explicit emergence of positive discrimination. However, in general terms the concept of positive discrimination did date from Plowden and was characterized as being mainly area-based.

The facility with which the 'new' concept was adopted owes much to the fact that what it described was already familiar. Indeed, the acceptability of positive discrimination throughout the late 1960s and the 1970s can be attributed to its characterization as an *area* policy and practice. As long as the benefits distributed were communal goods and so long as the beneficiaries were anonymously identified as 'areas', the practice remained uncontentious. By the beginning of the 1980s, however, both conceptions of and attitudes towards positive discrimination had changed – except, that is, in the academic social policy literature. Here we may note a strange divergence. While the press and politicians were now fulminating against a practice that was contrary to fair play and justice by advantaging ethnic minorities at the expense of the white ethnic population, a book published in 1982, summarizing the results of the 'cycle of deprivation' studies, was calling for more positive discrimination in education, health care, income maintenance, employment, and personal social services (Brown and Madge 1982: 293 ff.), and in 1985 Pinker was still supporting 'more positive discrimination in favour of the poor' (Pinker 1985: 200). In policy orthodoxy and common usage, positive discrimination was no longer about special help for special areas; it was about giving advantage on the basis of racial characteristics. Among academic social policy commentators, it would seem, it was still about non-stigmatizing selectivity within a context of universalism. Between

Plowden and Scarman there had been a transformation in the public and political mind, to which academics seem to have remained immune. We shall presently examine the shift in the valuation of positive discrimination in policy orthodoxy. But first, because it is an important part of the history of positive discrimination in Britain, attention will be focused on the concept's admission to the corpus of academic social policy thought.

Positive discrimination has, almost without exception, been treated by academic social policy analysts as a useful, progressive, and advantageous practice. It has been subjected to surprisingly little critical analysis. Its general characterization has been as a means of achieving a more penetrating intervention at points in the social structure where needs are greatest and most persistent. As such it has been treated as a valuable new weapon in the armoury of social intervention. It has, however, achieved this rarefied status largely because of its misrepresentation.

The scene was set by Titmuss, Pinker, Miller, and Rein. In 1966 Miller and Rein, in their essay on poverty, inequality, and policy, described positive discrimination as a means to intervene 'more directly at strategic points in the social structure' (Miller and Rein 1966: 516). They were talking about the situation in the United States, but theirs was an image that imprinted itself among British social policy academics. Most frequently cited is Titmuss's question in his lecture of 1967 on 'Welfare State and Welfare Society':

> 'What particular infrastructure of universalist services is needed in order to provide a framework of values and opportunity bases within and around which can be developed socially acceptable selective services aiming to discriminate positively, with the minimum risk of stigma, in favour of those whose needs are greatest?'
> (Titmuss 1968: 135)[7]

Pinker later expanded on Titmuss's formulation thus: 'In this sense, positive discrimination becomes a tactical exercise within a wider universalist strategy. Such discrimination is the only form of selectivity compatible with the idea of a welfare society because its ultimate goal is the achievement of optimal rather than minimal standards. Discrimination becomes a process of inclusion rather than exclusion' (Pinker 1971: 190). It is not immediately clear what Pinker means by his assertion of 'optimal rather than minimal standards', but I take it to reflect Plowden's view that positive discrimination must involve additional resources and not just a reallocation of resources at current levels (i.e. give *more* to the least well off without disbenefit to any recipients under existing distributions). If this is the case then all that is being claimed is that existing resource distribution formulas are inadequate in not being selective enough. Positive discrimination becomes a makeweight to compensate for the unselectivity of present distributions. Because if at *any* level of resource provision supplementary amounts are to go to the least well off, then this ought to be written into the formula so that the least well off become beneficiaries at any (and especially lower) levels of overall provision. The real substance of these scene-setting arguments however is that positive discrimination is a form of selectivity and the only form that is acceptable, and then only within a universalistic framework.[8] These arguments invite closer examination.

4.1 The universalism/selectivity debate

By about 1970 the universalism/selectivity debate was becoming threadbare. Apart from economic and political exigencies – which increasingly made universalism look like a luxury we could no longer afford – the universalist arguments, against the hard edge of selectivism, were beginning to expose threads of sophism. In this context, as I have argued above, positive discrimination presented a welcome and new dimension to the debate. It gave succour to the flagging troops of universalism. Thus Reddin was able to argue:

> 'They [positive discrimination practices] . . . enable us to proceed to an egalitarian society without too many explicit and individualised signposts of stigma, success or failure *en route*; they may prove in the long run to be part of a more generous and discriminating system than that augured by the superficial promise of selectivity.'
>
> (Reddin 1970: 35)

And in similar vein, M. Brown wrote that positive discrimination 'remains an important ideological step forward out of the universal/selective dilemma and a practical tool of great potential for evening-up standards of provision and directing extra resources to the most deprived without undue stigma' (1977: 229).

Others took up the same theme or variations on it. Hatch and Sherrott claimed that positive discrimination incorporated the advantages of selectivity – the ability to concentrate resources where they were most needed – without the disadvantages of the means test and low take-up (Hatch and Sherrott 1973: 223). Halsey noted that Conservatives welcomed positive discrimination as being consistent with selectivity (Halsey 1972: 33). Parker argued that positive discrimination is a form of selectivity to be distinguished from other forms that deny people's rights (Parker 1975: 152). Room noted that positive discrimination could not be 'justified as distinct in its rationale from universalism' (Room 1979: 234); and Foster goes further in claiming that universalists 'do not deny that the only way to ensure that the social services redistribute welfare to the poor is to positively discriminate in their favour' (Foster 1983: 145).

Stripped to its essentials, the argument being proposed here is that:

(a) universalism is to be preferred to selectivity;
(b) but universalism fails to concentrate help where it is most needed;
(c) selectivity does so only inadequately and then only at high cost in terms of stigma, low take-up, and negation of rights;
(d) positive discrimination does concentrate resources where they are most needed and without the costs (human and financial) of selectivity;
(e) the best of both worlds can therefore be achieved by maintaining universalism (with its respect for citizenship, dignity, and status) but giving it a cutting edge by supplementing it with positive discrimination.

There is a contingent rider to the argument. If the mutual benefit of the selective concentration of resources without the imposition of stigma was to work, beneficiaries must be identified in non-stigmatizing ways. And the most common solution to this was to use spatial location as the selection criterion to replace the individual means test. It is therefore to the question of areas that we must turn next. We shall then be in a position to assess whether these arguments for positive discrimination have any substance.

4.2 The spatial dimension

Spatial location was not the only selection criterion proposed – Titmuss mentioned it only along with others. But it was the most frequent, and in practice the only criterion operated throughout the 1970s. So, although we find reference to positive discrimination in respect of (special) areas or 'categories of special need' (M. Brown 1977: 228), 'groups of people in greatest need' (Higgins 1978: 38), and 'neighbourhoods and institutions' (Hatch, Fox, and Legg 1977: 242), other than where the target has been schools – as with Educational Priority Areas – no one has specified how the need categories or groups are to be identified and located other than on an area basis. Thus, while Pinker draws attention to the danger of too closely identifying positive discrimination with priority areas, he does not go on to explain how positive discrimination would operate in practice other than through some form of priority area designation or distribution. Similarly, Halsey notes that, even for the EPAs, whilst the targets were schools, for administrative convenience, area data were simpler and more available (Halsey 1972: 181). Again, for some commentators, discussion of positive discrimination is conducted solely in terms of area policies as if the two were synonymous, which in practice they almost were; see, for example, Cullingworth (1973: 140), Marshall (1975: 186), Robson (1976: 106), Coates, Johnston, and Knox (1977: 230 ff.), and Loney (1983: 17–18).

It is not difficult to see why areas became the most common means of selecting potential beneficiaries of positive discrimination policies. Firstly, there were plenty of precedents for area selectivity. Secondly, even at the small area level, which some saw to be the real novelty of priority area policies (see Hatch and Sherrott 1973: 223), data were readily available in the form of Census statistics for wards and enumeration districts to facilitate the identification of deprivation black spots with a deceptive ease (see Edwards 1975, Edwards and Batley 1978: 51). Thirdly, the selection of areas for priority treatment (even if there were seen to be an element of advantage involved) was acceptable to politicians and public. In fact, if you wanted to select beneficiaries for a practice or policy in a non-stigmatizing and politically acceptable fashion, then small areas provided the best and most anodyne method.

The public and political acceptability of area-based positive discrimination depends on just the same features as make it acceptable and welcome to despondent universalists. For the former, priority treatment is acceptable as long as no one is actually seen to benefit. For universalists, positive discrimination is non-stigmatizing for just the same reason. Area positive discrimination amounts in practice to not very selective selectivity. Whether it really is in fact positive discrimination we shall examine later.

The acceptability of area-based positive discrimination, then, and its attractiveness to academic policy analysts, lies in its crudeness as a means of identifying and concentrating resources on the deprived. No one is stigmatized, because the benefits go to generalized recipients and the benefits themselves are collective goods – community centres, law centres, housing aid centres, extra language teachers, subsidies for industry, and so on, rather than individual benefits.[9] If *in practice* priority area policies did deliver social goods to the most deprived, to most of the most deprived, and to only the most deprived, the relative crudeness of the selection process would be a real benefit in so far as this would be achieved without stigmatizing the beneficiaries. But the potential effectiveness of such practices depends upon the assumption that, in directing resources to the most needy or most deprived areas, these resources are truly getting to those individuals most in need of them. The assumption is false, as Holtermann and others have ably demonstrated (Barnes 1974, Holtermann 1975, Townsend 1976, Alnutt and Gelardi 1980, Hall 1980, MacLaran 1981). Although the degree of spatial concentration of different deprivations varies, most show a relative lack of concentration, so that resources directed at the most deprived areas would reach only a minority of the most deprived individuals and households, and would benefit many who could not in relative terms be described as among the most needy.[10]

Priority area policies are therefore a fairly ineffective and inefficient way of concentrating social goods on those most in need of them. Whilst they can be useful in some contexts (housing and general economic regeneration are examples) they are certainly not the ideological salvation that many universalists saw them to be.

4.3 The beneficiaries of positive discrimination

In a sense it is perfectly clear who the beneficiaries of positive discrimination are intended to be throughout the social policy literature: the most deprived and needy. What is less clear is *who* these individuals, families, households, groups, or areas are. Even less clear is how they are to be identified and how resources may be got to them in a non-stigmatizing way other than by the designation of the area they live or work in. The significance of this stems from our formulation of positive discrimination. If we wish to meet the needs of a particular body of people all of whom have identifiable needs, and if we direct resources to them (and them alone) to meet those needs, this is not positive discrimination. Thus when Titmuss speaks of positive discrimination in favour of 'the poor, the handicapped, the deprived, the coloured, the homeless and the social casualties of our society' (Titmuss 1968: 134), and Pinker identifies the focus of positive discrimination programmes as 'particular groups such as large families, disability groups and groups generally defined as social deviants, such as gypsies, barge families and some categories of immigrant' (Pinker 1971: 192), there are only two prima-facie senses – and I believe only one in practice – in which they can really be talking about positive discrimination. The first is that to discriminate positively in favour of such groups is to give them *extra* resources (extra, that is, to those that would satisfy their needs in accord with some concept of equality of welfare),[11] and thus advantage them in comparison with other need groups – which is not, I presume, what the commentators *do* mean. The second is that the potential beneficiaries would be identified on criteria *other* than their particular need. Since, as I shall argue in Chapter 5, the first of these arguments is flawed, only the second specifies action that would be positive discrimination.

Both Titmusss and Pinker have included in their lists of beneficiaries categories that are necessarily descriptive of need (the handicapped, the deprived, the homeless), as well as other categories that, while they may contain high proportions of the needy, are not themselves constitutive of need (large families and ethnic minorities, and probably barge families). To give additional resources in pursuit of meeting need to *all* large families, *all* ethnic minority members, and *all* barge families would be to discriminate in favour of these categories. But in the absence of any evidence that those categories that are necessarily constitutive of need would be identified in any way other than to benefit them and them alone, we must conclude that what Titmuss and Pinker are talking about is not positive discrimination.

Who or what else in the literature has been identified as a potential beneficiary of positive discrimination? We have seen that areas are often specified (and in terms of our formulation of positive discrimination this is a problematic case, to be discussed in the next chapter), but there are others, most generalized, and almost all specifying need or deprivation as the basis for action. Thus 'the most deprived' or 'the seriously deprived' have been specified by M. Brown (1977), Glennerster and Hatch (1974a), Kogan (1978), Brown and Madge (1982); 'groups in need' by M. Brown (1977), Higgins (1978), McLeay (1982), Foster (1983), Schuller (1983); 'ethnic minorities' by T. Blackstone (1980), Brown and Madge (1982), Cheetham (1982); 'women' by Hewitt (1980), and 'the children of deprived families' by Halsey (1972) and Webb (1980). Again, some of these are self-defining groups where, in the absence of identifying criteria such as areas, the same arguments apply, and what is being talked about is not positive discrimination. Others, like ethnic minorities and women, are not need groups *per se* and may involve some positive discrimination.

Almost all the beneficiaries are identified as *groups*, as in the above examples. Occasionally 'individuals in need' are also specified; see, for example, Titmuss (1968), Pinker (1971), Holtermann (1975), McLeay (1982). Halsey has argued that 'while insisting on the claim that the EPA is a viable administrative unit for positive discrimination, we would not wish to deny that, in the end, *the appropriate unit is the individual and his family*' (Halsey 1972: 181, emphasis added). Ultimately, the desired beneficiaries are of course individuals and families, but this is not the essence of positive discrimination. The use of generalized group criteria and communal benefits (which, in Britain, *are* the essence) is not necessarily, always, or even usually the best way of getting help to them. As Robson (1976), Hatch, Fox, and Legg (1977), and Young and Connelly (1981) have rightly pointed out, positive discrimination is *not* about delivering benefits to individuals; it is necessarily about giving benefits to *groups*, however they may be defined.

4.4 The benefits to be distributed

We have mentioned that, in Britain at least, the benefits that have been allocated by those practices which have been called positively discriminatory have been almost exclusively communal or collective goods. Whilst there is no clear and unambiguous distinction between a collectively and an individually consumed benefit, it is easy enough to see the difference between the nature of the benefit to be derived from a community centre on the one hand and a direct cash payment to an individual or the preferential allocation of a place in a medical school to a less qualified black or woman on the other. Certainly, in terms of political and public acceptability, the difference is clear and very significant. The British Urban Programme has not and could not result in Bakke- or De-Funis-type litigation (see below, pages 125–27).

What kind of benefit from positive discrimination practices has been alluded to in the social policy literature? For most, the benefits are given no more specifically than as 'resources' or 'additional resources'. As far as the Educational Priority Areas are concerned, Little (1974) claims that they involve the provision of more teachers and higher pay for teachers in EPA schools as a form of incentive. Halsey also is specific about EPAs; what positive discrimination is going to provide is more money, teachers, and buildings as well as a range of other incentives (Halsey 1972). For Titmuss and Brown and Madge positive discrimination provides more and better 'services' – including housing, education, health, and personal social services. The purposes to which the resources allocated under the Urban Programme were put have been documented by Edwards and Batley (1978: ch. 6), and Higgins (1978) among others has described the 'benefits' deriving from the Community Development Projects. In all these examples the benefits are all collective goods, and for none would it be easy, or even possible, to specify a particular benefit that had accrued to an identifiable individual. It is worth recalling the point made in the 1977 White Paper on policy for the inner cities that there could be no question of higher levels of supplementary benefit payment to residents of the inner cities, however they were defined. In terms of acceptability, there is a world of difference between inner-city policies that fund more community centres or provide infrastructure works for industrial estates, and ones that would put £*X* per week into the pockets of individuals because they lived in a specified area. As we shall see, the non-specificity of both beneficiaries and benefit has been a decisive factor in the political and public acceptability of what have been called positive discrimination programmes in Britain.

This brief review of the treatment of positive discrimination in British academic social policy literature indicates a high (though not unequivocal) level of valuation, and this accords with wider attitudes to it, so far as these are ascertainable, until the late

1970s. Whilst there has been a reversal in political and public valuations of positive discrimination since about 1978, however, it seems to have maintained its attraction to academics. Thus we find continuing calls for more positive discrimination in the social policy literature (see, for example, Blackstone 1980, Brown and Madge 1982, Foster 1983, Schuller 1983, Pinker 1985) at a time when public and political opinion, including that of the political left, had reacted against it. We shall examine this reaction in a moment, but we can usefully conclude this examination of the incorporation of positive discrimination into the social policy literature by noting that most academic proponents of positive discrimination have been content with a characterization of it that emphasizes its foundation in the needs principle and more willingly accepts the dubious efficacy of generalized benefits to anonymous beneficiaries because of the promise of no stigmatization. There are exceptions, but this formulation contains the essentials of the academic orthodoxy on what is considered to be positive discrimination, to much of which the term is however not usefully applicable.

5 How positive discrimination went sour

It is illuminating to compare the attitudes towards positive discrimination expressed during the debates in Parliament on the Plowden proposals in 1967 and during the second reading of the Local Government Grants (Ethnic Groups) Bill in 1979. The twelve-year gap between these two debates is sufficient for the fortunes of positive discrimination to have suffered a complete reversal.

In 1967, as we have seen, positive discrimination was welcomed on both sides of the House; on the political right because it was recognized for what it was – an extension of selectivity – and on the left because it appeared to provide a new weapon in the fight against deprivation. Hardly a voice was raised in criticism, although Lord Newton expressed the reservation that the policy should not 'be pushed too far' lest 'more generous staffing in priority areas . . . be allowed to result in levelling down over the whole field' (Hansard, 14 March 1967: cols. 177–78). Nevertheless, he welcomed the principle, as did his fellow peers Plowden and Eccles, who called it 'an admirable principle'. The feeling was reflected in the lower House, where positive discrimination was welcomed on both sides: 'let us endorse the

Plowden principle of positive discrimination and *recognise how widely it ought to apply throughout the range of public activity*' (Sir E. Boyle MP, emphasis added); 'a most radical recommendation, utterly convincing . . . we cannot rely on economic growth alone to even out gross social inequalities' (Mr A. Crosland MP). Twelve years later, in the same place, positive discrimination was being condemned as 'the most dangerous and insidious principle of all to introduce into the distribution of public funds or public favours' (Mr A. Clark MP, Hansard, 12 March 1979: col. 101), and as a part of the 'extremist activities' of the race relations industry, 'who put up the backs of so many fair minded citizens' (Mr Dudley Smith MP, Hansard, 12 March 1979: col. 78). Opposition came not only from the right of the Conservative Party, nor only from the Conservatives. No one had a good word for positive discrimination. Mr Brynmor John, Minister of State at the Home Office in the Labour Government and haplessly responsible for putting the 1979 Bill to Parliament, was at pains to argue that it was not about positive discrimination: 'It is a very short Bill and it gives the lie to those who have alleged that it involves a form of positive discrimination' (Hansard, 12 March 1979: col. 166).

What was the nature of the general opposition to positive discrimination, which expressed itself on the Conservative benches as an opposition to a Bill believed to be discriminatory and on the Labour benches as a denial that positive discrimination had anything to do with it? To answer this, we need to be clear what the Bill was proposing. It was intended to replace Section 11 of the 1966 Local Government Act, which enabled Exchequer grant to be paid to local authorities that had high levels of social need arising from concentrations of immigrants. This provision was outdated by 1979 in as much as the term 'immigrant' was meant to apply literally as 'new arrivals', and eligible authorities were those with high proportions of minority group members who had arrived within the previous *ten years* and not necessarily of ethnic minorities *per se*.[12] The new Bill was in effect an updating of Section 11 and a recognition that the high levels of social need in areas with ethnic concentrations arose not primarily out of 'newness' to the country (the assumption of Section 11), but out of the disadvantaged position of ethnic minorities in general, irrespective of how long their members had been resident.[13] The Bill was to make provision for grants to be paid to local authorities with high levels of need arising out of concentrations of ethnic groups *per se* and not new arrivals. It was this that formed the basis for opposition. To many MPs the new provisions were seen to incorporate an element to positive discrimination, which was now seen as giving aid and *advantage* to ethnic minorities at the expense of white ethnics. And so the old canard was resurrected; this would cause resentment among the white population of Britain and would therefore be counter-productive to good race relations; it was contrary to the English notion of fair play; it was selective in giving succour to the needy; if you were black and in need you got help, while if you were white and in need you didn't.

This view was expressed in a variety of ways, but the sentiments were similar:

> 'it is no good thinking that the ordinary white, working class people, who exist in all the inner cities and who feel that they are deprived, are not keenly aware that there is a form of discrimination that is likely to be codified and extended in the Bill which makes special provision for people simply because they are coloured.'
>
> (Mr A. Clark MP, Hansard, 12 March 1979: col. 100)

> 'The present proposals do not seem fair to many English people.'
>
> (Mr J. Stokes MP, Hansard, 12 March 1979: col. 112)

> 'The Bill is liable to incense our own countrymen who were born and bred here. They feel that they are being discriminated against.'
>
> (Mr J. Stokes MP, Hansard, 12 March 1979: col. 112)

> 'if this system of benefiting people is introduced, it will add to the resentment that is already felt.'
>
> (Mr N. Budgen MP, Hansard, 12 March 1979: col. 127)

> '[The Bill] inevitably seeks to identify and to single out what it calls "ethnic groups".'
>
> (Mr G. Gardiner MP, Hansard, 12 March 1979: col. 151)

In the face of such attacks, the response from the government benches was not to defend positive discrimination but to deny that the Bill had anything to do with it. Those who weren't attacking positive discrimination were rapidly trying to disown it.

Why, then, was a practice that twelve years earlier had been needed 'within the whole field of government expenditure' now 'the most dangerous and insidious of all to introduce into the distribution of public funds' in the words of two Conservative

MP's? The answer is that they were talking about different things. What Sir Edward Boyle had in 1967 taken to be selectivity was by 1979 more accurately recognized as being something significantly different. There was little talk about fairness and justice in 1967 because what was being proposed was something that had long been practised and, being simply selective allocation according to need, offended no one's canons of fairness. But it wasn't positive discrimination. By the end of the 1970s the distinguishing characteristic was more clearly recognized – the identification of beneficiaries on criteria other than the acceptable one of need. Issues of white backlash apart, this did raise the question of fairness and justice. Whether or not it was an insidious and dangerous practice remains to be examined.

The negative valuation of positive discrimination has not been, and is not, confined to Parliament. Much of the evidence to the Home Affairs Sub-Committee on Race Relations and Immigration also points directly or implicitly to a dislike of the practice, and much of the debate consequent upon the Scarman Report betrays reservations about 'advantaging ethnic minorities'. It is all the more strange therefore that the academic world seems to have remained immune to the change of perception and hence the change of heart. True, positive discrimination was increasingly discussed in the context of racial and gender disadvantage, and some noted its low public acceptability (see, for example, Young and Connelly 1981, Bindman and Carrier 1983).[14] But the old Fabian view of positive discrimination as concentrating resources on the most needy within a context of universalism and without stigma prevailed (see, for example, T. Blackstone 1980, Brown and Madge 1982, Mortimore and T. Blackstone 1982, Foster 1983). Whilst it is clear that those on the right of the political spectrum were readier and quicker to oppose the 'unfairness' of positive discrimination, and that academic social policy analysts are not on the whole noted for right-wing views, this does not explain why the very real issues raised by a changing perception of positive discrimination from a 'needs' to an ethnic or gender base have hardly appeared on the academic agenda.

Conclusion

Positive discrimination has for too long been a chimera in the language of social policy in Britain. It has done sterling service in the armoury of rhetoric; at once a valuable new weapon for universalists, and a club with which to beat the heads of those who would promote the interests of ethnic minorities over those of 'fair-minded Englishmen'; a banner of hope and a weapon of abuse. Whatever it is, we liked it in the 1960s and we dislike it now. But it has remained a phrase without substance. This is in marked contrast to the situation in the USA, where the equivalent notions of affirmative action and reverse discrimination have generated a vast literature and a body of moral debate that has added much to our ideas about distributive justice.

This chapter has examined the term 'positive discrimination' (one hesitates to use the word 'concept') as it has been used in Britain since the late 1960s. It has attempted to show that because no clear *idea* of positive discrimination has emerged much of the debate about it has been futile. We have indicated what really does constitute 'positive discrimination' if the term is to mean anything at all; and in the light of this we have been able to see that much of the debate has not in fact been about positive discrimination. For if positive discrimination is not to constitute a distinctly different practice from selectivity and allocation according to need using need criteria, then it is a meaningless phrase.

The contention of this book is, however, that there is a policy practice to which the term 'positive discrimination' can be applied and as such it is a distinct practice. What makes it distinct is also what makes it morally interesting and contentious. Indeed the moral issues raised by positive discrimination are reflected in the intuitive aversion to it in today's common orthodoxy, so that even though we are not sure what it is, we know we don't like it. A clear conception of positive discrimination has perhaps not yet emerged in Britain, but the growing aversion to it does reflect an increasing awareness of its particularity.

From the confusion of usage we can extract a picture of the history of positive discrimination in Britain. When first introduced, it was almost universally misunderstood. It was acceptable to all shades of political opinion precisely because it was misconstrued as a means of directing welfare resources more accurately at those in need without stigmatizing them. It was selectivity without stigma. What made it attractive to Fabian socialists also made it acceptable to Conservatives – that is, its relative *unselectiveness*. It did not stigmatize because its beneficiaries could not easily be identified, and it did not affront English 'fair play' for just the same reason. It could achieve this remarkable feat only because in practice the beneficiaries were to be identified by the area in which they lived. Positive discrimination was area discrimination, and the benefits received were to be collective goods.

It was when criteria other than areas were introduced (such as ethnicity and sex) that the moral implications of positive discrimination became more apparent and the universal acceptance of it began to disintegrate. Giving money for community centres in inner-city areas was one thing; giving benefits and preferential treatment to blacks and women was another. And so, with growing awareness of the particularity of positive discrimination, came an increasing opposition to it. Nevertheless even today much of the opposition to positive discrimination is based on misconceptions of what it is and why we might wish to pursue it.

We shall leave the British scene at this stage, returning to it later in the book. Having in the meantime examined the moral issues surrounding positive discrimination, we shall be better placed to assess how much of what is currently called positive discrimination and positive action in Britain can correctly so be called, and, more importantly, whether a case can be made in justice for the use (and extended use) of positive discrimination in Britain. We now turn our attention to the concept itself. In order to establish exactly what positive discrimination is and what distinguishes it from other distributive processes, we must set it in the context of social justice. This is the burden of Chapter 3.

Chapter 3

Positive discrimination and social justice

There has been a bewildering array of claimed justifications of and reasons for positive discrimination in Britain and the United States. Some are claims to justice, some to consequentialism, and others more particularly to utility. Because such claims are numerous and varied, and since much of the debate about positive discrimination in Britain and the USA concerns its 'rightness' or justifiability, the next few chapters subject the practice to critical moral thinking.[1] The value of this – apart, that is, from the obligation to subject all action, particularly public policy, to the test of morality – is twofold. Firstly, it will enable us to see better the nature of positive discrimination and what distinguishes it from, say, action in pursuit of the needs principle. The reasons why positive discrimination has been characterized in the way it has in Chapter 2 become clearer when the template of basic principles of distributive justice is imposed upon it. Secondly, positive discrimination has not been more than sketchily analysed in moral terms in Britain; and even though it has generated a vast literature in the USA, and has been the focus of much legal action, there has probably been no systematic critique of positive discrimination in moral terms in that country either. Such an analysis needs to make clear the moral standing of the arguments for and against positive discrimination, identify where these are purely expedient – and hence non-moral – and begin to tabulate which claims are apodictic or deontic in nature (i.e. founded on morality) and which are utilitarian or more generally consequentialist. Not until this is done and the nature of the claims for positive discrimination are recognized for what they are can we begin to weigh the claims of justice against those of utility. Only then in our pursuit of positive discrimination can we see if utility will grant what liberal justice appears to deny us.

We need to know whether positive discrimination is a just practice. But justice is not the whole of morality. Our treatment therefore will fall into two broad categories reflecting the division between deontic and teleologic ethics – the ethics of duty and the ethics of ends. This is not the place to discuss the value of this dichotomy but it is necessary to say why it is used here, how it is used, and how it helps to structure the argument. In general terms, I follow Frankena's characterization of the deontic and the teleologic: deontic principles being those concerned with duties, obligations, and the rightness of action or prescriptions to action in itself (Frankena 1963). Teleologic principles, a sub-type of consequentialist principles,[2] are those that in valuing the rightness of action take cognizance of the outcome or the net balance of 'good' and 'bad' results. Teleology in this sense is a broader category than utilitarianism. Utilitarianism is teleologic (and consequentialist) but not all consequentialism is utility maximizing (Mackie 1977: 149–57, Finnis 1983: 83). The arguments for and against elevating outcomes as the primary determinant of the rightness of action are familiar (Frankena 1963, Melden 1977, Hare 1978, Brandt 1979, Finnis 1983); all ethical systems comprise some admixture of the ethics of duty and of ends. Indeed, as Rawls makes clear in his definition of deontic principles as 'non-teleologic' ones rather than ones that take *no* account of consequences, to do the latter would be 'irrational, crazy' (Rawls 1972: 30). Any set of institution-based *apodictic* rules such as one that included 'promises ought to be kept' could be accepted by a rule utilitarian as necessary to the maintenance of a valuable or necessary institution – in this case the institution of promise-keeping. But despite the overlaps and the moral insufficiency of either system as a complete ethic, the division into deontic and teleologic is useful for our present purposes.

Many defenders of affirmative action in the United States have 'justified' it in utilitarian or consequentialist terms (Thalberg 1973–74, Glazer 1975, Dworkin 1977b, 1978, Goldman 1977, Nagel 1977, Gross 1978). Others, in seeing it as a form of restitution for past harm, treat it as a requirement of justice (Beauchamp 1977, Day 1981). Criticism in Britain, as we saw in Chapter 2, is a mixture of justice (unfair) and utility (white backlash) arguments. We need to be aware therefore of both 'duty-regarding' and 'consequence-regarding' claims. An important part of the moral critique of positive discrimination must consist in its subjection to tests of justice. Now I treat justice in this regard as a thoroughly deontic principle not easily open to the calculus of consequences. But whether or not positive discrimination is a 'just' practice cannot be the end of the matter since, as I have noted, much of its defence ignores questions of justice. We must also consider the calculus of consequences. I do not wish to maintain that justice can never be overridden by utility – such would be a foolish assertion – but I *do* wish to maintain that prima facie what justice requires should take precedence over the calculus of consequences or the balance of utility. (For a contrary view, see Ake 1975: 71 ff.) Where the requirements of justice coincide with what utility would dictate, that is a happy alliance; but where they do not, there must be very good reasons for preferring the latter over the former.[3] It is for this reason that I wish to maintain the importance of the distinction between deontic and teleologic ethics in a discussion of positive discrimination. Lest it be thought overly naïve to hold to this dichotomy, it ought to be said that I am aware of the arguments like those of Finnis that 'it fails to accommodate Platonic, Aristotelian, Thomistic, and any other substantially reasonable ethics' (Finnis 1983: 84). None the less, for the reasons given above, it is of analytical value to the task in hand. Thus Chapters 3 to 7 consider positive discrimination in the context of justice and its requirements, while the consequentialist arguments for it are dealt with in Chapter 8.

The language of moral thought does not always adequately reflect the distinction between arguments for the rightness of action (in this case positive discrimination) that derive from the teleological/deontological dichotomy, and the incongruence of 'the just' and 'the moral'. The verb 'to justify' is particularly vexatious. Often one comes across statements to the effect that positive discrimination (or affirmative action or reverse discrimination) is 'justified on grounds of utility'. This is very different from saying that positive discrimination is justified according to some set of principles of justice. What is meant in the first case is that positive discrimination is 'on balance the right thing to do given the balance of outcomes'; this is not at all the same as saying that it is right because it is just or because justice requires it. If utility arguments were consistently referred to as 'right-making' and justice arguments as 'just-making' or 'justifying' there would be no difficulty. But they are not, hence the potential for confusion. Frankena has provided a useful if inelegant answer to this particular problem by using 'justifying' to refer to (generally) right-making considerations and 'justicizing' to refer to specifically just-making considerations. Just-making or justicizing considerations are but one species of right-making or justifying considerations (Frankena 1962: 5, 25). Where it is necessary to make a clear distinction, I shall follow Frankena's usage.

Social justice consists in a set of principles to guide the allocation of burdens and benefits in a consistent way when they are not distributed according to other processes such as the market, bequests, gifts, charity, or lottery. Its use is confined not entirely, but mainly, to the allocation of social goods in the public sector of welfare. But not all public goods are allocated according to principles that could be said to be principles of justice (public transportation systems are an obvious example). None the less, enough of our lives is affected by considerations of social justice to make it of fundamental importance. Positive discrimination is one process by which burdens and benefits (albeit a small proportion) including public resources and places in schools, universities, and employments are distributed. It is a process that at least prima facie looks as though it uses different allocational criteria from those we are used to (and accept) in the public sector, which we take to characterize the principles of social justice. Is positive discrimination just? Clearly, justice features prominently in our concern about it. We cannot think about positive discrimination without thinking about justice.

1 What sort of justice?

It matters what sort of justice we have in mind and what sort is most relevant when we analyse positive discrimination. We shall have to say a word about this without undertaking an exegesis of classifications of it.

The most common distinction that is made between types of justice is the oldest – the Aristotelian division between distributive and corrective justice in *The Nicomachean Ethics* (Aristotle 1925: 110–17). This appears in a variety of guises such as conservative and reformative justice (Raphael 1976), conservative and ideal justice (D. Miller 1976), and comparative and non-comparative justice (Feinberg 1973). The essential difference common to all these formulations is that distributive justice is proportional (in the sense that what is distributed is in proportion to the degree of that quality which justified its distribution and comparable as between recipients), whereas corrective justice is not. What is distributed in corrective justice is dictated by the degree of harm that has to be corrected. The harm-doer must recompense to the extent that his actions have deprived the victim so that the status quo ante is re-established. The amount of benefit in corrective justice is therefore determined (in the pure Aristotelian form) by this consideration alone and not by any reference to other harm-doers or sufferers. In distributive justice, on the other hand, beneficiaries are to receive an amount proportional to the quantity they possess of that factor which justifies the benefit. People with the same quantity of the relevant factor (say, need or merit) should receive equal amounts of the benefit. In this sense, distributive justice is comparative (but see Sidorsky 1983).

Social justice is usually (though not invariably) equated with Aristotelian distributive justice (Feinberg 1973: 98). Corrective justice on the other hand is more often seen to fall in the province of conservative or legal justice and to be concerned with the guaranteeing of rights. The most common justicization of positive discrimination in the United States (though not in Britain) is on grounds of reparation, whether or not such a claim is supported (Bayles 1973b, Beauchamp 1977, W. T. Blackstone 1977). Blackstone is explicit on this point, although he thinks the balance of arguments is against such a policy, in arguing the case for and against reverse discrimination in terms of compensatory justice; this, he maintains, corresponds closely with Aristotle's corrective justice. By contrast, the main plank of the support for positive discrimination in Britain is, we saw in Chapter 2, a claim to 'needs' or 'special needs'. If need is a component of justice then it must be of distributive or 'social' justice. It would seem therefore that our analysis of positive discrimination must be carried forward on two fronts – the one in terms of compensatory or restitutive justice and the other on the different grounds of distributive justice. This makes the task inordinately complex (and possibly unnecessarily so) and I want if possible to avoid it. I believe there are reasonable grounds for doing so, and these must be explained.

One possible solution to the problem of two separate kinds of justice-consideration is to subsume one within the other. R. M. Hare claims that this can be done, and further maintains that it is what Rawls achieved (Hare 1978: 119 ff.). He asks whether distributive and retributive justice are reducible to a single sort of justice and goes on: 'Rawls . . . thinks they are, and so do I' (Hare 1978: 119). Rawls, he argues, successfully reduces all justice to distributive justice by means of the procedural vehicle of 'justice as fairness' whereunder impartiality is secured by the 'veil of ignorance' device. The fairness of course inheres in the ability of participants in the original position to arrive at principles of justice in a just way ('just principles, justly arrived at'). Behind the veil of ignorance, principles of justice cannot be tailored to suit individual interests, and impartiality is secured. It is this impartiality, claims Hare, that unites distributive and corrective justice:

> 'Therefore, the principles which govern *both* the distribution of wealth and power and other good things *and* the assignment of rewards and penalties ... will be impartial as between individuals and in this sense just. In this way Rawls in effect reduces the justice of acts of retribution to justice in distributing, between the affected parties, the good and bad effects of a system of retributions, and reduces this distributive justice in turn to the adoption of a just procedure for selecting the system of retributions to be used.'
>
> (Hare 1978: 119–20)

But in claiming that retributive and distributive can thus successfully be reduced to distributive justice, I think Hare makes the purely procedural notion of impartiality bear far more weight than it can stand or was meant to bear in Rawls's account. Impartiality is a minimal requirement of justice-making and implementation but it does not in itself (even as 'pure procedural justice') secure the congruence of distributive and retributive principles. Retributive justice has a moral basis: punishment for wrongdoing and restitution for those harmed by the wrongdoing. But justice-as-fairness rejects any notion of moral desert: 'There is a tendency for common sense to support that income and wealth, and the good things in life generally, should be distributed according to moral desert ... justice as fairness rejects this conception' (Rawls 1972: 310). The difference principle for the allocation of goods and resources has nothing to do with moral desert; rewards and punishment on the other hand most certainly do. The principles involved are quite different categories. Thus Rawls again: 'To think of distributive and retributive justice as converses of one another is completely misleading and suggests a moral basis of distributive shares where none exists' (Rawls 1972: 315). There can be no uniting of (Rawlsian) distributive justice and retributive justice on the grounds that Hare claims.

Rawlsian principles however do not exhaust the possibilities of distributive justice, and if Hare wanted a means of uniting distributive and retributive justice he might have done better to look elsewhere. The distinction that Rawls makes between a moral-desert basis for corrective justice and the non-moral basis of his own principles of distributive justice is not a universal one. Not all systems of distributive justice eschew moral desert as a distributive principle; indeed 'merit' in its various forms is often taken to be the cardinal principle for allocating benefits and positions. So the moral-desert divide that we find in Rawls need not worry us at this stage (although it will later) and need not necessarily constitute an inseparable barrier between the two kinds of justice. Both corrective and distributive justice may use moral desert as a relevant principle. This is of some help but it does not resolve the difference between the proportionality of distributive justice and the non-proportionality (Aristotle refers to 'arithmetic progression') of corrective justice. However, so far as compensatory reverse discrimination is concerned, even this distinction may be purely theoretical, as I demonstrate below.

The approach I wish to adopt to avoid analysis on two fronts is to argue that, as far as positive discrimination is concerned (but *not* for other areas of compensation or restitution), an Aristotelian notion of corrective justice is not the most appropriate or useful. The argument here is based in part on Blackstone's observation that the sense of compensatory justice as applied to reverse discrimination differs in two respects from Aristotelian corrective justice: '(1) It involves compensation between rather indeterminate classes of persons as opposed to compensatory actions between individuals. (2) It does *not* require that wrongful injury has been committed by the party obligated to pay the compensation' (W. T. Blackstone 1977: 54). There is yet another and I believe more important difference that Blackstone does not enumerate. It is this. There is no possibility in the case of restitution for past harm to groups (such as blacks and women) that the restitution to be paid can equal (in quantity or kind) the value of the harm that was (and is) done in such a way as to restore the status quo ante which is the distinguishing feature of Aristotelian corrective justice.[4] The requirement of corrective justice that differentiates it from distributive justice cannot be fulfilled in the case of reverse discrimination for groups. Certainly, *some* recompense can and must be made, but *what* this recompense is cannot be determined *now* by the canons of corrective justice.

Taken together, these three major differences between the present circumstances of compensation and Aristotelian corrective justice seriously flaw the useful application of the latter in an analysis of positive discrimination. The tenets of corrective justice cannot usefully prescribe what ought to be done now in matters of positive discrimination. But can distributive justice help? From earlier remarks it would seem not, but there is a way I think that *basic* principles of distributive justice can usefully illuminate some aspects of compensatory positive discrimination. Our present concern is to elucidate the characterization of positive discrimination that was given in Chapter 2, to identify its defining and peculiar features, and then to see whether and in what forms it might be justicized and whether justice would require it. The first part at least of this task – an examination of the peculiarizing features of positive discrimination – can I think be achieved for both 'distributive' positive discrimination and compensatory positive discrimination by means of a distributive principle: that of 'like treatment'.[5] How far this will enable us to fulfil the other parts of our task in respect of compensatory positive discrimination remains to be seen. In using a simple principle of distributive justice to elucidate some aspects of compensatory positive discrimination, no violence is intended – nor I think committed – to the fundamental distinction that some people would wish to make between the moral foundations of distributive and compensatory justice, which were noted above.

For the purposes of the present analysis we shall concentrate on distributive justice, or what is more commonly referred to as social justice. There are circumstances in which these two terms require to be distinguished (Lucas 1980: 163), but the present ones are not such. If the terms appear synonymous in the following accounts, this does not matter. 'Fairness' presents a slightly different problem. In everyday use it means broadly the same as social or distributive justice, and some philosophers use it in this way (for example, Raphael 1976: 172). Social justice and fairness do not mean the same thing, however; in common parlance 'fairness' is applied to *any* rule-governed procedures, some of which have nothing to do with justice. The distribution of burdens and benefits that results after a game of poker is fair (provided no one has cheated), but justice has nothing to do with it, (Barry 1967b: 193).

2 Social justice and the equality principle

There are advantages for our present purpose in taking as our critical model a very general formulation of social justice rather than any specific theory such as that of Rawls (1972) or Ackerman (1980) or Nozick (1974), simply because to take the latter course would tie our critique of positive discrimination to one particular formula. However, it must be acknowledged that the following analysis gives greater weight to distributive issues than to questions of rights, although these are dealt with within a distributive framework. This is largely a question of what weight to give to rights in a formulation of justice, and the approach adopted is one that does not elevate rights to primacy of importance (as would, for example, a Nozickian approach).

The basic formulation of social or distributive justice is the Justinian injunction to 'render to each man his due' or *suum cuique tribuere* (Sidgwick 1930, Frankena 1962, Von Leyden 1963, Honoré 1968, Lucas 1980). This is a purely formal statement, a corollary of which is the Aristotelian equality principle (see D. Miller 1976) of 'treat like cases alike and unalike cases differently'.[6] This oft-cited principle (for example, Benn and Peters 1959, Hart 1961, Feinberg 1973, Woozley 1973) is, like *suum cuique*, a purely formal principle that in itself yields very little guidance,[7] and to elevate it beyond the realm of tautology requires fleshing it out with what Feinberg calls material principles. Even at its most basic, however, it has led to some misconceptions, the most frequent and important of which arises from its sometimes being called the principle of equal treatment. The equality principle does not require, as Honoré for example has argued, that all men have a claim to an *equal share* of all advantages; it *does* imply that all have a claim to equal consideration. This is the distinction that Dworkin makes in his arguments against De Funis's claim against the University of Washington Law School. De Funis, argues Dworkin, did not have a claim to *equal treatment*; he did have a claim to *treatment as an equal* (Dworkin 1977a: 227). The distinction necessarily follows from the proportionality inherent in the Aristotelian principle; people should not have equal shares, but shares in proportion to particular qualities that would reflect their being equals. To treat people *as equals* requires us to recognize the inequalities between them and distribute accordingly. The needy should get *more* than the wealthy; they should not be treated equally (see Dworkin 1983, Narveson 1983). This consideration lies at the heart of arguments for and against positive discrimination.

To be any use, then, the equality principle must be filled out with a set of *material* principles that identify what qualities or actions justify us in treating people equally or unequally. As Feinberg (1973: 102) points out, despite its name there is no *presumption* of equality in the equality principle. Which of the multitude of differences between people justify us in treating them differently, and which similarities justify similar treatment? Immediate intuitive candidates come to mind; differences in skin colour, hair pigmentation, height, or IQ, do not warrant different treatment in the allocation of burdens and benefits. Nor do similarities in these characteristics alone justify equal allocations. On the other hand, we may feel justified in giving different allocations to people with different needs, handicaps, degrees of merit, or efforts undertaken. But already we are in difficulties. We do not want to treat IQ as justifying different treatment – but clearly we use it or variations of it all the time and without a qualm (or much of one). Places in higher education must count as an important benefit in technological and professionalized societies, and a relatively high IQ is a crucial qualification for the receipt of that benefit. Few people would argue that anyone, whatever their IQ, should have a place in a university; and even open-entry systems, as in some colleges in the USA, soon deprive the less able of the benefit by expelling them). The importance of relevant differences to the issue of positive discrimination needs no spelling out.

There have been several attempts at producing a principle that will distinguish relevant from irrelevant differences in a consistent fashion. Since a specification of what have sometimes been called *morally* relevant differences is central to our discussion of positive discrimination it is worth looking at the form such attempts take. Feinberg's 'fair opportunity test' is perhaps the best example; it also illustrates the inadequacies of such attempts:

> 'Let us consider why we all agree . . . in rejecting the view that differences in race, sex, IQ or social "rank" are the grounds of just differences in wealth or income. People cannot by their own voluntary choices determine what skin colour, sex or IQ they shall have . . . . To make such properties the basis of discrimination between

individuals in the distribution of social benefits would be "to treat people differently in ways that profoundly affect their lives because of differences for which they have no responsibility". Differences in a given respect are *relevant* for the aims of distributive justice, then, only if they are differences for which their possessors can be held responsible; properties can be the grounds of just discrimination between persons only if those persons had a *fair opportunity* to acquire or avoid them.'

(Feinberg 1973: 108, emphasis in original)

Feinberg then goes on to list five possible candidates as morally relevant differences that can be tested against the fair opportunity criterion: perfect equality, need, merit and achievement, contribution, and effort. We shall not pursue Feinberg's analysis of these five candidates here, but more briefly expose the fair opportunity test (which prima facie looks like a useful distinction) to some of our 'intuitive' expectations of a just distribution. Clearly, the test works for the sort of example Feinberg cites; we are happy to rule out (at least as a first-case argument) race, sex, and social rank as relevant differences. But one of the most common reasons (in social policy the main reason) why we might want to differentiate between people in the distribution of burdens and benefits is need. How does this fare against the test? Are we to meet only need for which its 'possessors can be held responsible'?[8] Intuition – and partly also practice – dictates the reverse; the notion of the deserving and undeserving poor is alive and well. And what of the handicapped, or at least the congenitally handicapped? They are not responsible for their need, nor have they had a 'fair opportunity to acquire or avoid' it. But we wish to, and do, treat them differently from the non-handicapped by a variety of grants and tax concessions. IQ does not pass the fair opportunity test, but as we have seen, we do not feel we have done great violence to justice when we benefit the more intelligent (in a number of ways). When pitted against intuition and practice, the fair opportunity test fails, and I do not think that in order to save it we would wish to abandon what we think is right and what we practise.[9] (It might be argued that helping the needy and the handicapped is an act of beneficence and charity and has nothing to do with justice; something of the fair opportunity test could be salvaged in this way. But although justice is but one moral virtue, I think it *is* the one to which the needy can claim.)

Other attempts to find a criterion for specifying relevant differences fare worse. Thurow (1979) in the particular context of redistribution to whole groups suggests, but subsequently rejects, the criterion of mobility. If it were possible for individuals to leave or join a group easily, then, suggests Thurow, members cannot claim to be unfairly treated in the distribution of burdens and benefits (Thurow 1979: 32). We need not dwell on the evident disadvantages of such a criterion. Nor need we delay over the only other attempt we shall mention, that by Gross. He identifies three 'traits', discrimination against which would or could be deserved: '(1) could be voluntarily eliminated or is incompetent at the activity in question; (2) *truly* offensive or morally negative; (3) relevant to the claim' (Gross 1978: 13–14). These criteria serve more to press Gross's strong objections to reverse discrimination than to provide a workable criterion of relevance.

The examples given here serve to demonstrate the difficulty of finding a criterion for relevance that will produce a list of material principles which, in Rawls's term, when pitted against intuition will settle into a 'reflective equilibrium'. Before proceeding to the next stage of our analysis, it is worth restating our problem. Positive discrimination (in its wide sense) is *par excellence* a way of treating people, as individuals or groups, differently in the allocation of burdens and benefits. There is a multiplicity of differences between people, only some of which justicize treating them differently. Are the beneficiaries of positive discrimination people who as individuals or groups are characterized by differences that we would count as justicizing receipt of those benefits (the benefits – of whatever kind – constituting the different treatment)?

We thus still need to know what counts as relevant differences before we can tell whether the beneficiaries of positive discrimination are among them or not. We have failed to find a criterion of relevance and must now look to other methods. What is required in establishing the grounds for different treatment involves two stages:

- a specification of those qualities, characteristics, or actions of people, differences on which will justicize different treatment;
- the identification of the actual differences (and similarities) in proportion to which the possessors of those qualities, characteristics, or actions may be benefited or disbenefited.

This two-stage process concerns those differences that might constitute *justicizing* criteria, and there is a second, separate but parallel two-stage process that will identify *justifying* criteria, but we shall for the moment concentrate on just-making differences and return later to right-making ones.

It is axiomatic that relevant differences are not derivable from *suum cuique* or from the equality principle itself, since it is a purely formal statement about comparabilities; it has no substance. The equality principle would be satisfied if we gave the same amount to everyone with the same quantity of a relevant characteristic (let us suppose for the moment 'need'), even if this amount were nothing. We have treated relevantly like cases similarly, and the formal requirement is satisfied. And even when, or if, we have identified relevant characteristics (again let us suppose 'need'), we still require to know what *ought* to be done about it. But it may of course turn out that answering the second question *ipso facto* answers the first. That is, if we can say (for whatever reason) that need *ought* to be met, *that* may be the reason why we count it as a justiciable characteristic or difference. In fact, I am inclined to think that this *is* the way in which relevant differences might be identified, but in order to advance the argument I wish for the moment to circumvent this issue and proceed to particulars. What characteristics, qualities, or actions have *in practice* been adduced as relevant differences?

Table 1 contains the grounds suggested by a number of writers that would allow departure from a strict principle of non-discrimination or constitute relevant differences allowing different treatment. The sum total of suggestions is bewilderingly long and for our purposes needs to be whittled down. To this end a number of caveats require to be entered. Firstly, the lists include justifying (right-making) as well as justicizing grounds. Secondly, there is frequent confusion between 'desert' and 'merit' and the specificity with which the term 'desert' is used. Thirdly, there is occasional confusion between material principles (relevant differences) and the formal injunction of the equality principle itself. Fourthly, authors differ on which if any principle is of primary importance, and if one is selected as being so, how its primacy is to be ensured in actual distributions. Fifthly, there is relatively little guidance about how conflicts between different or alternative principles are to be resolved in practice.

Our present purpose will not be served by a detailed analysis of these lists, but several points of relevance to the arguments about positive discrimination do emerge in the light of the caveats above. Although we have not yet specified a clear distinction

Table 1 Suggested grounds for 'rightful' discrimination between individuals

Benn and Peters (1959)	*Feinberg (1973)*	*Frankena (1962)*	*Honoré (1968)*	*Lucas (1972, 1980)*	*D. Miller (1976)*
desert	perfect equality	capacities	special relations	desert (as contribution)	rights
need	need	needs	rule conformity	merit	needs
property ownership (rights)	★merit and achievement	contribution	desert	need	★contribution
	★contribution or due return	desert or merit	need	entitlement	★effort
	★effort or labour		choice	status	★compensation
	(★all sub-categories of desert)				(★all sub-categories of desert)

Perelman (1963)	*Rescher (1966)*	*Ross (1974)*	*Vlastos (1962)*	*Von Leyden (1963)*
equality	equality	merit	need	need or hardship
merits	need	performance	worth	desert or merit
works	ability	need	merit	natural capacity or ability
needs	merit	ability	work	public welfare
rank	achievement	rank	agreements	
entitlement	effort	station		
	sacrifices	actual productive contribution		
	common good			
	scarcity of skill			

between just-making and right-making principles, it is clear that very different kinds of grounds for different treatment appear in Table 1. Thus some grounds are apodictic (needs 'ought' to be met; desert 'ought' to be rewarded) whilst others can make their appearance only on consequential arguments (public welfare, common good, etc.). Secondly, whilst some writers treat desert and merit as synonymous (Frankena, Honoré, Von Leyden), others distinguish between the two (Lucas) or treat desert as a broader category (Feinberg, Miller), or require that merit be confined to actions, or to qualities that must have been acquired (Vlastos). It does seem important that some distinction be made between qualities for which the possessors are not responsible (we do not 'deserve' our IQ, manual dexterity, or our 'bent for numbers') and those qualities that are acquired by dint of hard effort (the skills of the surgeon or the concert violinist) and deserving actions (bravery, hard work, effort, etc.). Following Lucas (1980), the use of 'merit' to refer to qualities an individual may possess, and 'desert' for actions, effort, and sacrifices, seems a useful distinction and will be followed here. Thirdly, it is more correct to treat 'equality' (Perelman, Rescher), 'perfect equality' (Feinberg), and 'rule conformity' (Honoré) as aspects of the formal equal treatment principle rather than as examples of *material* principles required to flesh it out. These can be ruled out therefore in our search for relevant differences. Concerning our fourth caveat, only two of the material principles are singled out by authors as of primary importance. 'Need' is specified as the first principle by Frankena, Vlastos, Honoré, and Feinberg, and 'desert' (as distinct from merit) by Lucas. The fifth caveat takes us into ground that is beyond the scope of the present discussion and will not be discussed further.[9]

The range of material principles contained in the lists can, with the aid of some suppositions and interpretations of intent from the texts that contain them (which space does not allow us to elaborate), be narrowed down to six general principles as follows:

- need: this is unequivocal and mentioned by all eleven writers;
- desert: if 'contribution', 'desert', 'work', 'effort', 'achievements', and 'compensation'/sacrifices' are counted as reflections or sub-categories of desert (as defined above), this principle is mentioned by all eleven contributors;[10]

- merit: as including 'capacities', 'merit', 'worth', and 'abilities' is mentioned by eight contributors;
- rights: as including 'rights', 'entitlements', 'agreements', and 'choice' (i.e. the right to choose to benefit or not) is mentioned by six contributors;
- position: as including 'special relations', 'status', 'rank', and 'station' is mentioned by four contributors;
- consequential or utilitarian reasons: as including 'common good', 'public welfare', and 'skill scarcity' is mentioned by three contributors.

Four further entries under 'equality' and 'rule conformity' are, as explained above, not material principles.

This represents a rough and ready classification, doing no great violence to reason or to the intent of the authors. No claim is made about this exercise other than to suggest that, given a little judicious collapsing of categories, there is, among these social philosphers, a degree of consensus over relevant material principles and that the prime candidates on this basis are need, desert, merit, rights, and more tentatively, position and consequential arguments. Need was counted as the primary principle by four writers, and desert by one.

There is one considerable drawback to such a crude counting exercise (though I believe the exercise does serve its purpose), which since it is of consequence to our subsequent argument, ought to be mentioned here. It was noted earlier that the lists evinced a degree of ambiguity on the part of some writers about whether the principles being adduced were right-making or more specifically just-making. Intent varies; some lists are confined to the latter, some include both. However, because a number of the authors cited were looking more specifically for *justicizing* grounds for different treatment, this has resulted in an under-emphasis in the lists, and in the subsequent collapsed categories, of consequentialist or utilitarian grounds, *compared with the frequency with which such grounds are in practice adduced* in respect of particular cases of different treatment, of which positive discrimination is a prime example.

2.1 *The moral foundations of material principles*

In an attempt to avoid an *ab initio* derivation of material principle (given that they are not derivable from the equality principle itself), I have adopted the ploy of seeing what social philosophers themselves have suggested. This of course is not only less than satisfactory, it is also philosophically bad form. However, this is ground better left to philosophers, and I shall stop short by simply mentioning what seem to me to be the three most common ways in which material principles such as need and rights are ultimately 'justified'. The first is by appeal to the Kantian categorical imperatives (indeed, the whole of deontic philosophy is sometimes equated with the Kantian ethic). Thus, for example, Raphael, in discussing what he takes to be the two main elements in distributive justice (equality of opportunity and the satisfaction of basic needs), argues: 'We think these two things are due to individuals as such, as being ends-in-themselves' (Raphael 1955: 93–4). And Blackstone, in defending 'need' and 'capacity' (by which he does not mean merit) as the two main relevant criteria, argues:

> 'Interpreted along these lines as primarily emphasising criteria of need and the capacity to achieve the minimally good life, the equality claim seems to amount to the principle of the equal intrinsic dignity or value of the individual, emphasised by Kant and others.'
>
> (W. T. Blackstone 1967: 242)

Similar arguments have been put by Vlastos (1962) and Frankena (1963) among others. Appeal to the imperatives of 'act so as to treat human beings always as ends and never merely as means' and 'act as if you were a member of a realm of ends' is fairly common while at the same time requiring a good deal of elaboration to limit its inadequacies.[11]

A second sort of appeal is that to intuition; that is, that the most likely candidates as material principles are those that would satisfy our intuitive feelings about justice. Again, this is not the place to enter an argument about intuitionism but simply to note its use as a foundation for establishing principles. For example, Honoré, in identifying his list of material principles, is 'guided by ordinary usage'; and Downie and Telfer (1976) argue that the idea of equality of treatment 'which ought not to be overridden by any degree of social utility' derives from 'ordinary moral judgements'.[12]

The third way in which principles could be established is by the mechanism of the contract, as in Rawls's work. It may be argued that this is really a form of 'constrained intuitionism' and, like intuitionism itself, tells us only what contractors behind a veil of ignorance (or East Coast or Hampstead liberals who had thought themselves into that condition) might in fact agree to. It is not, unlike Kantian imperatives, an ultimate foundation for just principles but a device for producing agreement. However, given the sense of desperation with which appeal to the Kantian ethic is sometimes made, perhaps this is the best that can be hoped for.

The Kantian ethic, intuitionism, and contract do not exhaust the bases upon which the justice of material principles is founded (a full account would, for example, require a discussion of the foundation of rights); but they are frequent grounds, and serve for present purposes to illustrate the sort of argument that might be required to underpin and give substance to the purely formal and comparative equality principle.

Whatever the basis of the claim for any particular material principle, there is, as has been shown, a degree of consensus over what such principles might be – although with a good deal of ambiguity of usage and intent. There may be others, but need, desert, merit, rights, position, and utility seem to constitute the main general types of principle, and such a list would be unlikely to incur much disagreement. I shall take these therefore as being the main material principles of the formal equality principle. Thus, when we say that 'like cases should be treated alike and unalike cases differently', the relevant likenesses and differences are to be found in this list. Now, given that the equality principle is exceptive rather than presumptive (see page 43), what it requires when fleshed out by these material principles is that we not only treat people with similar needs in the same way but also treat differently those with different needs (hence 'treatment as equals' rather than 'equal treatment'). Similarly, we should take note of people's differing deserts (efforts, sacrifices, etc.) in the allocation of social goods and benefits. Allocation should also take account of merits, and people's rights should be respected in distributions. Again, it is right or fair, though it may not be just, that relatives and friends rather than strangers benefit from gifts we might bestow and that the common good or welfare be taken into account in according benefits and burdens. All these things (and possibly some but doubtfully many others) justify us (and some justicize us) in treating people differently. These then are the dimensions, differences that justify different treatment; they constitute the first part of the two-stage specification we noted above (see page 45). We can reasonably say that, *taken as a group*, these material principles constitute both a necessary and a sufficient specification of the rightness or justice of actions in the allocation of burdens and benefits.

The second part of the specification – determining what kinds of difference on these domains call forth what *kinds* of different treatment – is more problematic and will vary as between material principles. It cannot, I think, be dealt with in isolation from the distinction between justicizing and justifying principles.

2.2 Justicizing and justifying material principles

It was noted earlier that the two-stage process for identifying relevant differences or material principles was one that required application twice over: once in search of justicizing principles, secondly for justifying ones. The specification of material principles undertaken above has in effect collapsed these two applications and produced a list that contains a mixture of both kinds of principle. Before we can apply this analysis to positive discrimination they must be sorted out.

It is clear that the six material principles do not all carry the same moral status. When we say that distributions *ought* to take account of people's needs, this is different to saying that people's relationships (or positions) one to another are relevant to distributions. In the latter case they are clearly relevant to *some* distributions but not to others. Position is a relevant criterion in the bestowal of gifts or bequests; it is not so in the allocation of supplementary benefit or jobs or housing. IQ (as in item of merit) is relevant in the granting of scholarships but not of housing benefit or rate rebates. Can we say that need, desert, or rights are *never* irrelevant? It all depends on what you mean by relevance, and this, I think, has caused some confusions in some of the United States debate on positive discrimination. Blackstone, for example, in his essay on reverse discrimination and compensatory justice, argues that 'Characteristics or conditions which are *relevant* to the differential treatment of persons or groups may hold in one context but not in other' (W. T. Blackstone 1977: 60, emphasis in original). In an earlier essay the same author makes the distinction between *prescriptive* and *descriptive* judgements of relevance, where the latter refer to factual questions about whether a particular characteristic is relevant to a particular goal, and the former to differences over goals – whether need ought to take precedence over merit, for example. What Blackstone is presumably arguing, if we take these two pieces together, is that while there will be normative judgements about desirable goals, the *relevance* of material principles will always be dependent on the context of their application – the nature of the burden or benefit being allocated and the circumstances of the allocation. This, I believe, is wrong. The material principles of need, desert, and rights are *always* relevant to justice irrespective of circumstances. It cannot be *unjust* to allocate any burden or benefit according to (some combination of) need, desert, and rights (although it may be unwise and even 'unfair' to do so given other goals than absolute justice, and hence *fiat justitia, ruat caelum*). It *is unjust* on the other hand to allocate *some* burdens and benefits solely on the grounds of merit, position, and utility (or some combination of them); they alone can never justicize any allocation (although to allocate on these grounds may be the 'right' thing to do in some circumstances).

The relevance of need, desert, and rights to justice therefore never depend on circumstances, but the relevance of merit, position, and utility to right behaviour always will. In terms of justice, therefore, we can say that differences in needs, deserts, and rights must always call forth differences in treatment. Whether differences in merit, position, and utility call forth differences in treatment in pursuit of right behaviour will depend on circumstances. In short, need, desert, and rights are justicizing and deontic principles; merit, position, and utility are teleological and may be justifying principles.

Talk about the relevance of criteria or characteristics can thus be misleading unless the nature of the relevance is specified. What we have are two general types of relevance: the *unconditional relevance* of needs, deserts, and rights to justice, and the relevance of merits, positions, and utility to right action, which is *contingent* upon ulterior goals. There is, however, a third use of 'relevance', which stands on a quite different plane and is concerned with purely factual and function-specific relationships. A real difficulty arises from the fact that this usage of relevance is sometimes marshalled in arguments about reverse discrimination *as if it were a moral criterion* and is in this capacity used to attack or defend *moral arguments*. Thus Blackstone argues:

> 'Race, sex, religion, national origin and so on are generally taken as invidious grounds of discrimination. . . . But are they always so? . . . courts have permitted racial classification for the purpose of overcoming past invidious discrimination. But race and racial characteristics

> may be relevant to differential treatment on other grounds. For example, race may be quite relevant to the choice of a candidate for a certain acting role in a movie.'
>
> (W. T. Blackstone 1977: 61)

In fact, defences of and attacks on reverse discrimination often take a similar form, which in caricature goes something like 'Race (or sex) is (or is not) a relevant criterion or characteristic in this sort of instance (racial classifications to monitor ethnic minority representation in the civil service, or selecting an actor to play a slave) and therefore can (cannot) be accepted as a relevant criterion in the implementation of affirmative action or reverse discrimination policies'. The flaw in the argument is that race and sex are not *relevant* criteria in either of the moral senses used above, but are relevant in the purely factual, descriptive third sense from which no conclusions about their relevance in one set of circumstances can be used to justify their application in others.[13] The status of characteristics such as ethnicity, sex, IQ, manual dexterity, height, and weight is as sub-categories of function-specific relevance, which are used to identify the relevant beneficiaries under one or more of the six material principles (which, making an heroic assumption, I take to be the *only* morally relevant differences).

Thus, once we have established the morally relevant differences, we still require to identify *who* are in need, *who* are deserving, *who* have what rights, *who* possess what meritable qualities, *who* stands in particular relations to others, and what is the good we wish to maximize or the aim we wish to achieve. It is in the identification of the 'who' in each case that we use sub-categories of function-specific relevance. When therefore Edel (1977) speaks of 'job-specific criteria' or Bayles (1973b) of 'task-competence' criteria, it is to this sub-category that they refer. Again, when Blackstone argues that 'If it were shown that a given race were particularly susceptible to a given disease, then equal treatment or distributive justice vis-à-vis medical services might require racial differentiation in public health policies' (W. T. Blackstone 1977: 62), all he is really saying is that, in this instance, race is a specifically relevant characteristic for identifying a particular *need*. The material principle involved is need; race is simply an identificatory sub-category and as such no conclusions can be drawn about its relevance (moral or otherwise) in other circumstances.

It is my belief that most (possibly all) of the *specific* criteria we use in allocating burdens and benefits are in fact sub-categories for identifying morally relevant beneficiaries under one or more of the six material principles. (As we shall see, it is the relationship between morally relevant material principles and the function-specific criteria we use to identify their beneficiaries that lies at the heart of the debate about positive discrimination.) We can now see that particular characteristics such as IQ, height, weight, and manual dexterity are all sub-categories of merit and/or relevant for utilitarian or consequentialist reasons. Height is a particular aspect of merit (a personal quality) that is *specifically* relevant to entry to the police force, and it may also be relevant for consequentialist reasons; very small police might not function so effectively as law-maintaining agents. Manual dexterity is a characteristic (constitutive of merit) that is specifically functionally relevant to being a brain surgeon; clumsy brain surgeons would cause frequent deaths. Physical handicap is a characteristic that is a component of the needs principle, as is unemployment or illness.

When the question of relevance is formulated in this way, we can more easily find the answer to such a question as 'Why are we prepared to accept characteristics such as IQ or fitness or height as relevant to the allocation of some burdens or benefits (scholarships, jobs as steeplejacks or in the police) that are just as arbitrary from a moral point of view as race, whilst we strongly reject race itself as a relevant characteristic?' The answer of course is that we *do* accept race as a specific relevance in particular circumstances. What we do *not* accept is race as a *blanket* qualificatory or disqualificatory trait; but our attitude would be just the same in respect of any of the other traits mentioned above.

3 Positive discrimination and the material principles

This chapter has considered in some detail social justice as characterized by the equality principle and the derivation of the material principles required to give it prescriptive force. We have also along the way found it necessary to distinguish between material principles that are justicizing and those that are justifying. This detour into social philosophy has been necessary in order to prepare the ground for our analysis of positive discrimination; without it our understanding of positive discrimination would be incomplete. The chapter will conclude by outlining the analytical questions that are posed when we set positive discrimination against the framework of social justice that we have outlined. Consideration of these questions will then form the substance of subsequent chapters.

Differences in the allocation of burdens and benefits can be justicized only on the grounds of need, desert, and rights, and may be justified on grounds of merit, position, and utility (or more broadly consequentialism). Positive discrimination is a process that allocates burdens and benefits differentially (it is in fact a paradigm case of this). How then do we justify positive discrimination? Is it used in pursuit of one or more of the material principles listed? If it is, what makes it different from other ways in which these principles are fulfilled? If it is not, is it necessarily therefore unjust or wrong? And a different question: does justice (as the fulfilment of needs, deserts, and rights – but *not* of merit, position, or utility) *require* positive discrimination?

Firstly, then, what have been the grounds upon which positive discrimination has been justified in Britain and the United States? We saw in Chapter 2 that in Britain the common claim for positive discrimination has been on the basis of need or 'special need'. Even where positive discrimination is claimed to be 'compensatory' (as, for example, in Plowden 1967, Pinker 1971, Donnison 1974, and Weale 1978) it is, as we have seen, a claim to need – that is, compensation as 'making up for a deficiency' rather than as restitution. There are occasional claims for positive discrimination as a means of achieving 'racial justice' (Bindman and Carrier 1983), and these would represent a claim to compensation as restitution, but such claims are rare. The only other argument that has been put for positive discrimination is a consequentialist one, as in Lord Scarman's report, but this is done almost apologetically (Scarman 1981: 135).

In the USA, on the other hand, positive discrimination (or affirmative action or reverse discrimination) is justified more often on the grounds of compensation as restitution (Bayles 1973a, Bittker 1973, O'Neil 1975, Banner 1977, Goldman 1977) or for utilitarian or consequentialist reasons (Thalberg 1973–74, Dworkin 1977a, 1977b, Nagel 1977). A third argument that is sometimes put in the US context is that affirmative action is required in order better to fulfil the equality principle itself – that is, to counter unjust negative discrimination in the present. This case has been argued in respect of women by Ruth Ginsburg

(1977) and in respect of blacks by Bayles (1973b) and Beauchamp (1977).

Taken together, these constitute the only grounds on which positive discrimination has been and could be claimed to be just or right. Thus we have as the possible justificatory grounds for positive discrimination: needs, compensation as restitution, utility, or consequences, and as a counter to negative discrimination.

The task that lies before us is to examine whether positive discrimination is in fact justified, or in the stricter sense justicized, on these grounds; and further, whether on any of these grounds it is a *required* practice. A prior difficulty that must be dealt with is the seeming incongruence between the material principles that we have identified and the second of these claimed justifications. Compensation as restitution does not appear among our list of material principles. Is the list incomplete, or is positive discrimination being 'justified' on a ground that is apparently neither just nor even moral? I think neither is the case. Compensation for past harm is a matter of rights. That is, we have a right to compensation for past harm that has been caused us and to restitution for the denial of rights in the past. This is the line of reasoning that is adopted in most US treatments of positive discrimination as compensation (see, for example, Goldman 1977, 1979, Nagel 1977). We can therefore treat compensation as restitution as a matter of rights, and as such bring it clearly within the fold of our material principles.

The *claimed* justifications for positive discrimination, then, fall under the material principles of needs, rights, and utility or consequence. The fourth claim is a more general one and will be dealt with separately. The first two of these are deontic and justicizing grounds, the third a teleologic and (possibly) justifying ground, and the treatment of positive discrimination in respect of these principles in subsequent chapters reflects this distinction. Our immediate concern in the remainder of this chapter and in Chapters 4 to 7 is with the deontic principles of need and compensation as rights. Utilitarian and consequentialist considerations are the subject of Chapter 8.

3.1 Positive discrimination, needs, and rights

Our characterization of positive discrimination is of a practice in which the criteria used to identify beneficiaries and potential beneficiaries are different from those for which the benefit is being given (see pages 17–18). We can now specify this more precisely in the light of our discussion of relevant differences. If we wish to allocate on the basis of need, and if we use as *functionally* specific criteria qualities that are constitutive of need (i.e. have clear function-specific relevance to it), then we are not positively discriminating. To identify the beneficiaries of allocations on the grounds of need by the application of a means test to identify these with low incomes, or to identify a sub-category of the handicapped or the sick, is not to discriminate positively. If on the other hand we use qualities that are not themselves constitutive of need (such as race, sex, or IQ), then we do positively discriminate. Similarly, if in the pursuit of restitution for past harm or rights denied we identify groups or individuals who have actually been harmed (accident or crime victims, thalidomide children, wrongfully convicted prisoners), we do not positively discriminate. We *do* do so if we restitute groups or individuals whose identifying characteristic (race or sex, for example) is not one that immediately identifies them as a harmed group. And if, in the pursuit of one principle (or aim or goal), we give to groups or individuals identified by one set of qualities or characteristics, benefits that are usually allocated on function-specific criteria used in pursuit of a second principle, then we positively discriminate.

It may perhaps be argued that this is a quixotic characterization of positive discrimination and one that necessarily makes it appear (at least prima facie) unjust. But, as was argued in Chapter 2, we are forced to characterize positive discrimination in this way if it is to retain any peculiar identity. Because to give 'extra' resources to the deprived or the educationally disadvantaged, or to hospitals in run-down areas with high morbidity rates (all of which have been called examples of positive discrimination), is simply to allocate on the basis of need and is not distinct from any other way of meeting need. To characterize positive discrimination in this way is to define it out of existence.

Positive discrimination, then, as a practice that allocates burdens and benefits to beneficiaries who are identified on criteria which are not specifically functionally relevant to the material principle justifying the allocation, is prima facie necessarily incompatible with the equality principle. It treats people differently according to morally irrelevant differences.

This, however, is the beginning and not the end of the argument. A great deal hinges on the relationship between justicizing material principles, on the one hand, and the characteristics of the groups who benefit from positive discrimination, on the other. It is to these questions that we must now turn.

Prolegomenon to Chapters 4, 5, 6, and 7

Chapter 3 has shown that the two deontic principles to which claim is most often made in arguments for positive discrimination in Britain and the United States are need and compensation (as a right). We have also noted what the distinguishing feature of positive discrimination must be if it is to survive as a peculiarly distinct means of meeting needs and fulfilling rights to compensation. The distinguishing characteristics of positive discrimination however turn out to be ones that bring it into conflict with the requirements of the equality principle (it discriminates on grounds that prima facie have no relevance to the material principles being pursued) and therefore make it an unjusticiable practice. Justice and positive discrimination appear to be incompatible. The 'intuitive' aversion to it that we noted in Chapter 2 in respect of Britain and the large body of opposition to it in the USA reflect this apparent incompatibility.

The argument summarized here revolves upon the apparent *irrelevance* of the criteria usually used to select the beneficiaries of positive discrimination policies (i.e. ethnicity, areas, and sex) to the material principles in pursuit of which the positive discrimination is being made – need and compensation. Our exploration of the justiciability of positive discrimination beyond the first-case argument with which we concluded Chapter 3, summarized above, must therefore concentrate on this issue. Chapters 4 and 5 consider the question in respect of the needs principle, and Chapters 6 and 7 as it affects the principle of compensation as rights.

One caveat must be entered before we look to the defence of positive discrimination. This is that the practice relates to *groups* rather than to individuals. This is necessarily entailed in our characterization whereby *group* characteristics (race, sex, area of residence) are used to identify beneficiaries. To benefit one individual who has been found to be in need or to make restitution to an individual who has been wronged has nothing to do with positive discrimination.

There are two main lines of defence of positive discrimination in the light of the prima facie conclusion of its unjustness:

(1) It may be claimed that positive discrimination does not fall foul of the equality principle because *all* the members of the groups that it selects for benefit have legitimate claims against one or other of the two material principles of need and compensation. The group characteristics (race, sex, area) therefore constitute criteria that are functionally relevant to the material principles, and no incompatibility exists between justice and the positive discrimination practice.

Such an argument will require us to say that *all* blacks, *all* women, *all* inhabitants of an area have needs or have suffered harm or rights denied in the past. (We shall in fact require to say rather more than this, as subsequent chapters demonstrate.) The strength of the argument will vary between beneficiary groups and between the needs and compensation principles. However, if the argument is empirically true, two important consequences follow:

(a) what we would be doing would not be positive discrimination;
(b) that *all* members of the identified groups ought to have their needs met or wrongs righted, and if positive-discrimination-type *practices* were followed (even though *pace* (a) they would not be positive discriminaiton), this would be unlikely to be the result.

(2) It may be claimed that whilst not all members of groups identified for benefit under positive discrimination practices have legitimate claims of need or for compensation, sufficiently large proportions do to make the use of their group characteristics reasonable surrogate criteria relevant to the claim. Furthermore the advantages to be gained in terms of reduction of stigma, administrative ease, efficacy, and efficiency, by using easily identifiable surrogate criteria such as race, sex, or area, are such as to produce a greater on-balance justice than would be achieved by treating individuals by means-tested selectivity or by individual recompense through the courts. In short, the degree of correspondence between the possession of a legitimate needs or compensation claim and particular group characteristics is such that no great injustice is done in using the latter to fulfil the former, and the advantages to be gained tip the balance in favour of a greater sum total of justice.

There is a third argument that the essence of positive

discrimination has nothing to do with the identification of beneficiaries but rather lies in giving 'extra' resources – in the sense of 'more than average' (or 'more than due'?) – to those in greatest need. It is this, the argument goes, that gives positive discrimination its distinctiveness and makes it important. This is the 'Plowden' argument mentioned in Chapter 2; I think it is empty, and I show why in Chapter 5.

These, then, are the issues that we must address in the next four chapters.

Chapter 4
Social justice and the needs principle

When a claim is made that positive discrimination is justified by the needs principle, what is meant is that positive discrimination is a practice that can be used to meet needs. The needs principle asserts that variations in need constitute one of the differences between people that justify us in treating them differently. It asserts more than this however. It is an injunction, as we have seen, that 'needs ought to be met'. Not only do needs allow us to treat people differently, they lay on us the moral requirement to do so. That this is the case, and why it is so, is disputable ground; but if it is the case, and if positive discrimination turned out in any given set of circumstances to be the only, the best, or the least-cost way of meeting need, then justice would not only permit its use, it would also require it. And whether positive discrimination *is* the only, best, or least-cost means of fulfilling the needs principle depends in large measure on the issues raised in the Prolegomenon to this chapter.

1 The basis of needs claims

In Chapter 3 it was noted that there were three obvious candidates as the bases upon which the material principles of needs, deserts, and compensation could be 'justified' in the sense that we might say that needs 'ought to be met', 'deserts ought to be rewarded', and 'wrongs ought to be righted'. These were appeals to the respect for persons as ends, intuitive notions of rightness or justice, and various forms of contractual arrangements. Whilst the three material principles of need, desert, and compensation were identified (among others) in the previous chapter by means of a review of what philosophers have claimed to be material principles, and whilst these three at least accord with our intuitive judgements, their strength as material principles – indeed their *being* material principles – must depend upon their moral prescriptivity. So it is necessary to examine the bases for these claims a little further. Can we ascribe the 'oughtness' of need or compensation claims to respect for persons, intuition, or contract? Our concern here will focus on the basis of need claims.

It may seem that the most obvious contender as a basis for need claims has been ignored. That is, that we have a *right* to have our needs met and an obligation to meet the needs of others. Indeed, it may be argued that the basis for all material principles of justice is that they are founded upon rights and that justice consists in meeting needs, rewarding desert, making compensation, etc., *because* these *are* rights (see, for example, Vlastos 1962). This is at odds with the argument developed in the previous chapter where rights were identified as but one of the material principles of justice. This is not the place to examine the concept of rights and its relation to justice, and we must content ourselves with a few brief comments. There is, I believe, no fundamental contradiction between the views that rights underpin all material principles and that rights constitute one of the material principles. The former argument is really a restatement of the prescriptivity of material principles. To say that justice *requires* that needs be met and that people have a right to have their needs met is but to argue the two sides of the same coin. But however desirable and necessary the concept of social rights, it is not as strong nor as unambiguous as the rights of compensation and restitution for past harm. Where rights are held to be one material principle of justice, what is most often argued is that one of the relevant differences between people, which permit and require their different treatment, is that between people who have clearly established rights (usually of contract, implicit or explicit) and those who do not. Thus the fulfilment of contractual rights is one factor that justice must take account of. And compensation or restitution falls, I believe, into this category of contractual rights. Purely in terms of *rights*, then, the right to compensation or restitution for past harm or denial of rights is a stronger, clearer, and more definite claim than that of social or welfare rights. It stands independently as a material principle of justice, whether or not the bases of needs or deserts claims are seen to rest in rights.

None of these arguments denies the existence of social rights, or the right to have needs met. There is a clear implication however that social rights, except where these are contractual as in effective social insurance policies, are much less self-evident, and therefore less defensible against attack, than contractual rights. None the less, the claim that needs ought to be met because social rights require it is now well established both in the literature of social policy – from T. H. Marshall's seminal article of 1950 to the more recent articulations of Mishra (1984: 164–65) and Foster (1983) and in the literature of social and moral philosophy; see, for example, Feinberg (1973), D. Miller (1976), and Plant, Lesser, and Taylor-Gooby (1980).[1] But while such arguments are necessary if the claim to justice is to have force (if justice requires that needs be met then it cannot be left to altruism or supererogatory action), they do not provide an answer to the question of *why* needs ought to be met. They are complementary to justice statements, not explanatory of them. The question of *why* needs ought to be met can be turned round to ask *why* there are social rights; and again, the answer to this question is not nearly so obvious as the answer to why contractual arrangements should be kept, promises be honoured, or harm be rectified.

Whilst social rights are a necessary complement to social justice, therefore, they do not provide *in themselves* a foundation for need claims. We must return to our original three contenders of respect for persons, intuition, and contract. For present purposes it is not necessary to survey the arguments and evidence for each of these but merely to establish that there is a reasonable case for claiming that needs ought to be met and thus to give confirmation to need as a material principle that not only *sanctions* different treatment but also, in justice, *requires* it. Such a case would seem most convincingly to rest upon a recognition of persons as moral beings and in respect for persons as ends in themselves – that is, on some formulation of the Kantian categorical imperatives. Such a case, as we saw in Chapter 3, has frequently been made, although not always explicitly in Kantian terms. Thus Plant has argued that 'any moral code must be able to recognise two fundamental features of human life as valuable in order to make sense of any other moral prescriptions such moral codes may make', going on to identify the two features as basic survival and human autonomy; 'any moral view, to be coherent, must recognise the maintenance of human life and the development of autonomy as basic obligations . . . the needs for life and autonomy provide the logically basic human needs which have to be recognised by any morally self-consistent point of view' (Plant 1980: 115, 120; see also Plant, Lesser, and Taylor-Gooby

1980: 93). Although not couched in Kantian terms, the arguments here are clearly in the same mould: that recognition of people as autonomous moral agents and as ends-in-themselves obliges us as holders of any moral code to maintain both the basic existence of moral agents (without which there could be no moral code) and their moral autonomy (without which any moral code would be barren). Hence the obligation to maintain life, to which end 'needs ought to be met'. Whether this lays an obligation only to meet survival needs and whether and to what extent the maintenance of human autonomy requires the meeting of further needs remains to be considered.

One final point on the moral bases of need claims is worthy of note and it brings us back to the question of needs and rights. It was remarked above that the assertion of social rights does not in itself provide an answer to the question of why needs ought to be met; it simply poses the question in a different form. The ultimate claim to the Kantian ethic however does provide such an answer, but it also gives us a reason for asserting social rights. The argument here has been put by Fried:

> 'The needs of our fellow citizens are thought to make a peculiarly urgent claim upon us not just because they are susceptible to objective measurement but for the deeper reason that they relate to the development and the maintenance of the moral capacities of freedom and rationality, that is, the capacities to develop a conception of the good and to respect the moral personality of others. That we must maintain life and some modicum of vigour if these capacities are to persist is obvious and is a corollary of our corporeal nature. . . . It is links such as these to the physical and moral integrity of the person that explain why needs – unlike wants – are thought to generate positive rights, rights measured in terms of their actual satisfaction.'
> (Fried 1978: 120–21; see also Fried 1983)

Appeal to the Kantian ethic provides convincing reason why welfare should be treated as a right and why justice requires that needs be met rather than that they be subject to the vicissitudes of beneficence and supererogation, as Lucas (1966), Acton (1971), and Hayek (1976) among others have argued they ought to be. It is on grounds such as these that need may be established as one of the material principles of justice.

We are now in a position to restate the problem in so far as positive discrimination is concerned. If justice requires that needs be met, and if positive discrimination turned out to be the best, the most efficient or effective, or the only way of meeting needs, then despite its prima facie unjustness it would be a justiciable practice. Whether or not positive discrimination is the best or only way of meeting needs in the circumstances in which it has been applied or could potentially be applied is largely an empirical issue. What we have done so far is to pose the theoretical or philosophical problem in such a way that a partial answer at least may be sought on empirical evidence. The next chapter will be concerned with a review of some of this evidence in respect of need, and for that reason our attention will focus on the practice of positive discrimination in Britain.

Our discussion of need is as yet incomplete in so far as the concept itself has been treated as unproblematic. This has suited our purposes so far, but is inadequate for the ensuing arguments. The complex concept of need requires further examination.

2 The boundaries of need claims

If we are effectively to assess the justificatory force of positive discrimination as a means of fulfilling the needs principle, we shall require a more definitive interpretation of what constitute needs, which needs fall legitimately to be met in the public domain, what distinguishes needs from wants, and what, in particular, the needs principle enjoins us to do. This and the subsequent sections examine the variety of interpretations of need and attempt a specific formulation of the needs principle that can be used as a yardstick by which to test the justification for positive discrimination.

Need is one material principle of the purely formal equality principle that justifies us in treating people differently. In this elemental form however it offers no particular prescription for action; the equality principle is fulfilled if people with similar needs, and levels of need, are treated alike even if this treatment is nothing more than refraining from doing anything. In order to progress from this purely formal standpoint, we have attempted to show in the previous section why we would treat the needs principle as prescriptive – by demonstrating that needs ought to be met and that people have rights to have needs met. Thus, if we now combine the equality principle with the prescriptive material principle of needs, we are able to say that justice is done only when people with equal levels of need are treated similarly and that this treatment consists in actually meeting the needs they have. The corollary is that people with different levels of need should be treated differently and that those with greater needs should receive more resources (of whatever kind) in order to meet their greater needs. Ideally, under such a formulation, resources should be differentially distributed according to different levels of need, until all needs are met. Such an ideal formulation, however, bears little resemblance to the real world, assuming as it does that (a) there is a consensus about what constitute needs; (b) needs are static; (c) needs are finite and measurable; (d) all needs can be met; (e) it is possible to say when all needs have been met. Clearly, if we are to be able to say in any particular set of circumstances that positive discrimination is the best or only way of fulfilling the needs principle and it is thus justicized, we must specify more clearly what constitute needs.[1]

One of the main problems that arises in needs-talk is that the concept of 'need' is philosophically multiform. This can be illustrated by the example of Barry's (1965) claim that needs statements do not constitute independent justifications for resource distribution because their justificatory force depends upon the aims or goals for the achievement of which the need is simply an instrument (thus, *X* needs *Y in order to* . . . achieve an end *Z*). Clearly, there is a sense, as Plant (1980: 105–06) points out, in which all need statements are triadic in structure, requiring a subject to have the need, an object that is needed, and a purpose for which the subject needs the object, and in this sense any requisite for any purpose will constitute a need (you need health care if you are ill, but you also need a horse to play polo and cards to play poker). What matters, as Scanlon in his essay on 'Preference and Urgency' (1975) points out, is the 'importance' or 'urgency' of the purpose or end for which something is needed. To claim, as Barry does, that need cannot represent an independent justificatory principle seems to ignore the significance of the ends involved, and this is precisely what is at issue. What is required, therefore, is some differentiation of ends.

There have been a number of classifications of need that use, with varying degrees of explicitness, a differentiation of the ends to be served. Such classifications are useful for present purposes in that they help to narrow down the range of needs that are of concern here and provide the necessary distinctions within the concept of need that Barry's analysis lacks. Thus D. Miller (1976) distinguishes between three types of need statement: 'instrumental', 'functional', and 'intrinsic'. Whilst Miller's claim that only the first of these conforms to Barry's characterization seems less than convincing, the division he makes is a useful one. Instrumental needs, he argues, are those that require to be met solely and directly in pursuit of a further end – such as needing a key to unlock a door. Functional needs are those requiring to be met in the course of performing some function – such as surgeons needing manual dexterity. Intrinsic needs are those that require to be met for normal human functions – the need for food, shelter, health care, and so on. A second typology is that of Benn and Peters (1959: ch. 6), who distinguish between biological, basic, and functional needs. Biological needs are those relating to survival maintenance; basic needs are those that are relevant to the maintenance of a decent level of life (which will to some extent be normatively defined); and functional needs are akin to Miller's instrumental and functional needs – that is, those that require to be met in the pursuit of an immediate end of a social role or function. A third classification is that noted by Braybrooke (1968: 90) into course-of-life needs and adventitious needs. The former represent more urgent needs, in the sense that Scanlon (1975) uses the word – those requiring to be met for normal species functioning (including social functioning). The latter are those more immediate but lesser-order needs requiring to be met in the course of fulfilling some immediate project.

All these classifications are in effect elaborations of a more simple division into 'basic' and less 'basic' needs, and all enable us to begin to whittle down the concept to a more manageable core. If, for example, we were to make a distinction between action in the private and public domains, then it becomes clear that the public domain (the area of social and public policy) is *mainly* concerned with 'intrinsic' needs (Miller), 'biological' and 'basic' needs (Benn and Peters), and 'course-of-life' needs (Braybrooke).[2] Such a division enables us to surmount Barry's argument that needs do not constitute an independent justificatory principle because, if we accept the prescriptive principle that needs ought to be met in order to sustain survival and autonomy, then 'intrinsic' or 'biological and basic' or 'course-of-life' needs would constitute just such a principle. Useful as this is, it is only a first step; it leaves unresolved what are to count as needs even when we have eliminated those that are purely instrumental. Needs, or social needs, beyond the minimum requirements for survival are normatively defined, socially relative, and extensionable, and what might count as a need may well at any given time depend upon what are considered to be the legitimate bounds of the public domain. It is for this reason that any coherent needs-talk must admit of the public/private domain division. How then to specify the constitution of social needs? It would deflect us too far from our central concern with positive discrimination to elaborate an answer to this in the detail that it really requires, but the bare bases of an argument will suffice for present purposes. (These arguments are given further treatment in Edwards 1983, 1985.)

Let us assume that whatever may count as needs falls on a continuum that merges with wants and preferences.[3] Let us further suppose that the public domain of social, economic, and public policy is concerned with meeting need and that the satisfaction of wants is to be left to the private domain of the market. If we can now find a boundary between needs and wants we shall have specified, at least in general terms, the constituency of social need. Any talk of distinctions between needs, on the one hand, and wants and preferences, on the other, is of interest only in the context of a distinction between the public and private domains. What we are concerned with essentially is a specification of these things that we consider it reasonable should be provided by state action in the public domain. If it were not a question of states' obligations to meet the needs of their citizens, if there were no socially actionable consequences to these obligations, and if the needs/wants debate did not engage the public/private domain division, then needs-talk would be uninteresting. It is precisely *because* we accept that the ultimate responsibility for meeting need is a public one that the boundary between needs claims and wants is as important as it is.[4]

One of the most common means by which philosophers have tried to distinguish between needs and wants is the 'harm principle' (Benn and Peters 1959, Feinberg 1973, D. Miller 1976). In its simplest form, the harm principle holds that needs (as opposed to want or preferences) are those things that, if they remain unmet, cause harm to individuals who have them. If an unmet 'need' causes no harm, it is more likely to be a 'want'. There are several varieties of the harm principle (Edwards 1983) but most acknowledge that 'harm' must be interpreted to include not only physical harm (such as would result from health-care needs or housing need remaining unmet) but also psychological and emotional harm (such as would be incurred if, say, the need for good social-work counselling remained unmet, or if the need for the maintenance of self-respect were denied, or if people's standard of living fell so far below the common standard as to isolate them from the mainstream of social life).

Whilst any coherent formulation of the harm principle must include psychological and emotional harm as well as physical harm, once these are admitted they deprive the concept of its cutting edge by allowing of that relativity that makes of need the endlessly extensionable concept that we are trying to put fences round. If, for example, the inability to possess some things causes us psychological or emotional harm because most people do possess them, then the range of things the absence of which will do so will increase the more widely available they are in society. And the more that happens, the less convincing does the harm principle become as a means of distinguishing between needs and wants.

In an attempt to provide some stability to the harm principle and thus retain its cutting edge, Miller has allied it to the notion of 'life plans'. Thus, rather than allowing any transitory want or deprivation or thwarted preference to be the cause of harm, only deprivation of those things essential to people's life plans can be taken to represent serious potential causes of harm. In Miller's formulation, everyone has some form of 'plan of life', since people's identities are in part determined by their conception of their own good.[5] Everyone has some conception of the sort of person they want to be and what they wish to do with their lives. Elsewhere (Edwards 1985: 35) I have cited the case of the budding young musician; for her, going to concerts and hearing musicians play are essential to her life plan. She *needs* to do these things, and the inability to do so (as a result, say, of lack of money) would cause her harm to the extent that her life plan would be thwarted. The fact that she also feels deprived, 'left out', because she does not have a sports car when most of her peers do is purely incidental to her life plan as a musician; it constitutes a want rather than a need, however much she desires it. We may wish therefore through taxation or social policy to subsidize her concert-going, but not her car. In Miller's formulation a *need* is the lack of something that is important or essential to the fulfilment of life plans, the want of which will cause harm by thwarting the fulfilment of life plans. Whilst there is much that is questionable about the notion of life plans (which space does not permit us to examine), it does appear to be at least potentially useful in providing an answer to the problem of specifying the constituency of social needs. Unfortunately, it turns out in the end to be an unsatisfactory solution, as I will show in the next section.

3 Equality of welfare

The use of life plans to distinguish needs from wants ultimately founders on the problem of inter-personal utility comparisons (along with most other subjective assessments of welfare). This is immediately clear when we consider the question of distribution. Let us suppose that we can identify needs as those things that, whilst unfilled, cause harm by thwarting life plans. Let us also assume that there is a consensus that 'needs', so identified, should be met within the public domain – that is, out of taxation, social insurance, and so on. What then must be done? Ideally, we should meet all need until no harm remains and no one faces insuperable obstacles to the pursuit of their life plans. In the real world, not all needs can be met (unless 'needs' are so restrictively defined as to constitute only those things that could be met at any given level of resources). The range of accepted need is far greater than given resources will allow to be met. Thus, as Weale (1978: 70) has argued, the satisfaction of need is itself a good to be distributed. Some set of distributive principles must be applied to determine *what* needs to meet and to what degree of satisfaction. How is need satisfaction to be distributed? The equality principle enjoins us to treat similar cases alike and different cases differently. Greater needs call forth greater resources. The only way in which such a formulation can be given coherence in distributive terms is by using some such notion as equality of welfare. Thus, given that some have greater needs than others, that we must treat cases differently according to the degree of need, and that not all need can be met, we must distribute in such a way as to bring everyone to the same level of satisfaction, and dissatisfaction, of their needs; or, in terms of life plans, so as to bring everyone to an equal level of attainment of their life plans.

The problem with this formulation is that life plans will not be static; they will be in part socially determined, and the degree of satisfaction of them will be subjectively determined (all elements of life plans to which Miller gives insufficient emphasis). In this respect they will share the same shortcomings as subjective assessments of need and inter-personal comparisons of welfare. We know, for example, from the work of Runciman (1966) and

Coates and Silburn (1970) that subjective assessments of need will be strongly influenced by past experiences and present reference groups, and that it is usually those *most* in need who have the most modest assessments of their requirements. So it is with life plans. It will be the better-off who will tend to have the most ambitious life plans with the highest harm-avoiding costs, with the poor and deprived tending towards modest plans and cheap harm-avoiding costs (or needs). To fund both to an equal level of satisfaction of life plans will build inequality of resource distribution into our need-meeting policies. It is these characteristics of life plans – their social relativity and personal subjectivity – that deprive them of the ability to give stability and focus to the harm principle and in consequence deprive us of the means of defining a boundary between needs and wants. Useful as attempts to define such a boundary are, and valuable as such a distinction would be (especially when tied to the public/private domain division), all such attempts have so far failed. Where needs become wants remains a matter of political and policy expediency.

We have noted that the problem is not peculiar to the concept of life plans; it is common to any system that involves subjective measures of welfare, satisfaction, utility, happiness, or need. If we are to distribute in order to produce equality of welfare, then we shall allow our resources to become hostage to those with champagne tastes, high utility functions, and high levels of dissatisfaction. Dworkin has examined the issue at considerable length in two papers on the nature of equality (Dworkin 1981a, 1981b). The dilemma as he poses it is that the equalitarian must choose between two forms of distribution: an equality of resources or an equality of welfare (or some combination of the two). The notion of equality of welfare, he argues, despite its superficial appeal, is seriously flawed not only because of the problems of measuring equality of satisfaction or welfare, and the heavy commitment we must make to inefficient users of resources, but also as a result of the difficulties thrown up by measuring and combining people's personal, impersonal, and political preferences. In the second of the two papers Dworkin argues in favour of a distribution to promote equality of resources. A similar conclusion is reached by Fried, who argues:

> 'there are grave difficulties in accepting a subjective standard of fair shares. Some people derive great happiness from the simplest pleasures ... others require the most extravagant expenditures of

> resources before they are moderately happy. A subjective standard makes the first group the hostage of the second.'
>
> (Fried 1978: 119–20)

It is a feature of most formulations of equality of welfare that they involve subjective assessments of welfare. This, as Fried notes, is responsible for much of the difficulty, and it certainly underlies many of the problems that Dworkin identifies. It is for this reason, I believe, that in the assessment and meeting of need, the principle of equality of welfare must for practical purposes be tied to a set of *objective* measures of need satisfaction.[6] As Scanlon notes:

> '[It] is not that there is anything wrong . . . with egalitarian doctrines *per se* but rather that a subjective criterion of well-being seems insensitive to differences between preferences that are of great relevance when these preferences are taken as the basis for moral claims.'
>
> (Scanlon 1975: 659)

In claiming the necessity of objective assessments of need satisfaction, I do not wish to deny the force of Dworkin's or Fried's arguments – that distributions aimed at achieving greater equality of resources are ideally to be preferred to any attempts at equalizing welfare or satisfaction, even though the concomitant is that at adequate resource levels individuals must then be responsible for their own welfare. And it should be noted that distribution of resources according to need, towards some notional equality of resources, is just as consistent with the requirements of the equality principle as distribution of resources according to need, towards equality of satisfaction. But we don't live in that sort of world. All merit-based systems (and not only capitalist ones) have gross inequalities built into them, and there is no evidence, certainly in either Britain or the United States, that redistributive policies that would result in anything like equality of resources could or would be implemented. Clearly in the realm of social policy in the mid-1980s our enquiries are consumed not by grandiose schemes of economic redistribution, but with affording even an adequate standard of living to the victims of capitalist economies. We have, therefore, to lower our sights from the desirable schemes Dworkin and Fried have to offer and to pitch our attention to meeting even fairly basic social needs in as just a manner as possible.

What this more modest proposal entails is a distribution of resources according to needs to effect some overall equality of welfare as measured by objective criteria of housing, education, employment opportunities, social and economic security, health status and health care, and, more generally, quality of life. This, I believe, is the most practical scheme of need-meeting against which we must test policies of positive discrimination. However, such a formulation is not without its shortcomings. We have escaped one form of social hijacking of resources – by those with champagne tastes – by requiring objective specifications of satisfaction. Those with champagne tastes but not the resources to enjoy them will have to drink 'plonk' or learn to love their deprivation. Objective measures of need satisfaction nevertheless expose us to another form of social hijacking – by those with the greatest needs. Strict adherence to equality of welfare must result in the allocation of a very large proportion of welfare expenditure to those with great need, and the overall level of need satisfaction within a given resource ceiling will be relatively low. (The area of health care is one that immediately springs to mind in this context: see Daniels 1981.) The result would be a rough equality of welfare at a very low level with more unmet need and greater inequalities above that level. It is ironic, as Scanlon points out, that only rich societies (and, we might add, those willing to commit large resources to need-meeting) can afford to buy equality. There really seems to be no way out of this dilemma; we have to accept an uneasy approximation whereby we trade off more overall needs met for less equality of welfare or vice versa. The situation is exacerbated by the unwillingness to forgo private want satisfaction in order to fulfil obligations to the needy.

4 Equality of opportunity and the needs principle

The promotion of equality of opportunity is sometimes cited both in Britain and the United States as a reason for pursuing policies of positive discrimination.[7] Goldman, for example, draws the distinction between backward-looking reasons for promoting positive discrimination, such as compensation for past harm, and forward-looking reasons, such as creating equality of conditions or equality of opportunities (Goldman 1979: 9–10). It is important not to confuse this distinction between forward- and backward-looking reasons for positive discrimination with the distinction made earlier between deontic and teleologic justicizations and justifications. Utilitarian and other consequentialist arguments for positive discrimination are teleologic and forward-looking; compensation is deontic and backward-looking. But equality of opportunity, though forward-looking, is not a teleologic ground for positive discrimination but rather, as I argue below, a function of the needs principle and hence morally apodictic rather than prudential.

I believe that we can treat equality of opportunity as a function of the needs principle for the purposes of our examination of positive discrimination for the following reasons. Equality of opportunity is considered to be a good in itself in meritocratic and unequal societies. Indeed, the more unequal the distribution of rewards and the more that these inequalities are justified on grounds of meritocratic principles, the more important it is to ensure that the opportunities of gaining these rewards are equally distributed. So long as some members of society do not enjoy equality of opportunity, therefore, steps ought to be taken to ensure that they do, and such steps will consist of making provision to meet the additional needs that such people have to bring them to a position where they can compete equally. Thus, as Plowden (1967) argued, some children do not have equality of opportunity because of deficiencies or wants in their social and physical environments. These deficiencies represent needs that must be met before equality of opportunity is achieved. Promoting equality of opportunity involves meeting those needs that act as a barrier to its realization.

Does this mean that the ultimate ground for wanting to promote equality of opportunity is the same as the one identified earlier as the foundation of need-meeting – namely, some formulation of the Kantian categorical imperatives? I think the answer is yes. To deny people equality of opportunity is to treat them as less than ends in themselves.[8]

Given this prolegomenon, the arguments for or against positive discrimination as a means of promoting equality of opportunity follow the familiar line: that, although positive discrimination is prima facie unjustified, it can be justified, and justice may require it, if most of the members of the beneficiary group have greater needs (than others with needs) that ought to be met if they are to have equality of opportunity. If in such circumstances positive discrimination turned out to be the only or best way of meeting the needs principle, then justice would require it.

To acknowledge equality of opportunity however as a function of the needs principle, and thus as a potential ground for positive discrimination, immediately introduces a potential conflict with our formulation of the needs principle as meeting needs to some level of equality of welfare. It is a conflict at a more general level, between equality of opportunity and equality of reward, which has been noted by a number of commentators (for example, Raphael 1955: 90 ff., Honoré 1968: 90 ff., Nagel 1977: 10–11). In an attempt to resolve this conflict, we shall need to treat equality of opportunity as a more complex, and ambiguous, concept than we have so far assumed it to be.

There are two sets of ambiguities involved in the concept of equality of opportunity. The first revolves upon the question of what it is that people should have an equal opportunity to be or to do. The second concerns what is involved in promoting equality of opportunity. There are two, not mutually exclusive, interpetations of the first: equality of opportunity to compete fairly for desired positions and rewards, and equality of opportunity to fulfil life plans, lead the good life or fulfil one's personality (Benn and Peters 1959: 118), or fulfil one's natural capacities (Goldman 1979: 171). We have already noted the shortcomings of the concept of life plans, and since the alternative formulations are really fancy ways of saying 'doing what you want to do' – and, as such, a meaningless basis for policy – the following remarks will be confined to the more concrete notion of competing for rewards and positions.

When we speak of equal opportunity to compete for rewards, positions, and goods, what we mean – as Williams (1969: 165) points out – is that some goods, such as high-status or highly remunerated occupations, are highly regarded and desired (by most, if not all, members of society), that these goods are acquired by competition and the exercise of skills and attributes, and that they are in short supply relative to the numbers who would wish to obtain them. Williams then further identifies three ways in which valued goods can be in relative short supply. They may be *necessarily* limited – for example, positions at the top of professional or commercial enterprises. They may be *contingently* limited, in that there are conditions of entry that not everyone can satisfy, as with places in universities. And they may be *fortuitously* limited, where, although a large number of people satisfy the entry requirements, there are not enough places or positions to provide for everyone who qualifies. The way in which valued goods are limited will affect the opportunities of achieving them and the nature of the skills, aptitudes, and efforts required, which in turn will influence the way in which equal opportunity of obtaining these skills can best be effected.[9]

More significant are the ambiguities surrounding what is, or should be, involved in promoting equal opportunity and what genuine fair equality of opportunity would consist of. At the risk of over-simplification, we can identify a range of interpretations of equality of opportunity, from the 'minimal' to the 'radical'.[10] A minimal view would hold that arbitrary barriers (either moral or functional) to equal opportunity should be removed. No one should be arbitrarily excluded from the opportunity to advance him- or herself. Such a view would be represented by what Rawls terms 'careers open to talents' (Rawls 1972: 65). The natural objection to such a formulation is that the mere removal of arbitrary barriers, such as policies of racial exclusion, will not achieve genuine equality of opportunity. We know only too well that a wide range of social factors influence people's ability to compete – and, in particular, children's abilities to perform well in school at those tasks and tests that are the hurdles on the way to the glittering prizes. So, the argument goes, we must either remove the inequalities and deprivations (such as poverty, bad housing, and 'poor parenting') that depress people's abilities to compete equally, or, failing that, we must compensate (make up for them) by more and better schooling. This is the more liberal interpretation that has formed the basis for much equal opportunity policy in Britain and the USA, and was one of the foundations of forward-looking affirmative action in the latter.

But why stop there? There are many other non-social factors that influence people's ability to compete effectively. There are the obvious ones such as mental and physical handicap, dexterity, and intelligence, and many others, less tangible, such as drive, energy, and ambition. And so we arrive at the radical view of equality of opportunity: that genuine fair equality of opportunity cannot be achieved just by removing barriers and compensating for social disadvantage; we must compensate also for 'natural' handicaps. I do not want to pursue the more radical line of argument, partly because I do not think it leads very far, partly because some of the factors that it is argued ought to be compensated for are in practice deemed to be at least functionally (if not morally) relevant to the award of the prizes and partly because it is of little relevance to our concern with positive discrimination.

Equality of opportunity therefore may be seen as a 'necessary' component of a meritocratic system; 'necessary' in the sense of being required by liberal justice in order to make an unequal distribution of burdens and benefits more fair (though not necessarily more just). The objective to be achieved by equality of opportunity is to rule out morally arbitrary characteristics from the determination of chances, and hence to rule out such factors as sex, ethnicity, and social background. However, as we have seen, there are many other characteristics that affect life chances and ability to compete, that are also arbitrary from a moral point of view and ought also therefore to be corrected for. Where the radical interpretation of equal opportunity proves to be unrealistic is in its assumption that a truly fair meritocratic system requires the elimination of all morally irrelevant chacteristics from the determination of chances. In reality, in a meritocratic system, we do accept some morally arbitrary characteristics (such as drive and intelligence) as being at least functionally relevant to winning the prizes and achieving desired offices.[11] To say that such factors are 'acceptable' (meaning that there is a general consensus that it is fair to let them play a part in the distribution of burdens and benefits) is *not* to say that they are morally relevant or that to distribute rewards differentially in proportion to their possession is just. It merely demonstrates that in liberal democratic societies we do not live by justice alone. It also demonstrates that equality of opportunity is not only concerned with making society more just, it is also a means of making inequalities more acceptable and of increasing utility and efficiency in a meritocratic system.

Given this sort of analysis of equality of opportunity, I believe that the purpose of positive discrimination in promoting equal opportunity is also a means of promoting the randomization of losers and winners of the race for prizes over those sections of society defined by characteristics that are both irrelevant from a moral point of view and deemed to be irrelevant from a functional point of view. Ethnicity and sex would be clear examples of such defining characteristics. What sort of deficiency would we be correcting for in promoting equality of opportunity through positive discrimination? By definition, positive discrimination is concerned with groups in the population, not individuals, whereas equality of opportunity is usually taken to refer to equality as between individuals. Positive discrimination will therefore cover only a part of equality of opportunity – that concerned with performance ability deficiencies which vary significantly between relevant groups. This means in effect that 'natural' deficiencies such as mental and physical handicap and ill health will *not* be the subject of positive discrimination programmes, unless (as would be highly unlikely) they were very highly correlated with race, ethnicity, and sex. What would be the subject of positive discrimination efforts would be social factors, such as bad housing, poor social and physical environment, and poverty, which acted as brakes to people's ability to compete fairly and equally, if (and only if) such factors were highly correlated with the defining characteristics of the beneficiary group – ethnicity, for example – in such a way that all or most members of the group suffered such deprivations to a greater extent than all others so suffering.

Finally, in our treatment of positive discrimination and equality of opportunity, we come to the problem noted earlier of the potential conflict between the concept of meeting need to equality of welfare and the idea of equality of opportunity. The problem is simply that, if our purpose is to promote equality of opportunity to compete for unequal rewards, we are not promoting equality of welfare. If, therefore, we adopt a policy of positive discrimination (assuming it were just) to meet needs to some level of equality of welfare *and* at the same time to meet those needs that prevent people from competing with fair equality of opportunity, we are acting inconsistently and contradictorily. The answer to this I believe is that meeting needs to promote equality of opportunity necessarily entails meeting need to some level of equality of welfare, but that the latter does not go all the way to satisfying the former.

Thus justice requires that before all else we meet needs to an objectively stipulated level of equality of welfare. This is apodictic and founded on an assumption of individuals as ends in themselves. Such a procedure would also be a necessary first step in the promotion of equality of opportunity; without it, there could not possibly be equal opportunity. Further than this, however, because we live in a meritocratic society in which inequalities are justified (though not necessarily justicized), and because the injunction of 'the kingdom of ends', *because* it is a universal injunction, knows no political boundaries, we ought also to ensure that even within the inadequacies of a meritocratic system people are still treated as ends in themselves. This entails ensuring that everyone (or, so far as positive discrimination is concerned, all groups of people) has a fair and equal opportunity to go beyond this level of equality of welfare and to compete equally, so far as this is possible, for the further benefits that may be available. Put more simply, if there is a surplus left over after all needs have been met to equality of welfare, and if this surplus is going to be distributed unequally, we ought all to have a fair equality of opportunity of getting our hands on some of it. The purpose of positive discrimination would then be to ensure that no particular groups in society were disproportionately denied that opportunity.

Conclusion

It has been our purpose in this chapter to consider some of the theoretical and philosophical questions about the complex concept of social need as a material principle of justice. Much needs-talk fails adequately to acknowledge that the concept is a complex and problematical one, and it has been necessary as a preamble to our more empirical discussion in Chapter 5 to put down some markers to guide our way. Armed with these, we now turn to consider whether positive discrimination can be a justiciable practice in pursuit of the needs principle.

Chapter 5
The needs principle and positive discrimination

1 Needs, special needs, and greatest needs

Need is the most common – almost the exclusive – justification for positive discrimination in Britain, as was demonstrated in Chapter 2. Subsequent chapters made out a case for need as a material principle of distributive justice. The vernacular arguments for positive discrimination in Britain however go further than this in frequently claiming the necessity of positive discrimination for those with 'special' needs, or 'additional' needs, or the 'greatest' needs; or synonymously for the 'least advantaged', the 'most deprived', the 'least privileged', or the 'least fortunate'. Variations on this theme are to be found in a number of reports (Plowden 1967, Seebohm 1968, Cullingworth 1969, Black 1980, Scarman 1981), in numerous contributions to debates in Parliament (see Hansard, House of Lords, 14 February 1967: col. 209; House of Commons, 16 March 1967: cols. 738, 789, 824), in Community Relations Commission and Commission for Racial Equality reports and annual reports (CRC 1974, CRE 1977, 1978, Little and Robbins 1982), and with undiminished frequency in the social policy literature.[1]

This particular sort of rendering of the necessity for positive discrimination is revealing about the nature and conceptions of it in the minds of policy-makers and analysts whilst at the same time remaining coy about the details such as who has special or additional needs, what these consist of, and how those who have them are to be identified and located. The picture of positive discrimination that these formulations reveal is of a special practice designed to allocate resources (or 'additional' resources) to those in greatest need and whose needs are not being met by mainstream policies. It is thus an argument, as we noted in Chapter 2, for more selectivity of a kind, or for a greater concentration of resources on those with greatest needs. This is fully in keeping with the formulation of the needs principle that we have outlined – allocating resources according to degree of need towards some level of equality of welfare. One exception to this generalization must be mentioned, however. This is the case of 'special' needs, as opposed to 'additional' or 'greatest'. The latter two formulations clearly imply that positive discrimination is intended for those who have greater needs than *other people with needs*, and, as we noted earlier, distribution to equality of benefit will leave some needs unmet. This is not necessarily the case with *special* needs. People with special or peculiar needs may well be free from other needs, and their overall 'needs quotient' may not put them among the most needy (either within a particular realm of need or if overall needs could somehow be totalled). The equality of welfare principle does not require us therefore *ceteris paribus* to give priority in the allocation of resources to those with special needs, so long as they are not also additional needs. (It is not immediately obvious, for example, that handicapped people with special housing needs should take priority over those in appallingly overcrowded or poor-amenity dwellings, unless they are also living in such conditions. If the latter is the case then we can probably argue that they should be given priority since their handicap combined with their appalling conditions would constitute 'greatest' or 'additional' need.)[2]

If what were being called for were a greater concentration of resources, either by redistribution within an existing resource ceiling or by the addition of resources, on those with greatest needs, and if this is what in practice were achieved, then it would not be exceptional; but nor would it be positive discrimination. As we have seen in our discussion of universalism and selectivity, the attraction of positive discrimination is its apparently non-stigmatizing nature, which it achieves only by being relatively unselective – that is, by identifying beneficiaries by group characteristics that do not bear any necessary relationship to need itself. In practice, the group characteristic that has most often been used in Britain (as was demonstrated in Chapter 2) is that, at first sight rather odd, of area of residence (and less frequently of area of employment). Hence the almost complete association in Britain of positive discrimination (but not positive action) with priority area policies. However, I do not wish to confine the analysis to the group characteristic of areas; ethnicity, although it has been an explicit criterion to only a limited extent until recently,[3] has been the subject of debate (see Chapter 2, pages 28–31) and is at the back of most people's minds when positive discrimination is under discussion. It must also therefore be a strong contender. Sex is also the subject of positive action policies but is as yet highly marginal so far as positive discrimination is concerned in Britain.

Apart from the practice of positive discrimination being largely area based, the claim basis for positive discrimination is also often couched in terms of areas. Thus, whilst we have noted that vernacular arguments for positive discrimination frequently refer to people with special or additional needs, this is often put in the language of areas. For example, the Seebohm, Cullingworth, Black, and Scarman reports all call for positive discrimination for *areas* of greatest need, areas of racial disadvantage, or areas of greatest health needs. This is probably no more than a reflection of the close association that has developed between positive discrimination and priority area policies; but whilst the use of 'area' may serve as a synonym for 'concentrations of ethnic minority group members', this is not necessarily the case. There is an overlap between 'areas of greatest need' and the 'needs of ethnic minorities', but they do not entirely coincide.

What then are the additional (and special) needs that are being referred to? This is not always, or even often, made explicit, but we can make some assumptions. I take 'areas of greatest need' to by synonymous with 'areas of deprivation' or 'multiple deprivation' that have been the subject of inner-city policies since 1968. I have shown elsewhere (Edwards 1975, 1984) that urban deprivation is a portmanteau term into which can be (and is) thrown any and every social problem. There can be no doubt that there are some areas in some cities that exhibit high concentrations of a wide range of problems, from bad housing and unemployment to wife – and baby-battering and mugging, and this no doubt has been the attraction of small-area programmes – that such areas are like festering ulcers on the body of the welfare state which cry out for localized injections of resources to cure their problems. This is not the same however as saying that all the inhabitants of such areas are multiply deprived or have multiple problems and therefore constitute the most needy. Where problems are additive, then they may well constitute the basis for greatest need, but this is not manifestly the case for all, or perhaps even most, residents of inner-city areas. The calculus of needs is highly complex (as Davies 1968 has shown), and the concatenation of problems if these are relatively minor does not necessarily outweigh gross deprivation on one dimension (e.g.

extreme poverty). We shall have more to say on this when we consider the arguments for positive discrimination in respect of areas, but our attention will in general focus on needs in the major social policy areas of housing, education, employment, health, income, and personal social services. The same will be the case when we look at some ethnic minorities; that is, our concern will mainly be with the extent of needs in some of these main areas (housing, education, employment, and income), but with the necessary addition of respect and status – which, although they are to a large extent 'special' needs of some minorities (as a result of racial discrimination), do constitute an important area of need.

2 The requirements for justiciable positive discrimination

In the light of the discussion of need as a vernacular argument for positive discrimination, we can now specify the requirements that have to be met for positive discrimination to be a justiciable need-meeting practice. The justicization for positive discrimination so far as it is based on need and to the extent that the needs principle is interpreted (as here) as distribution according to degree of need to some level of equality of benefit, must be this. There is a sufficient concentration of people living in the area or who are members of a particular ethnic minority group, who have greater needs than others with needs who do not live in the area or who belong to non-preferred groups, to warrant the use of the group criterion as the best or least-cost way of allocating resources to bring such people nearer to equality of welfare even talking into account the injustice incurred by benefiting people in that area or ethnic group who do not themselves have greater needs than others not so defined. Furthermore, we must require of positive discrimination, if it is to be a justiciable practice, that in using whole-group criteria it does in fact bring nearer to equality of welfare all, or most, of those with greatest needs and not only some of them. The equality of welfare principle requires that we treat like cases alike, and we must therefore benefit all those with greatest needs to the same extent. We are allowing (for 'best' or least-cost reasons) that some will benefit who do not have great needs, but this cannot be compounded by leaving many of those with the greatest needs without benefit.

A further consequence of our formulation of positive

discrimination must be that if *all* the residents of selected areas or *all* members of an ethnic group are the most needy (of *all* with needs) then the use of the group criterion (area or ethnic group) to select beneficiaries is *not* positive discrimination. In the circumstance of a complete coincidence between the most needy and a particular ethnic group, say, the use of that group's (exclusive) characteristics to identify beneficiaries is simply a way of selecting those who ought to benefit under the needs principle and does not constitute a distinctive practice that warrants the distinct title of 'positive discrimination'.

One further consequence of the way that positive discrimination is characterized was alluded to in Chapter 2. This is that the assertion to be found in Lord Scarman's report (1981) and in the literature of social policy (for example, Titmuss 1968, Pinker 1971, Brown and Madge 1982), that ethnic minorities may be equated, for the purposes of positive discrimination, with other need groups such as the handicapped and the deprived, is misconceived. Need groups, or special need groups, are defined in ways that are constitutive of need (handicapped, the infirm, elderly, the sick, battered wives, etc.); 'ethnic minority' on the other hand is not a term that is itself constitutive of need (even though members of some ethnic minorities have high levels of need). So when we use the term 'to discriminate' in its colloquial and normative as opposed to its literal meaning, we cannot 'positively discriminate in favour of the most needy' in the sense that we can in respect to ethnic minorities or bus drivers or red-heads. Positive discrimination must mean using non-justice-relevant criteria or it means nothing.

We turn now to an examination of the three claims for positive discrimination that were outlined in the prolegomenon to this chapter:

(a) that positive discrimination does not fall foul of the equality principle because all members of preferred groups have *higher* need claims (and not just need claims) than people outside the groups;
(b) that positive discrimination does not contradict the equality principle because the degree of correlation between higher need claims and the group membership is so high as to make the use of whole-group criteria the best, least-cost, or on balance most just way of meeting needs;
(c) that positive discrimination is not about beneficiary selection

but rather about giving 'more' or 'additional' resources to the most needy.

The first two claims will be examined in respect of areas and ethnic minorities in turn, and our attention will focus largely on the second claim. The first claim is relatively uninteresting because it is manifestly empirically unsound; and if it *were* true, the practice involved, as I have shown, would be neither contentious nor positive discrimination. The third claim I shall argue is empty, it is a sleight of hand.

2.1 The area criterion

Are priority area policies positive discrimination? On our characterization of positive discrimination they must be. Behind the bland phraseology, 'giving resources to areas of greatest need' means 'giving resources to people who live in a spatially defined unit'. The intended beneficiaries (although not always the actual ones) are people defined by a group characteristic – that of residence or employment. Nevertheless, there are qualitative differences between discriminating on an area basis or according to, say, ethnicity or colour that make the former acceptable and the latter less so in common orthodoxy. Since these differences are relevant to our discussion of the three claims, they must be outlined here.

Area positive discrimination is acceptable because it is an anodyne or 'soft' form of positive discrimination, and this stems in part from its characteristics as a group appellant, partly from the way, as we have seen, it allows social problems to be characterized, and partly from the nature of the benefits that in practice it allocates. We have discussed the second of these reasons above; the first and third require some elaboration.

Unlike ethnicity or colour, area of residence is not an inherent human characteristic; it does not easily or readily mark people off from others. It is less easy therefore to attach to people, because of their place of residence or work, such negative (and therefore 'undeserving') characteristics as common prejudice may attach to particular ethnic groups – (although this is not to deny that people do suffer discrimination because of the reputation of the area in which they live, as the difficulties of getting a loan or hire purchase or a mortgage with a Toxteth or Moss Side or Brixton address will testify). We are therefore more likely to accept as a reason for having a need that 'it is the fault of the area' than that it is our fault for pursuing racially discriminatory practices.

Secondly, 'area' can more easily be equated with need than can ethnicity. We are more easily convinced of the deprivation suffered by people who live in some inner-city areas than that need is a strong correlate of ethnicity. And if we do associate need with ethnicity, common orthodoxy is more likely to attribute this as a fault on the part of its possessors than is the case with areas.

Thirdly, 'area' is a characteristic that everyone could in theory possess (where by 'area' we mean a deprived area), whilst ethnicity is not. All (or most) of us may fall on hard times; we cannot change our colour.

As important as its particular characteristics as a collective description in making 'area' an acceptable group definition for positive discrimination is the sort of benefit to which it lends itself, particularly when it is combined with the kind of problem definition we noted above. Area policies by their nature prescribe generalized and collective rather than individualized benefits. Thus if the problems are seen to be general and collective ones of 'multi-' or 'urban' deprivation the sort of solution they suggest will also be collective in nature. This is in fact the case, although not without exceptions, as is clear from the kind of provision that has been made under such area-based positive discrimination programmes as Section 11, the Traditional Urban Programme, the Community Development Projects, and the Inner Area Programmes of Partnership and Programme Authorities. The emphasis has been on provisions such as community centres, advice centres, play-groups, nursery schools, environmental work, and job creation programmes. The advantage of such forms of benefit from a 'public acceptability' point of view is, as we noted in Chapter 2, that they do not allow of the identification of particular beneficiaries nor of quantifiable benefits. It is the difference between setting up a benefit claims advice centre in an area on the one hand, and paying higher rates of supplementary benefit to all the people in that area on the other. The first is 'acceptable', the second is not. Whether the sort of provision that area policies promote is the one that is most likely to meet the needs of the residents is doubtful, but that is an empirical rather than a moral issue.

For these reasons, then, area-based positive discrimination

policies constitute a 'soft' and acceptable form of positive discrimination. This inheres partly in the nature of 'area' as a group appellant and partly in the nature of the benefits area designations promote, in both theory and practice. However, area policies would become a 'harder' form of positive discrimination (and less acceptable) if individualized benefits were given to people defined on an area basis. Examples would be higher supplementary benefit rates, higher pensions, better housing benefit, and housing waiting-list points given solely on the basis of residence within a designated priority area. None of these, although entirely feasible, would be politically thinkable.

How extensive are area positive discrimination policies in Britain today? We should have to include all those policies and programmes that fall under the general rubric of inner-city or urban deprivation policies. These currently (1986) number twelve and comprise the following:

Partnership Authorities
Programme Authorities
Other Designated Districts
Traditional Urban Programme
Section II Grants
Industrial Improvement Areas
Enterprise Zones
Urban Development Corporations
Local Enterprise Agencies
Derelict Land Grants
Urban Development Grants
Freeports[4]

In addition, Housing Action Areas, General Improvement Areas, and Priority Estates Projects might be included, although they do not generally fall under the label of inner-city policies.

The strategies used in these programmes take two main forms: the direct allocation of capital or revenue funding to (mainly) local authorities and voluntary agencies to establish projects of a variety of kinds; and the use of incentives,[5] such as tax and rates concessions, subsidies, relaxed planning regulations, and the provision of physical infrastructure, to attract industry and commerce as a means of generating employment.[6] These two strategies do not differ in principle, both having the effect of increasing, if only marginally, the resources going into areas of need – although not necessarily to *people* most in need.[7] However, allowing area incentives as a form of positive discrimination does widen its scope to include many urban and regional policies that are not normally included under its label. Certainly, incentive policies do enable the state to distance itself from the benefiting process by using private enterprise as the intermediary and hence provide a form of positive discrimination that, as S. M. Miller (1973) points out, conforms more closely to free market values.

In addition to the specific programmes mentioned above there are a range of policies that, although not normally called positively discriminatory, must be regarded as marginal cases, because they do not differ in principle. Such would be allocatory policies such as Rate Support Grant and the Resources Allocation Working Party formula for distributing health resources between the health regions (see Department of Health and Social Security 1976, Buxton and Klein 1978). There is little point in debating whether or not such policies are examples of positive discrimination. It doesn't really matter. My view is that they are not. The 'areas' involved are incidental, they are administrative (as opposed to designated) units, and they are large enough (local authorities and regions) to allow a high *overall* correlation between need levels and levels of resources allocated. They constitute straightforward allocation according to the needs principle at an aggregate level.

We have noted the sorts of area-based positive discrimination policy that do exist in Britain and the kind of benefit that they provide; but we have not so far considered how the beneficiary areas (which on our interpretation of the needs principle ought to be the areas of *greatest* need on one or more dimension of policy provision) are selected. This we shall need to do when we analyse whether area-based positive discrimination policies represent the best and most just ways of bringing those with high levels of need closer towards some notional equality of welfare. As a prelude to this analysis, it is necessary to hypothesize the form that 'harder' area positive discrimination might, but does not, take. The examples given below are intended to be illustrative rather than comprehensive of all possibilities.

Let us suppose that an area the size of half a dozen enumeration districts has been designated on the basis of a range of social indicators as one of high need. What might we do in each of the main areas of policy provision to meet the needs of people in the area that would constitute 'hard' positive discrimination?

In the field of housing, as we have seen, we might provide higher housing benefit for residents in the area (although this might be seen as an income maintenance provision). We could allocate more housing waiting-list points for residence in the area. Or we could simply give area residents first priority for rehousing elsewhere should they wish.

In education, it is more difficult to hypothesize hard cases ('soft' cases are easy). The chance of extra years of schooling for children in the area might be an example. Lower entry qualifications for jobs, further, and higher education certainly would be.

Again, in the field of health care, 'soft' cases of positive discrimination are easy to come by – more health centres, more intensive preventive health and health education programmes. But given the nature of health care, it would not lend itself to 'hard' positive discrimination. It is possible to envisage priority placement on waiting-lists for area residents, but this would be difficult to defend in logic, let alone in morality. Perhaps preferential screening for morbidity for the area residents might count, but this falls at the margins of 'hard' and 'soft' positive discrimination.

The same goes for personal social services, where the distribution of resources – mainly in the form of social-work labour – is largely dictated by the exigencies of crisis work. Giving priority in terms of casework effort and time might count as 'hard' positive discrimination, but again would be difficult to defend in logic. Community work would be, and has usually been, a straightforward example of 'soft' positive discrimination given the generalized nature of its benefits. (It was the rhetoric rather than the practice of the Community Development Projects that ruffled feathers in the Home Office.)

Income maintenance provisions on the other hand are very much personalized benefits. As we have noted, higher supplementary benefit rates for area residents would be a paradigm case of 'hard' positive discrimination.

Although employment has not been included here as a major social policy area (with no good reason other than that, perversely, it has not been traditionally considered as such), it is worth considering what might constitute 'hard' positive discrimination in this field. We have already noted job-generation policies as a common form of 'soft' area positive discrimination; giving preference in job hiring, or requiring lower qualifications for area residents, would constitute a 'hard' form.

How much of the actual 'soft' and the hypothetical 'hard' positive discrimination that has been outlined above could be justicized against the requirements that we have set – that the degree of coincidence of 'greatest need' and area of residence (or employment) is such that the use of the area designation as the identifier of beneficiaries represents the most effective and most just way of meeting need? This really translates into a question about the degree of spatial concentration of greatest needs and the size of areas that might be designated for positive discrimination. Given the nature of the distribution of many deprivation indices in British cities, it is possible to increase the proportion of the population of an area who have high needs by reducing the size of the defined area – say, to one street or block. The problem is then that in order to pick up the majority of those in need many such areas would have to be identified, with consequent loss of efficiency. Conversely, you can catch more of the deprived by designating larger areas but you then increase the proportions of resources going to the non-needy.

There is a considerable amount of data now available and processed on the spatial distribution of deprivations (rather less on their concentration) in the UK, and it is not the intention to reproduce these data here.[8] Some illustrative points will suffice to show what is evident from studies of the distribution and concentration of needs in the UK: that whilst we all know that many deprivations are relatively concentrated (usually in the inner areas of large cities), the degree of concentration is not nearly as high as is often assumed, and on most measures of deprivation the great majority of those with greatest needs do not live in the areas of greatest concentration.

The best analysis of the degree of concentration of a selection of deprivations, indicators of which were derived from the Census, is that by Holtermann (1975) using 1971 data.[9] Holtermann was able to show, for example, that the 5 per cent of enumeration districts in urban Great Britain with the highest percentages of overcrowded households contained 33 per cent of all overcrowded households in Great Britain.[10] The equivalent figure for unemployed males seeking work was 16 per cent; for heads of households in socio-economic group II, 18 per cent; for children aged up to fourteen and for pensioners (both measures of high potential demand for services), 11 and 9 per cent respectively. The need indicator showing the highest degree of spatial concentration was households sharing a dwelling, where the equivalent figure was 51 per cent; and if we take New Commonwealth ethnic origin as a potential indicator of high need levels (assuming for the moment what we shall later need to test), then it shares 'first place' with households sharing.

Thus if we wished to use area-based positive discrimination to attack overcrowding and to lift overcrowded households nearer to equality of welfare, and if we did so by concentrating our efforts and resources on the 5 per cent of enumeration districts with the highest concentrations, we could hope to reach only a third of overcrowded households. If, on a similar basis, we wished to tackle male unemployment, we would reach only 16 per cent of our target population. And whilst precise estimates are impossible, a reasonable 'guesstimate' would be that current priority area policies probably target no more than 3 to 4 per cent of all urban enumeration districts.

Furthermore, if our concern is with overall need rather than with needs of single dimensions, the degree of spatial concentration of multiple needs indicators is considerably less than the figures we have quoted for single needs. Certainly, our 'intuitive' picture is one of heavy concentrations of deprivation in inner-city areas, and such a picture is supported by the most recent census analyses (see Department of the Environment 1983). But what we forget – or what present policy concerns seduce us to ignore – is that the vast majority of the deprived don't live in the urban black spots, or even in 'deprived areas'. To catch them all, or most of them, we should have to designate large tracts of urban and rural Britain as 'priority areas', a point that has been argued by Townsend (1976).

If these illustrative data are any indication of the degree of spatial concentration of deprivations, then area designation as a means of delivering benefits – either collective or individual – must be relatively ineffective. Equally, however, some benefits – mainly collective ones such as housing and environmental improvements, community centres, advice centres, sports and leisure facilities, and job generation schemes – must necessarily be provided on an area basis, either because they are specifically spatial themselves (as with environmental works) or because they serve a catchment area (as with community centres). Such area collective benefits are non-problematical for positive discrimination because justice would be satisfied if allocation were on a proportion-to-need basis. This is a matter of territorial justice (see Davies 1968), which requires only that levels of provision *as between areas* are proportional to variations in need as between areas; and this, we saw, is not positive discrimination. It would not necessarily be best achieved however by specific area designations. Of more significance is whether expenditures to guarantee territorial justice in the distribution of facilities such as community and advice centres and leisure complexes would create such a burden on welfare expenditure as significantly to reduce the resources available to meet other needs that *may* be thought (by providers or recipients or both) as being more important.[11] This is not a debate we can enter into here.

Hard-case (individualized-benefit) positive discrimination is a more paradigmatic test of the justiciability of area-based positive discrimination. Given the situation briefly outlined above and our earlier arguments, can a case be made in justice for the kind of hard-case positive discrimination of which hypothetical examples were presented on pages 90–1? Perhaps a prior question in this respect must be 'Why would we *want* to pursue the sort of example given?' There are several possible answers to this, but the main one would probably be that we would want to get relatively more benefits to those with greatest need in order to bring them closer to equality of welfare (by, in effect, squashing the bottom of the distribution), and to do so without imposing more or greater stigma. That is, we would want to be *more* selective without being stigmatizing. Secondary reasons would concern effectiveness, efficiency, and administration costs.

It is not my intention to conduct a cost-benefit or balance-of-justice analysis. The following remarks are intended only to indicate what considerations would have to be taken into account in assessing the justiciability of area positive discrimination. None the less, it behoves us to provide at least the rudiments of an answer.

Firstly, then, assuming a desire to concentrate greater resources on those in greatest need, area positive discrimination is not the only way in which it could be done. More detailed selectivity on an individual basis, combined with a more rigorous redistribution within a given resource ceiling to individuals and households thus identified as in greatest need, or increased welfare expenditure with all the 'extra' going to those most in need, would be an alternative. We cannot justicize area positive discrimination on the 'only way' criterion.

Secondly, given the picture of the spatial distribution of deprivation sketched earlier, it is highly unlikely that area positive discrimination could be more effective or more efficient than the individual selectivity alternative. The degree of concentration of deprivations (at least the ones we have examined) is such that too few of the most needy and too many of the not so needy would benefit to fulfil the equality principle. We would be treating too many like cases differently and too many different cases alike.

Thirdly, on the matter of administrative costs, given that much of the data relevant to the identification of deprived areas are readily available and relatively easily processed, identification costs could be relatively low. However, they would still represent additional costs if area positive discrimination were to top up existing forms of selectivity or if current means tests were maintained and additional resources given to those in greatest need. The only circumstance in which area positive discrimination would produce a cost saving would be if the alternative were more detailed and investigatory individual means tests.

Finally, in order to assess on-balance justice, it would be necessary to weigh the injustices involved in area-based selection of recipients (which would inhere in the transgression of the equality principle) against the costs in stigma and the violation of status, self-respect, and respect by others. This constitutes a complex piece of moral calculus and would require consideration of the following: that the empirical evidence suggests that the equality principle would be massively contravened; that the positive discrimination would have to substitute for the alternative of more detailed and invasory individual means tests; and that it would probably also have to substitute for some, at least, of the existing means tests.

On the basis of such tentative assessments, it seems likely that hard-case area positive discrimination would not satisfy our requirements and must remain unjusticized. As for soft-case area positive discrimination, characterized (except in the cases of jobs, housing, and environmental improvement) by collective and less tangible benefits, the issues are at once less clear but, as indicated earlier, more marginal. So far as employment generation and environmental and housing improvement are concerned, there is no clear alternative to an area approach *if there is to be any selectivity according to need at all*. In these circumstances, concentrating resources and effort in the areas of greatest need seems unexceptionable. What must be at issue is whether the areas of greatest need are the ones actually selected and whether the benefits go to those in greatest need. As we noted earlier, there is too much doubt on both these counts to be sanguine.

When we consider the other kinds of collective benefit that

have been provided by priority area programmes (including educational, health, and general community benefits), justice would be better served by area allocations proportional to area needs, or at least to potential demands, than by designating priority areas. The only exception to this of any real substance would be if an argument could be sustained that a concentration and multiplicity of deprivations in a particular area somehow created an additional 'area effect' – that is, some substantiation of the 'urban black spot' thesis. Other than for that reason many current area positive discrimination policies seem more important for their symbolic and political functions than for the reality of any benefits they bring to the most needy.

2.2 The ethnic minority criterion

There is very little positive discrimination in favour of ethnic minorities in Britain today. Some area programmes such as the original Urban Programme used area selection as a surrogate for ethnic minority selection;[12] Section 11 provides for some collective benefits for ethnic minority groups; and since 1982 the Inner Area Programmes of the Partnership and Programme Authorities have included – at ministerial behest – more approvals for ethnic-minority-specific projects providing collective forms of benefit. But none of this represents what in the previous section we called hard-case positive discrimination – that is, positive discrimination that provides quantifiable benefits to identifiable beneficiaries. This section considers the justiciability of hard-case positive discrimination for some ethnic minority groups in Britain today. This is our primary concern rather than a discussion of what *are* the best ways of meeting the needs of ethnic minorities, but this will of necessity be considered in our analysis of the most effective and efficient, least-cost, and on balance most just ways of so doing.

Since there is virtually no hard-case ethnic minority positive discrimination in practice, we must consider the justiciability of hypothetical rather than extant examples, and the form that these might take would be similar in principle to those given above in respect of areas.[13] So far as selected ethnic minorities were concerned this would mean for example awarding additional housing points to all members of preferred minority groups on housing waiting-lists, giving them priority in rehousing, requiring lower entry qualifications for education, professional training (including as doctors and lawyers), apprenticeship, and employment purposes, giving higher rates of supplementary benefit, housing benefit, and family income supplement, and so on. Lest it might be thought that *any* argument for any form of priority treatment for ethnic minorities is damaged by citing what might seem to some – and what 'common orthodoxy' might see – as 'extreme' and 'patently unjust' examples, it should be said that this is in fact what positive discrimination would consist in. And neither is it self-evident that common orthodoxy is right in assuming such practices to be unjust. If it were found that some ethnic minority groups were consistently more badly housed and educated, consistently poorer, and consistently to be found in the worst and worst-paid jobs, then in the absence of good reason (such as that all members of the group are qualified only to do the worst jobs), positive discrimination of the sort evidenced above would not be unjust.

Conversely, some might argue that it is self-evident that blacks in Britain should get some priority in the allocation of social goods and benefits and that testing the justiciability of positive discrimination is a moral nicety and an indulgence. In response to that, it has to be said that the self-evidence must have some foundation; it cannot be for purely quixotic reasons that we should want to prefer ethnic minorities in welfare distributions, and that foundation must presumably lie in assertions about the greater disadvantage and the racial discrimination suffered by ethnic minority group members. And it is just such assertions that a test of the justiciability of positive discrimination sets out to examine.

Following the pattern of our previous analysis, a test of the justiciability of positive discrimination for ethnic minorities would require an examination of the extent to which members of some ethnic groups have greater needs and suffer greater deprivations than the rest of the population. The justiciability of using ethnicity as a group criterion for identifying welfare beneficiaries will depend on whether this proves to be the only, the best, or the most just way of bringing minority group members nearer to equality of benefit. Again, as with our analysis of areas, space does not permit of more than an illustrative treatment of the degree of concentration of needs among ethnic minorities, and this has in any case been covered comprehensively elsewhere (D. J. Smith and Whalley 1975, D. J. Smith 1977,

C. Brown 1984, as well as the reports of the 1981 Census and continuing coverage in *Social Trends*). A completely adequate test of the justiciability of positive discrimination for ethnic minority groups would require a more comprehensive data analysis than is provided here; but it is unlikely that data other than those summarized below would paint a very different picture.

The most recent substantial study of the condition of the main ethnic minority groups in Britain is that undertaken by the Policy Studies Institute during 1982 and published in 1984 (see C. Brown 1984), and it is from this that the illustrative data in *Table 2* are drawn. These data enable at least a tentative comparison of the needs and deprivations of different ethnic groups (whites, West Indians, and Asians, and subdivisions within the Asian population), in respect of housing, education, employment, and income; they do not however enable us to say very much about the other major areas of policy provision, health and personal social services.

A number of caveats would need to be attached to the table for a full explanation of the data to be found in it. But for present purposes the data are presented as illustration only, and it is doubtful that the overall picture presented would alter very much when all qualifications and caveats had been taken into account. There is nevertheless one significant aspect of relative ethnic deprivations that the table does not illustrate but the PSI study (Brown 1984) emphasizes. When the data are analysed by area, and the patterns of relative ethnic deprivation in inner London, Birmingham, and Manchester are isolated from the national picture (as Brown's analyses allow), it is found that many of the differences between white ethnics and minority ethnic groups all but disappear, especially in respect of housing and unemployment. In short, the patterns of deprivation in the inner cities were typical for many West Indians and Asians; for whites, they were very atypical. On the whole, whites in the inner cities were as deprived on most dimensions as the ethnic minorities were.[14] If *any* positive discrimination were to be practised, therefore, a selection of beneficiaries by area rather than by ethnicity would be more just.

Perhaps the most disquieting of Brown's findings was that relative patterns of deprivation as between the ethnic groups had not changed in any significant degree since people of Afro-Caribbean and Asian origin arrived in Britain in any numbers.

We have not, it would seem, made much progress in reducing social and economic inequalities between the races over the past three decades. Patterns of inequality in respect of ethnicity, as in relation to the inner cities, have become fossilized. This must be a consideration in our evaluation of positive discrimination as a means of fulfilling the requirements of justice.

In the light of the extent and degree of concentration of greatest needs among ethnic minority groups revealed by these data, what can we now say about the justiciability of positive discrimination as a measure for bringing minority group members closer to equality of welfare and nearer to genuine fair equality of opportunity? Is the degree of correlation between minority group membership and greatest needs such as to make the use of ethnicity as the identifying characteristic of welfare beneficiaries the only, best, most efficient and effective, least-cost, or most just way of meeting the needs and hence of promoting equality of opportunity for those in greatest disadvantage? With the possible exception of the Bangladeshi and, to a lesser extent, the Pakistani population, the evidence is not such as to allow us to say that ethnic minorities in Britain are consistently and *entirely* more disadvantaged than the white majority, in the sense that *all* or *almost all* minority group members of either or both sexes are worse off than the white population. This is patently not the case. Inequalities between ethnic groups do exist, and persist, but they are not so great as to make positive discrimination for ethnic minorities the most effective or efficient and certainly not the most just way of bringing *all* those with greatest needs nearer to equality of benefit. Too many whites share the same deprivations – especially, as we saw, those who live in the same sort of area as the majorities of ethnic minority groups – and their needs would go unmet. If positive discrimination on any criterion were to be implemented, on the basis of these data it ought to be area-based and concentrated on the inner cities. Such action however would be subject to the criticisms of area positive discrimination we noted earlier, as well as being discriminatory against deprived ethnic minority members outside the inner cities. Similarly, too many ethnic minority members are not among the most deprived and they would gain the same benefits as those of the minority groups who were among the most disadvantaged, which would be denied to the whites who share this disadvantage. There would (as with the use of areas as the group criterion) be a massive

Table 2 Relative needs and deprivations of the main ethnic groups in England and Wales

	main ethnic groups (Bangladeshi and Pakistani included in 'All Asian' but some data also given separately)														
	White			*West Indian*			*All Asian*			*Bangladeshi*			*Pakistani*		
need or deprivation indicator	*M*	*F*	*All*	*M*	*F*	*All*	*M*	*F*	*All*	*M*	*F*	*All*	*M*	*F*	*All*
% in private rental accom.			9			6			6			11			
% in flats			11			27			12			43			
% in LA sector in flats			27			54			54						
% in LA sector in buildings (5+ storeys)			6			22			22						
% in pre-1945 dwelling			50			60			74						86
% in pre-1919 dwelling			24			23			34						44
% households share dwelling			1			4			5			12			
% households at > 1 p.p.r.			3			16			35			60			
% households at > 1½ p.p.r.			1			3			12			32			
% households no exclusive use ams.			6			6			6			18			
% terminate education at 16 yrs	23			39			18								
% continue education beyond 17 yrs.	17	21		16	25		43	31							
% 16–24 continue education beyond 16 yrs	29	47		41	51		58	50							

% 16–24 with O-level or ONCD	21			32			28					
% 16–24 with no academic or vocational qualifications	27	22		35	21		35	50				
unemployment rate	13	10		23	16		20	20		29	50	29
% unemployed > 1 year	5	2		13	9		13	9				
% semi-skilled manual	13			26			34			57		35
% unskilled manual	3			9			6			12		
% with O-level but in unskilled or semi-skilled work			5			17			34			
median gross weekly income £	129	77.5		109	81.2		110	73				
% households receiving child benefit			34			60			75			
% households receiving unemployment benefit			7			17			16			
% households receiving F.I.S.			1			5			2			
% households receiving S.B. + pensions			14			20			11			

Notes

1 Source: C. Brown 1984.

2 Data are for 1982; Scotland is excluded.

3 All percentages are rounded.

4 Data for Bangladeshi and Pakistani populations are selective; only where marked divergencies from the 'All Asian' figures occur are separate data shown.

contravention of the equality principle. Too many like cases would be treated differently, and too many unalike cases the same. It may well be argued that positive discrimination would not result in every member of an ethnic minority gaining an advantage, and neither would this be its purpose. Preferential access to universities or polytechnics would be an example. However, whilst selective beneficence such as this might be pursued for purposes of utility it is fundamentally unjust because it would contravene the equality principle and, as we shall see, it would give greater benefits to the less needy – especially in the case cited.

A possible exception to this general conclusion might be made for the Bangladeshi and, to a lesser extent, the Pakistani populations. The data show that Bangladeshis are more concentrated in the privately rented sector of housing than any other ethnic minority group. They are far more likely to live in flats; they have the highest levels of sharing with other households and by far the highest rates of overcrowding and serious overcrowding; and they are far more likely to lack the exclusive use of basic housing amenities. In education, again, the Bangladeshis are among the most educationally deprived and suffer far more than any other group from English language difficulties that exacerbate other disadvantages such as those in employment. The latter show up in unemployment rates, which are highest for Bangladeshi women (although now closely followed by West Indian males), and in the proportions of Bangladeshi males in semi- and unskilled manual work, which far exceed those for any other group. This evidence would support at least a prima facie case for concentrating more resources and better quality benefits on the Bangladeshi minority especially in housing, education, and employment. However, this is only a prima facie case and would have to be supplemented by an account of the reasons why Bangladeshis suffer so disproportionately from a variety of disadvantages. Not least among these would be the apparently strong desire of the Bangladeshi community to remain close-knit and spatially concentrated. This closeness of the community must at least in part account for the limited extent to which the Bangladeshi group has shared in the wider benefits of society, and any remedial action must take account of it.

Despite these general conclusions about positive discrimination for ethnic minorities in Britain, the fact remains not only that there are considerable inequalities between the majority white population and the main ethnic minority groups, but that these inequalities have persisted ever since West Indians and Asians arrived in this country. Need and deprivation are not randomly distributed across the ethnic groups that make up the population. The lesson that must be drawn from this is that so far as we have relied upon the straightforward operation of the needs principle – allocating welfare in proportion to the need for it – this principle has not proved to be adequate in equalizing welfare. The needs principle has not been indiscriminate in its effects in respect to ethnicity and has not produced the results that in theory it ought. If positive discrimination represents too gross a violation of the basic canon of justice, what then should be done in the face of the manifest inadequacy of current strategies? We must leave this crucial question hanging for the present, but it will be part of the subject-matter of our final chapter.

3 The argument for additional allocations

We turn now to the third claim for positive discrimination outlined in the prolegomenon to this chapter. This is the claim that the distinctiveness of positive discrimination lies not in the relevance or irrelevance of the criteria for selecting beneficiaries but in the allocation of additional resources to those with the greatest needs. It is a common theme in the literature of social policy and has its roots in Plowden's (1967) call for giving schools in deprived areas 'priority in many respects', and a new 'cutting edge' to the principle that special need calls for special help. We have seen (Chapter 2, pages 6–9) that Plowden's call was not unambiguous; but whatever her intent, it has often understandably been interpreted as a call for 'more' or 'extra' resources to be allocated to the most deprived or most needy schools. And once the particular claim in respect of schools became generalized to one about the whole spectrum of welfare, positive discrimination became characterized as 'the direction of *additional* resources to areas or categories of special need' (M. Brown 1977: 228, emphasis added), 'the allocation of certain *extra* resources towards specified areas of need' (Barnes 1974: 9, emphasis added), '*extra* help for the few' (Higgins 1978: 38, emphasis added), the allocation of '*extra* resources for deprived individuals and groups' (Pinker 1971: 108, emphasis in original), giving 'a greater priority to the most deprived' and '*extra* help' to disadvantaged groups (M. Brown and Madge 1982: 293, 315, emphasis added), and distinguishing people for 'unusually favourable treatment' (Parker 1975: 152).

To characterize positive discrimination thus is a sleight of hand. The argument for additional resources as a distinctly different practice turns out to have no substance. In the field of education it appears to have more substance than in other areas of welfare, but even there, there is nothing in the 'more resources' argument. We shall take the general case first and then consider education.

If the argument for more resource concentration on the most needy is really one about the inadequacy or maldistribution of existing levels of provision, and if distribution proportional to need requires more resource concentration on the most needy, there is nothing distinctly different about what is being called for. It is an unexceptional demand based on the straightforward operation of the needs principle and is certainly not positive discrimination.

Unfortunately, the calls for 'more', 'extra', or 'additional' resources on such occasions tend to be the social administrator's equivalent of Pavlovian salivation. Ring the 'most deprived' bell and out pours the 'extra resources' response. Rarely, if ever, is it explained what the resources should be extra to or why they are required. We must assume that such calls are based on one or more of the following arguments: that the needs principle is not properly in operation and more resources at the bottom end are required to make it so (the unexceptionable argument above); or that the most needy ought to get resources additional to those they are due under the needs principle (for whatever reason); or that they should get resources additional to what they are due under the needs principle in one area of welfare because of the knock-on (or directly causal) effects or simply as substitution for a deprivation in another area of welfare that cannot be made up.

What do the second two arguments amount to? The first seems to require that we divorce the formal from the material principles of justice and attempt a justification in terms of the material needs principle without reference to the formal equality principle. But can it make any sense to separate the two? Can we claim that needs *ought* to be met *without* the correlative claim that similar needs ought to receive similar treatment? It is hard to see how such a claim could be sustained if the equality principle is to have any apodictic force. It is not a claim that the needs of *some* be met or that *some* needs be met. The material principle of need – and indeed any other material principle – has no prescriptive power unless it is tied to the formal principle of equal treatment. A defence of the 'additional resources' argument could be attempted in the terms of the equality of welfare principle by arguing that those with the greatest needs be carried beyond the level of equality of welfare that applies to others with lesser needs. Diagrammatically, the argument could be illustrated as in *Figure 1*.

Figure 1 'Additional allocations' and equality of welfare

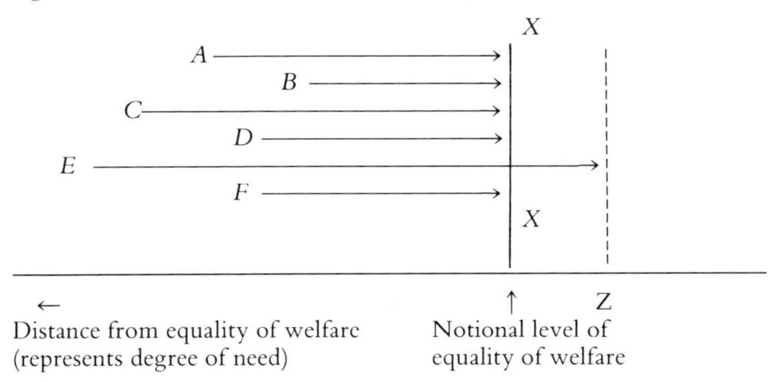

In *Figure 1*, if X represents some notional equality of welfare (either on a single dimension or on some composite measure), the principle of equal treatment to produce equality of welfare would require the allocation of resources proportional to the distance from equality of welfare. Thus A would receive $A–X$ resources, B would get $B–X$, and so on, with $D–X$ and $F–X$ representing equal amounts of resources. One possible interpretation of the 'additional resources' argument might be that E, the most needy, ought not to get just $E–X$ resources but should be taken beyond equality of welfare by receiving in addition $X–Z$ resources. (Within any given resource ceiling, this would have the effect of pushing line X backwards – that is, meeting fewer of the needs of A, B, C, D, and F. This is the 'social hijacking' phenomenon that we noted earlier.)

But why should we want to do this? We have already recognized the greater needs of E by giving them more resources than anyone else, so it cannot be on the grounds that they are the most needy. Yet this is just what must be implied by 'additional resources' arguments if they mean anything but the obvious and uncontentious claim that the needs principle be fulfilled – in which case it has nothing to do with positive discrimination. If the 'additional resources' argument means anything other than that the needs principle requires a greater weighting to the most needy in the allocation of resources, it means something that is indefensible in logic and justice.

This is not what Plowden meant in respect of education, and we must consider this apparently more substantial argument. It is essentially one about substitutability between different dimensions of welfare. If we strip the Plowden argument to its essentials and reformulate it in terms of equality of welfare it goes something like this. Some children have greater educational needs than others because they also suffer from greater needs or deprivations in other dimensions of welfare such as home background, housing, and social and physical environment. To allocate educational resources to these children on the basis of the needs principle will leave them with unmet need because of the compounding effect of the other deprivations. Because these other deprivations cannot be or are not being made good, the children should be given additional educational resources to make up for[15] their other unmet needs. In short, additional resources in one field of welfare should substitute for those that cannot be or are not being provided in others.

The question we must now ask is whether such practices of substitutability of resources constitute a distinctive practice that we can call positive discrimination. Even if the answer to this question is affirmative, it is not relevant or applicable to all areas of welfare. Causal links between deprivations on different dimensions of welfare have been established in the field of education (Halsey 1972), health, and housing; but it is far from clear that such causation links deprivation in all areas of welfare or that a substitution of resources in one area can make up for a want of resources in others. And it would hardly make sense in any case continually to boost, say, health expenditure to meet the health costs of bad housing rather than to improve the housing. Even if substitution did constitute positive discrimination in the field of education, it does not follow that it should or could be promoted as a process applicable across the whole spectrum of welfare provision.

More significantly, the argument even in respect of education that substitution constitutes a distinctive practice of positive discrimination cannot be sustained. Firstly, the substitutability argument is not an argument for going beyond equality of welfare in education. If children have greater educational needs because they suffer from other deprivations, they fall further from equality of welfare and ought simply in terms of the needs principle to get more resources to bring them up to it. The needs principle will do the job, and there is no necessity for anything that might be called positive discrimination. The additional resources are just those resources required by the needs principle to meet the housing, home-background, and environmentally induced education needs to bring the children to equality of welfare.

Secondly, even if it were a matter of taking the most educationally deprived children beyond equality of welfare in education, the very notion of substitutability implies that this is to make up for a want in other areas. The ultimate aim therefore would be to achieve some *overall* equality of welfare by making up in education what could not be done elsewhere. It is still a matter of evening up *overall* equality of welfare, not of going beyond it.

In any case, the substitutability argument is a dubious one, and our second counter argument here is probably unnecessary since the 'additional resources' claim falls with the first counter-argument. The 'additional resources' characterization of positive discrimination is a sleight of hand; it has nothing to do with positive discrimination.

Chapter 6

Positive discrimination and rights to compensation

Of the material principles of justice that we identified in Chapter 3, rights to compensation and need constitute the two most commonly claimed foundations for positive discrimination. If need underpins positive discrimination in Britain, rights to compensation most commonly form the basis for those practices in the USA that would conform to our characterization of positive discrimination. It is worth reminding ourselves, before we embark on an analysis of positive discrimination and rights, of the connection made earlier between rights and justice. Rather than treating compensatory rights or rights of restitution as elements of corrective justice, we have for the reasons enumerated in Chapter 3 adopted the more elementary approach of counting rights to compensation as one of the differences between people that justifies us in treating them differently. (But see Raphael 1955: 62 ff.) In short, compensatory rights are one of the material principles that put flesh on the purely skeletal equal treatment principle.

This suits our purposes as far as positive discrimination is concerned since one of the problems that most exercises us in this repect is that of morally relevant differences. Differential entitlements to compensation for past harm or rights denied clearly constitute differences that would justify us in discriminating in our treatment as between individuals or groups. Our problem regarding positive discrimination is to explore the prima facie injusticiability of the practice in selecting beneficiary groups on apparently morally non-relevant criteria in pursuit of differential treatment based on different rights claims. To this extent, our analysis will parallel that in our consideration of the needs principle. However, just as in that analysis we required some formulation of *what* needs to meet and to what degree of satisfaction, so in treating compensatory rights as a material principle of justice we are faced with the problem of the degree of compensation or restitution that justice requires. Indeed, it was one of our arguments for not treating compensatory rights in the context of positive discrimination as an element of *corrective* justice that, in dealing with whole-group compensation for harm suffered over long periods of time, one of the principal requirements of Aristotelian corrective justice – the restoration of the status quo ante by the granting of specifiable quantities of compensation – could not be fulfilled.

How much compensation, for how long, and to what end state is one of the central issues in the United States debate about reverse discrimination for blacks and other ethnic minorities and for women. Treating compensatory rights as a material principle of justice helps to illuminate the issues in the debate about the justiciability of positive discrimination; it does little to solve the problem of what compensation should consist in, for how long it should last, and how we shall know when all the debts have been paid. (See, for example, Lustgarten 1980: ch. 1.) We shall none the less have cause to address these problems, as well as several others, in the course of this chapter.

1 Positive discrimination and compensation

The right to compensation for past harm (or restitution, or reparations)[1] is the most usually cited basis for programmes of affirmative action or reverse discrimination in the USA. But, as we saw in Chapter 3, it is not the only ground; nor is there universal agreement that it is a sufficient or even a legitimate basis for reverse discrimination. Dworkin, for example, thinks that arguments asserting entitlements to compensation as the basis for affirmative action programmes are simply wrong: 'the programs are not based on the idea that those who are aided are entitled to aid, but only on the strategic hypothesis that helping them is now an effective way of attacking a national problem' (Dworkin 1977b: 12).[2] Again, Beauchamp (1977), while acknowledging compensation as the most commonly cited ground for positive discrimination, does not think it the most important – both because, in his view, positive discrimination does not achieve this end and also because there are firmer grounds on which to justify practices of positive discrimination.

Other commentators have noted the important distinction between compensation as restitution or rectification and compensation as 'making up for', which as we have noted is but another formulation of the needs principle (S. M. Miller 1973, Heslep

1977, Goldman 1979). As far as positive discrimination practices in the USA are based on the needs principle, we need add nothing more about them to our discussion of this principle in previous chapters save to say that, empirically, the balance-of-justice arguments will be different to those we examined in the British context in Chapter 5.[3] Equality of opportunity has nevertheless also assumed considerable significance as a goal of positive discrimination practices in the USA, as is evidenced in the titling of the agency in which primary responsibility for its implementation is vested (the Equal Employment Opportunities Commission). Thus Goldman, in his division of the grounds for positive discrimination into forward- and backward-looking, places the promotion of equality of opportunity firmly in the former (Goldman 1979). Our approach here has been different in that we have treated the promotion of equality of opportunity as a component of the needs principle (see Chapter 4), and this applies as much in the USA as in Britain.

Again, as remarked in Chapter 3, another formulation of the grounds for positive discrimination in the USA has been that its principal function is to promote racial justice by countering negative discrimination and ensuring the proper application of the equal treatment principle; and that this function is more important than, or prior to, that of compensating for past harm. (For varieties of this argument see Thalberg 1973–74; Beauchamp 1977, Dworkin 1977a, Ginsburg 1977, H. E. Jones 1977.)

A further set of arguments for positive discrimination in the US context revolve upon issues of utility and more generally consequentialism, and these will be considered in later chapters.

Despite the variety of reasons for which positive discrimination might be pursued in the USA, compensation for past harm remains the most often cited and the most important. As such it has generated a considerable volume of debate and soul-searching in both academic and legal circles. The purpose of this and the subsequent chapter is to examine the most important components of this debate. We shall then consider the British situation to see if similar claims to rights to compensation for past harm could be sustained by minority groups and women in Britain. If this turns out to be the case, we shall want to know whether positive discrimination in Britain could be justicized on these grounds.

In essence, the argument that positive discrimination is justicized or that justice requires it on the grounds of rights to compensation is a simple one. Condensed to its essentials, it is an argument that some groups in the population – how many and which groups remain a matter of contention – have suffered in the past from unjust negative discrimination on the part of the majority. Their rights to treatment as equals, and to equal treatment, have been overridden in many areas that affect life chances such as education, access to employment, housing, and health care. Furthermore, they have not been accorded the equal respect that is due to all people. Such groups have, so the argument goes, suffered harm as a result of having had their rights overridden and of not having been accorded equal respect. In consequence, the *present* condition of such groups in terms of their socio-economic status and their representation in the professions and the higher reaches of business and commerce is less than it would have been had they not suffered unjust harm in the past. In short, an unjustice has been done to some groups (and to some extent is still being done), and justice requires that the wrongs be righted by some form of compensation. Positive discrimination is one way in which compensation can be administered.

It is essential to see that a key element in the argument must be that those who have suffered harm and whose rights have been denied or overridden have a *right* in justice to compensation. They have a right to have the wrongs done to them righted. This right to compensation can be sustained in terms of rectificatory or corrective justice. But, for the reasons outlined above, the same claim can be made in terms of social or distributive justice; and, given the peculiar features of the claim (in terms of the nature of the harm, the form of the compensation, and the relative indeterminacy of the identity of the claimants and the wrongdoers), the right to compensation is in fact better treated in terms of the latter rather than the former. The right to compensation is one characteristic of people that justifies us in treating them differently in the distribution of burdens and benefits.

1.1 Compensation, restitution, and reparations

Thus far we have used the terms 'compensation', 'restitution', and 'reparations' as though they mean more or less the same thing. Although they are frequently used synonymously, along with 'rectification' and 'recompense', in the United States literature, they do in fact carry different connotations and as we noted earlier they ought to be distinguished. We are unfortunately faced with a variety of interpretations, and our solution to the terminological problem must to some extent be an arbitrary one. (For the sake of simplicity, however, we shall continue to use the term 'compensation' throughout our analysis except where something clearly different is meant.)

In general terms we can make a distinction between compensation and reparation on the one hand and restitution on the other. By the latter is meant restoring that which a victim of wrongdoing has lost – that is, what he or she has actually lost, be it property, position, status, etc. (Gross 1977: 383 ff., Honoré 1968: 64–5). There will be many cases in which pure restitution is impossible but where justice demands that some recompense be made (physical injuries are a case in point). In such cases we may validly talk of compensation or reparation for harm done, when what is given back is not what is actually lost but some approximate equivalence of value. (We shall not here examine the problems involved in calculating equivalences for non-restitutible harm but simply acknowledge that they exist and that compensation and reparation often provide only rough justice.) Goldman, however, argues that the distinction between restitution and compensation is not that the latter may substitute where the former is not possible, but that compensation is 'payment' *in addition to* restitution to the status quo ante. Thus we may wish not only that wrongdoers give back what they have taken but that they also make compensation for having caused harm (Goldman 1977: 72). It is not clear whether the primary objective here is to benefit the victim or to impose punishment on the wrongdoer. Clearly, there is a case that those who have been wronged ought to be compensated for the harm done to them as well as having restored to them that which they have lost, and in this sense 'compensation' can be seen to carry a useful and peculiar meaning of its own. However, this does not help us in those cases where restitution is not possible – and this, as we shall see, includes most of the circumstances in which we might want to exercise positive discrimination – so the simpler distinction between compensation and restitution would seem to be preferable. Goldman's formulation nevertheless brings to our attention one of the key problems that has made reverse discrimination in the USA so contentious a matter. This is the problem of how much compensation should be paid and in what form and for how long; and more particularly, whether when we exercise positive discrimination we are 'simply' trying to re-establish the status quo ante or whether in addition to this some compensation is required for the harm suffered at the time of, and since, the wrongdoing.

There is a further and somewhat different interpretation of the relationship between these terms. Day has noted that 'compensation' and 'reparation' (which we have so far treated synonymously) in fact represent the reverse sides of the same coin whereby compensation is a right and reparation is the correlative duty or obligation. Thus victims *are* compensated and wrongdoers have a duty to *make* reparation (Day 1981: 61). The distinction may be linguistically useful but does not challenge our usage of the terms as fundamentally interchangeable for the same idea.[4]

A fourth term sometimes enters the literature on positive discrimination: 'rectification' (W. T. Blackstone 1977: 53, Gross 1977: 3). We need not delay long over this; for present purposes its meaning can be taken to be broadly synonymous with compensation and reparation (but see Gross 1977: 383 ff.), and its most common usage is in the context of 'rectificatory justice'.

For our analysis we shall therefore retain the use of 'compensation' to cover those actions and purposes of positive discrimination that pertain to the rights to have past harm or wrongdoing put right. We can safely include reparations and rectification within its meaning but shall require when necessary to distinguish compensation from restitution. The latter is a more limiting concept, which if strictly applied should occur only rarely in discussions of reverse or positive discrimination for whole groups over time. It must be emphasized once more that when we talk about compensation we are referring to the right that people possess to have the wrongs done to them put right, and *not* to compensation as making up for a deficiency (as in 'compensatory education').

2 Compensation, rights, and justice

Most of the debate in the USA about compensatory reverse discrimination begins with the practice and argues its justification in terms of the rights of compensation. An alternative, though more problematical, perspective would be to begin with the wrongs committed and the harm done and argue from this what the most appropriate, practical, and effective form of compensation would be.[5] The answer might turn out to be some variety of affirmative action, but it might not. The benefits of such a perspective would at least be to force a contextual examination of affirmative action and to raise some of the more fundamental questions about its purposes and its moral standing. Since our concern is with positive discrimination, however, we shall keep it at centre stage; but it is worth casting a brief sideways glance at some of the issues that from the alternative perspective would force themselves on our attention. Two of these concern primarily what kind of right is involved and what the requirements of compensation consist of.

We begin with the indisputable fact that certain wrongs have been – and, to a lesser extent, still are being – committed against some sections of the population, primarily minority ethnic, nationality, and religious groups, and women. The victims, taken as whole groups, have in most cases suffered harm as a result. From this point two separate but linked lines of argument can be pursued. Compensatory justice requires that the wrongs be put right and that the victims of wrongdoing should be (re)instated in the status they would hold had the wrongs not been committed. And to the extent that this remains undone, justice is not satisfied. The second line of argument is more compatible with distributive justice. It is that the victims of wrongdoing now have a right to claim compensation for the harm done to them. They can claim just what compensatory justice would require. However, having that right also bestows on them the right not to exercise it, and if they chose so to do, the wrong would remain but presumably distributive justice would be satisfied. Therein lies a crucial difference between corrective and distributive justice. The former requires atonement by (and usually punishment of) the wrongdoer; the latter does not, although if the right to compensation *were* exercised it would (or ought to) be at their expense. We shall pursue the second line of argument – of rights to compensation constituting a legitimate ground for different treatment and a claim on resources.

If the victims of wrongdoing have rights to compensation, we must ask what sort of a right they have and what are the general principles of compensation that must be invoked to fulfil the right. Discussion of such questions is logically prior to any discussion about positive discrimination as a suitable compensatory practice.

There are numerous and often cross-cutting taxonomies of rights, but we may usefully begin by establishing whether the rights we have in mind are legal or moral ones. The distinction is usually taken to be that between rights that are enshrined in law and legally enforceable, and those that custom, practice, and morality argue ought to be, or indeed are, rights but which for whatever reason (usually impracticability or unenforceability) the law does not lend its shoulder to (see, for example, Benn and Peters 1959: 93 ff., M. Ginsberg 1965: ch. 3, Feinberg 1973: ch. 6, D. Miller 1976: 52 ff., Danto 1984, Gewirth 1984). Compensation for injury or harm is a well established legal right both in the USA and in Britain. It is also, of course, a moral right.[6] Whether in the particular case with which we are concerned a legal right is established is more debatable in the USA, but in Britain it certainly is not. It does not follow however that it could not be so established. There would be many difficulties, and the British legal system at least is not comfortable with class actions, but if it were to be established beyond doubt that wrongs have been done and that people (even though they be *groups* of people) had suffered as a result, then it is not inconceivable that legal remedies could be established. Group compensation for past harm is at least a suitable candidate for legal rights. Furthermore, in terms of Hohfeld's classic analysis of legal rights into claim rights, liberties, powers, and immunities (see Hohfeld 1923), rights to compensation clearly constitute claim rights; they represent a claim against a wrongdoer in the form of an individual or body of people. (We consider below against whom claims may be made in the circumstances where positive discrimination is or may be applicable.) Thirdly, we can continue the classification by asserting that the claim rights with which we are concerned are positive rather than negative rights (Fried 1978: 82) – that is, they are rights *to* something as opposed to rights of forbearance. Additionally we may say that rights to compensation are both formal and substantial rights (a distinction drawn by D. Miller 1978: 3) in so far as wrongs *in general* ought to be righted (a formal right), and that, in theory at least, the amount or degree of compensation that is due can be specified. Thus not only does the right exist in general terms, but we can, or ought to be able to, specify just what it is the claimant has a right to.

We can say, then, that the rights of groups to compensation for past harm or wrongdoing to the group are moral, and potentially legal; they are claim rights; they are positive rights and they constitute both formal and substantial rights. In short, they are positive claim rights to specifiable amounts of compensation that could potentially be enshrined in law. What is significant about such a specification is that the kind of right involved (in particular, positive claim rights) is one that is particularly correlative with duties. This is not the case with other *in rem* rights (such as some rights of forbearance), which are 'claims' against no one in particular but everyone in general. A positive claim right is one that is made against some specifiable actor or actors upon whom a duty rests to meet the claim. The problem immediately arises therefore, in the sort of case with which we are concerned, of *who* such claims can be made against. If claim rights and duties of compensation are correlative, there must be, for each claim to reparation, a party whose duty it is to fulfil this obligation. As we shall see subsequently, this raises particular and peculiar problems for cases where positive discrimination might be invoked.

Before we consider this issue, however, there is one further point in respect of rights that remains problematical for our present concerns. This relates to the issue of the exercising or non-exercising of rights, to which we alluded above. There is a sense in which rights-talk fails us in that it emphasizes the right to claim compensation and assumes the exercise of this right or the considered decision not to exercise the right, which must also be a component of possession of the right. But what of circumstances where a right to compensation exists – simply by virtue of a person having been harmed or of having had prior rights overridden – but where this right is not exercised, not in virtue of a considered decision but for any one of a number of non-voluntary reasons, which may include ignorance of the possession of the right, lack of motivation, or the impracticalities involved in exercising *group* claim rights? Is either compensatory or distributive justice satisfied in such circumstances? The question has significance because this is the situation that would appear to exist in the United States, and possibly in Britain. The pressure for affirmative action programmes has largely come from white liberal factions in the USA unlike the earlier movement for civil rights (which with the benefit of hindsight we can now see was of great significance in the history of black Americans). There would appear to be no concerted pressure for compensation for past injustices (in the form of positive discrimination or any other practice) from those who may lay claim to it. And it would be specious to argue that this is the result of a collective decision not to exercise a right that all potential claimants recognize they possess. There is a sense then in which rights-talk, in (implicitly at least) putting the onus on claimants to exercise their rights, falls short of a prescription that fully satisfies the requirements of justice. Of course, it may be argued that the state, in its role of protector of the rights of its members, carries an obligation to see that justice is done, and this it often does in the case of reluctant compensators. Empirically however it does not seem to be the case that states are particularly anxious to press claims that are not already being presented by those who hold them. This function *is* to some extent performed in modern Western democracies but usually by fourth parties (the first three being claimant, potential compensator, and state), in the form of voluntary agencies and pressure groups, which seek to sensitize and alert unwitting claimants to the rights they have and to cajole the state into recognizing them.

There is also the possibility of voluntary reparations. An argument in favour of these has been put by Silvestri. It would be an impropriety, he argues, to coerce whites into making reparations to blacks on the grounds that 'we are less afraid of unjustly giving too much [by voluntary action] than of hurting the innocent' (Silvestri 1973: 31). However, voluntary reparations are of minor importance in the case of black reparations; they are rarely forthcoming, their impact (whatever form they took) would be minimal, and, as Goldman points out, the costs could not always be confined to the guilty – especially in the case of preferential treatment: 'preferential hiring is never voluntary for those white males who apply for, and do not get, the job' (Goldman 1975: 169, fn. 1).

We shall not pursue the matter of rights to compensation any further at this stage, but must satisfy ourselves with having raised some of the more general issues involved. They will crop up again in the course of our analysis, but for the moment we must turn our attention to the second of the broader considerations we mentioned earlier; that of the requirements of compensation.

We have already noted the fundamental principle of compensation – that those who have suffered injustice or been harmed or had their rights denied or overridden have rights to compensation. Compensatory rights therefore constitute one characteristic of people that justifies us in treating them differently. As with the needs principle, however, the equal treatment principle requires a firmer foundation before it satisfies our requirements. Thus not only must like cases be treated similarly (a demand that could be satisfied by making no compensation to anyone who had suffered harm) but a further, and 'external' requirement must be that rights denied and harm suffered *ought* to be compensated. And whereas in the case of need we identified the ultimate foundation in the Kantian categorical imperatives, in the case of compensation we need look no further than the language of rights itself and the demands of compensatory justice.[7]

The basic statement of compensatory rights must be further elaborated by the assertion that the compensation must be proportional to the harm suffered (see Beauchamp 1977: 87, W. T. Blackstone 1977: 67, Hoffman 1977: 268). We may derive the proportionality requirement either from the Aristotelian principle of compensation or, indeed, from the equal treatment principle, since to treat like cases alike and dissimilar cases differently necessarily involves treatment that is proportional to the degree to which the material principle is possessed by potential beneficiaries. Formulated in this way, the principle of compensation is philosophically uncontentious and well recognized when applied to individuals. It is problematic however when applied to groups in circumstances where it is not self-evident that all members of the group, without exception, have suffered harm. As we shall see, this problem lies at the heart of the debate about positive discrimination.

There remain in relation to compensatory rights two further issues that are less unambiguous than the simple assertions made so far. Both are germane to the debate about positive discriminaton. The first raises the question of what exactly compensation is for. Despite the voluminous literature that has contributed to the debate about positive discrimination is the USA, this question remains to be answered satisfactorily. There is a general assumption (which we have so far shared) that compensation is due because of the harm suffered as a result of past injustice or the violation of rights. We might also assert that the violation of rights is itself something that ought to be compensated; and whilst there is a close connection between rights violation and harm or injury suffered, the two are by no means coterminous. Intentional injury inflicted on another, without their consent, would constitute a violation of their rights of forbearance, but not all injury results from rights violation (being struck by lightning, for example), nor does all rights violation result in injury (except definitionally). Ought we than to accept that compensation is due in *all* cases of injury or rights violation? So far as injury is concerned, the answer is a simple 'no'. We may wish as an act of supererogation to help the injured, or indeed we can argue that we all have *in rem* rights to assistance when we suffer hurt, and carry the correlative duty to help all the afflicted; but these are not rights and duties of compensation, even though the language of compensation is often used in such circumstances. The answer in respect of rights violation is by no means as self-evident. Surely if we take rights seriously (in Dworkin's happy phrase) we must be concerned when they are overridden or violated even if no harm is done. In practical terms we must take cognizance of the importance of both the rights involved and the degree of their transgression, and we have better things to do than to compensate and punish for trivial infractions of trivial rights, but this would be taken care of by the application of the like-treatment principle, following which, compensation would be proportional to the significance of the rights violated and the extent to which they were violated, irrespective of the harm caused.

This is a more contentious argument but not normally one that we find particularly troublesome, because we rarely have to face up to it in practice. However, it takes on a pronounced significance in the context of positive discrimination, where our concern is with whole groups and a longer time span than is normal in compensation claims. For example, we are usually willing to entertain a claim to compensation from groups who have clearly suffered harm as a result of their rights being violated in the past – even if we dispute the particular nature of the claim and the form that the compensation should take. But what of claims from groups who have suffered rights violation in the past but who in the longer term appear not to have suffered significant harm or injury? (The Jewish community in the USA or Britain might be an example of such a group; their representation in the professions and the higher reaches of commerce and business is not, unlike that of blacks, such as to indicate that they have suffered great harm *as a group* from past injustices.) In practice, it would seem that we are not prepared to entertain such claims – no one, so far as I know, has called for affirmative action or reverse discrimination for Jews – but if we take rights seriously, then it is not self-evident why we do not.

Why should rights violation be a matter for compensation only when it has caused harm? (I leave aside for the moment the question of the nature of harm and how it is to be measured. It is an issue that will arise later.) The answer, a practical rather than a philosophical one, would seem to be that our catalogue of concerns is full enough as it is with cases where rights violation *has* caused harm; and such claims should, perhaps rightly, take precedence.

Much of the difficulty that arises in this debate derives from the imprecision of the term 'compensation'. Morally it would seem necessary to make a distinction between injury that results from accidental events or unintentional or even negligent acts, and injury occasioned by harmful intent. It is an intuitive distinction that we make in everyday life when even the injured will say, 'It's all right, don't worry, it was only an accident.' Yet we use the same language to refer to the benefits that we think the injured party should receive in both types of case, namely, that they should receive 'compensation' for their injuries. And this difficulty is not simply overcome by arguing that the same thing *is* meant in both cases and what matters is only who is liable for the compensation. It often matters to the injured whether the harm they have suffered was intentional or accidental. It is also relevant to the amount of benefit they should receive; 'compensation' for intentional hurt ought to be greater than that for accidental injury, requiring, as it does, an additional element for having harm 'willed upon them' rather than simply 'happening to them'. 'Compensation' therefore is an inadequate vehicle for conveying the moral distinctions that we may wish to make. This imprecision allows Fried, for example, to argue that there is no necessary connection between compensation and wrongful acts. Injury, he says, may be occasioned by acts that are not wrong (not worthy of condemnation or punishment), and contrarily wrongful acts may occasion no harm to specifiable victims. The former, he argues, would warrant compensation whilst the latter would not (Fried 1978: 105). Such an argument treats morality as a sort of social balance-sheet and, as such, fails to capture what is meant by talk about rights and duties.

This connection between compensation and intentionality is one that exercises much debate in the context of group harm over long periods of time and the justicization of positive discrimination as a method of making up for the past. Fried recognizes – indeed, it is the essence of much of his argument – that *wrong*, as opposed to harm, is occasioned only by intentional actions: 'If I have a right that you do not harm me physically, you wrong me in respect to that right only if you harm me intentionally' (Fried 1978: 82).[8] But this seems not to affect his judgement that compensation is due for injury resulting from both wrongful and un-wrongful behaviour. It would seem rather that the case for 'compensation' is much stronger where harm is the result of intentional (wrong) actions than where it is the unintended consequence of actions that are not wrongful, or the result of accidents, and I shall confine the use of 'compensation' to cases of the former kind.

The distinction between intentional and unintentional actions applies equally to the benefits derived from actions or circumstances. We cannot attach the same degree of guilt (and hence duty to compensate) to those who have knowingly and intentionally benefited from past actions and those whose benefit has been unintended or inadvertent. Thus I believe Boxhill, for example, to be wrong when he argues the case for collective responsibility on the part of white ethnics to compensate blacks for past harm. Merely by being white, he argues, 'an individual receives benefits to which others have at least partial rights'; simply in virtue of receiving such benefits, whites are held to owe reparation to blacks, irrespective of culpability or blame (Boxhill 1977: 276–77). Boxhill's argument is however inconsistent, because he earlier asserts that 'when reparation is due, it is not the case that no one is at fault, or that everyone is innocent; in such cases, necessarily, *someone* has infringed unjustly on another's right to pursue what he values' (Boxhill 1977: 273, emphasis added). He acknowledges here, then, what he later denies: that reparation does require culpability or blame (the unjust infringement), although he glosses over the inconsistency by seeming to imply that guilt attaches to all whites by virtue of the wrongful past actions of some. It sets a dangerous precedent to visit the sins of the fathers on their children even if the latter have inadvertently and unwittingly, benefited from those sins. Hoffman, among others, has argued the opposite – and probably sounder – case that 'it is morally absurd to penalize [someone] for an evil that he could not have prevented'; and 'Surely there is something immoral in punishing someone for something that happens to him in contradistinction to something that he does' (Hoffman 1977: 348, 368).

Goldman also is inconsistent on this point. He makes the

useful distinction between guilt and liability, wherein guilt implies liability but not the reverse: 'Having unwittingly benefited from acts of injustice may create a liability to compensate them, at least to the degree of relinquishing the undeserved benefits, but it does not generally imply any guilt for the acts' (Goldman 1979: 108). Yet he later claims that victims of injustice 'cannot demand, as their right, compensation from unrelated or innocent third parties' (Goldman 1979: 140). If this is the case, wherein lies their liability to compensate? Surely if no claim right exists against innocent third parties, they cannot be held liable for compensation, let alone be guilty.

It remains the case, however, that someone, or some groups of people, has suffered harm and been treated unjustly and as a result is worse off now than they would have been had no injustice occurred. Justice remains unsatisfied so long as the victims remain disbenefited; something ought to be done to right the balance. The dilemma of positive discrimination is how to effect such compensation when the particular circumstances (involving whole groups and injustices committed over long periods of time) throw into greater relief the problems of intentionality, guilt, and liability. We shall pursue this problem in the next chapter.

The second area of debate revolves upon the nature and extent of the compensation that justice requires when rights violation has left groups less well off. Orthodox reasoning would prescribe that compensation should ideally restore the status quo ante with possibly an additional element of compensation for the hurt suffered. Such reasoning, however, fails to satisfy the requirements of justice in those cases where positive discrimination might be applied, both on practical and moral grounds. The time span over which injury has been inflicted on blacks and other minority groups in the USA, for example, renders restitution to the conditions existing before the injustice impossible in practice and morally inadequate in principle. The injury has been a continuous process, and the status quo ante would even predate the arrival of blacks in America as slaves; clearly, strict restitution (as opposed to general compensation) would be meaningless in such circumstances. So what is required by justice is not restitution but reparation for past harm along the lines proposed by Nozick (1974: 152) in his principle of rectification for injustices in holdings. This requires that compensation establishes the victims of past injustice to the positions they would now hold had the injustice not occurred. The principle, as it might apply in circumstances where positive discrimination might be relevant, has been clearly stated by Goldman: 'An individual harmed in violation of his rights should be restored by the perpetrator of the injury to the position he would have occupied had the injury not occurred' (Goldman 1979: 67). The complexity of the counterfactual calculus involved in establishing what that position would be for, say, blacks in the United States is horrendous, and in practice is side-stepped by the simple but probably inadequate assumption of approximate proportionality; that is, that the distribution of blacks (or Hispanics or Puerto Ricans or Amerindians) across the employment and socio-economic spectrum would reflect their representation in the population as a whole. The argument for proportionality is perhaps a necessary evil given the impossibility of real counterfactual reasoning but it sets a dangerous precedent, as we shall see. There are probably no sub-groups of the US or British populations who would fully meet the proportionality argument. None the less, it would seem that anything less than enstatement to a 'counterfactual situation' would fail to meet the requirements of justice, and it is to this end, rather than the status quo ante, that practices of positive discrimination must aspire.

3 The United States experience

Some of the issues we have identified in the preceding pages concerning positive discrimination as rights to compensation for harm have been argued out in the course of policy-making and implementation in respect of affirmative action in the United States, and in challenges to it in the court room. Indeed, as we have mentioned, the experience of positive discrimination in the USA has occasioned a moral debate that has hardly begun in Britain. For this reason, and because it provides some essential footholds for our subsequent discussion of the justiciability of positive discrimination as compensation, we must say a little about the US experience of positive discrimination. Our remarks need only be brief because there are several useful descriptive accounts available (Glazer 1975, O'Neil 1975, W. T. Blackstone 1977, Blackstone and Heslep 1977, Gross 1977, Eastland and Bennett 1979).

The principle of what today we call affirmative action was first established by the Wagner Act 1935, under which the ruling in the Jones and Loughlin Steel case required not only that discriminatory action against union members must cease but that members be reinstated with back-pay and that non-discrimination notices be posted (see Sowell 1977). What union members partially gained in 1935 it took another thirty years for ethnic minorities and women to achieve. The Civil Rights Act of 1964 established some fundamental rights for minority group members and in many respects proved to be the jumping-off point for further advances, but it could not provide what many were now demanding – *group* rights to compensation for group harm in the past. It was a milestone on the way, but by no means the end of the road.

Although the phrase first appears in 1961 in Executive Order 10925 of 6 March, the legislative foundation of affirmative action rests on Titles VI and VII of the Civil Rights Act (which also established the Equal Employment Opportunity Commission, subsequently to be an important instrument in the promotion of affirmative action). More directly, affirmative action has its particular foundation in a later Executive Order (number 11246, issued in 1965 by the Johnson administration), which required federal contractors to take 'affirmative action' to ensure non-discrimination in hiring policies. However, 'affirmative action' as yet remained undefined and was to remain so until its specification in Revised Order No. 4 of Executive Order 11375. Under this order 'affirmative action' should be taken in setting 'goals' and 'timetables' for the employment of minority group members in those jobs in which they were currently 'under-utilized' – that is, where their representation in the workforce was less than would be expected from their availability. Where such action was not taken or good faith efforts not made to comply, contract holders risked having their contracts rescinded. An earlier exemption for universities from the requirements of Title VII was subsequently removed under the Equal Employment Opportunities Act of 1972, which also gave powers of enforcement of affirmative action to the EEOC.

The various Executive Orders are legal instruments and as such have the force of law; but over a number of years they have been supplemented and filled out by a series of explanatory guidelines issued by the various and sometimes overlapping enforcement agencies, including the Office of Civil Rights of the Department of Health, Education, and Welfare, the Office of Federal Contract Compliance Programs of the Department of

Labor, and the EEOC. These guidelines have attempted to give substance to such vexed, though crucial, abstractions as 'under-utilization', 'targets', 'goals', and 'quotas'.

It was in the judicial system however that the principles and constitutionality of non-discrimination and affirmative action were often worked out. Over a long period of time – and still today – policy vied with legality as the ambiguities of Executive Orders and their attendant guidelines were tested out. Sometimes, as in the *Griggs v. Duke Power Company* case in 1971, which established the 'Griggs Doctrine' of indirect and unintentional discrimination, it was the courts that took the advance, with policy trailing behind. At other times the judicial system was used, as in De Funis, Bakke, and Weber, in an attempt to put a brake on policy. It is ironic that these three white males should have used, in testing the limits of affirmative action, the same constitutional and statutory foundations upon which non-discrimination and positive discrimination were based.

Much has been written about *De Funis* v. *Odegaard and the University of Washington, Regents of the University of California* v. *Allan Bakke*, and *United Steelworkers of America* v. *Weber.*[9] We need not go over this well worked ground other than to say that it was in these cases, and in the large number of briefs *amicus curiae* submitted, that much of the argument about the legality and constitutionality of affirmative action programmes was developed. The De Funis case never came to a decision since the claimant, having been admitted to Washington Law School pending an appeal by the university to the Washington Supreme Court, had completed his course by the time the case had passed to and been heard by the United States Supreme Court. The case was declared moot. The findings in Bakke and Weber however were in some measure contradictory, although, as Dworkin (1978) has argued, this had much to do with whether it was a statutory issue involving Title VII of the Civil Rights Act that was being tested, or a constitutional one under the 14th Amendment. One widely accepted interpretation of the majority finding in Bakke, which is of relevance to our later analysis, was that whilst fixed quotas for minority group admissions were deemed unconstitutional, milder forms of affirmative action, and in particular the setting of targets or goals, were permissible. However, whilst the Civil Rights Act and subsequent Executive Orders neither require nor permit fixed quotas, and whilst policy orthodoxy has consistently maintained the practical and moral distinction between goals and quotas (see, for example, Pottinger 1977: 42–4; Pottinger was the first head of the Civil Rights Office), the moral distinction between the two has been seriously questioned – as, for example, by Black 1974: 94–5, Greene 1977: 185, Dworkin 1978: 22, and Goldman 1979: 211). Certainly, as Goldman maintains, whatever the administrative differences between goals and quotas (which are real enough), the moral and practical consequences especially for whites who fail as a result to obtain positions or jobs are the same.

The Bakke case was chronologically prior to Weber (as was De Funis to Bakke), but this cannot wholly account for why many people have heard of Bakke but considerably fewer of Weber. Unlike De Funis and Bakke, which were concerned with graduate school admissions, Weber was about on-the-job training for blue-collar workers in Kaiser Aluminum & Chemical Corporation, and as such was of much greater potential significance for the vast majority of ethnic minority manual workers.

It may be, as Eastland and Bennett have argued, that familiarity with Bakke and the obscurity of Weber are related to issues of class and professional self-interest:

> 'It is not too daring to suggest that those in the media so interested in exploring Bakke and those in academe so outspoken on the issue in Bakke were more concerned with rites of passage to a professional career than with the particulars of on-the-job training programs for blue-collar workers.'
>
> (Eastland and Bennett 1979: 197)

Whether or not there is any truth in this – and there would seem to be more than an element – it is unfortunate to say the least that the potentially more far-reaching consequences of Weber should have been relegated to a footnote in the history of positive discrimination.

What then is the essence of positive discrimination in the United States that has occasioned so much government activity, legal disputation, and academic debate? Ruth Ginsburg has provided a useful summary, which we cannot do better than reproduce here. Something more positive and affirmative is required than simply desisting from negative discrimination if the aims of compensation for the past and the promotion of equal opportunity for the future are to be met. This 'something more' will include, in Ginsburg's words:

> 'special efforts to seek out and recruit qualified members of groups once excluded or subjected to disadvantageous treatment; elimination of employment tests, standards and qualifications that are not reliable predictors of requisite performance; in-service training programs; back pay and "front pay" (compensation during training at the pay rate for the post to be achieved); and, in settings where other measures will not accomplish the necessary alteration, numerical remedies – goals and timetables or outright quotas for a transition period.'
>
> (Ginsburg 1977: 138)

Affirmative action, or more generally, positive discrimination, therefore, includes a variety of practices other than the quota, target, or goal programmes with which it is usually associated. It comes in a variety of forms and in varying degrees of affirmation, of which quota-setting is but the extreme end of the continuum, just as in Britain positive discrimination and positive action form a continuum of 'assertiveness'.

There is much more that could be said about the US experience of positive discrimination, but the detail and the facts can be found elsewhere. Our concern is with the justiciability of positive discrimination, and these few brief comments will suffice to prime us for that examination, to which we now turn.

Chapter 7

The justiciability of positive discrimination as compensation for harm

Is the use of positive discrimination in fulfilment of rights to compensation for past injury a just practice? Furthermore, does justice require it, and under what circumstances? In the previous chapter we examined the claim for positive discrimination as an instrument for compensating for past harm, and briefly commented on the United States experience of implementing such a claim. The claim itself must now be tested.

In the prolegomenon to this and the previous three chapters we identified the starting-point for such a debate as the prima facie injusticiability of positive discrimination in so far as it uses (by definition) criteria that are morally irrelevant to the aims it allegedly pursues – meeting need and compensating for harm. The subsequent discussion was then centred upon the two claimed justicizations of positive discrimination: (a) that since all members of the target groups (women, blacks, etc.) have greater needs than all non-members, or since all members have suffered harm, there is no moral inconsistency in using criteria of sex or ethnicity in pursuit of these moral ends; or (b) that although not all members of the groups have greater needs or have suffered harm, a sufficiently large proportion have done so to make the use of positive discrimination justicized as the only or best way of fulfilling the requirements of justice in meeting the needs or compensation principles.[1] This chapter will examine these two claimed justicizations in respect of positive discrimination as a means of fulfilling the compensation-for-harm principle and will do so in the context of the US programmes of affirmative action and the debates they have generated, which have already been outlined.

The context of the US debate, however, forces us to begin our discussion one stage further back from our earlier starting-point. This is because the assumption upon which our discussion has so far been based – the prima facie injusticiability of positive discrimination – has itself been challenged during the course of the debate in the United States. We must first examine this challenge.

1 Relevant criteria for compensation

It has been the substance of many of the attacks on affirmative action, particularly in so far as this is thought to involve the use of quotas, that it must necessarily use morally irrelevant criteria (sex, ethnicity, etc.) to select beneficiaries of compensatory programmes, and that this is not only wrong in itself but will also perpetuate racial distinctions. The charge has been made in various forms, and a variety of consequences have been alleged. Thus O'Neil, in considering some of the critiques of affirmative action,[2] notes that one of the strongest and most persistent of these is the claim that its use of race as the identifying characteristic not only helps to maintain racial distinctions and hence the salience of race in society at large, but also represents a departure from the principles of equality and neutrality whose promotion it seeks to ensure (O'Neil 1975: 129 ff.).

The case against reverse discrimination on the grounds of the moral irrelevance of the criteria used has been spelled out at greater length by Blackstone. Although, race may be a functionally relevant criterion in some circumstances, he argues (but see Chapter 3, page 52), it is normally taken to be morally irrelevant. He continues that if race is used simply as a convenient means of identifying *individuals* who have *actually* suffered harm and ought therefore to be compensated, this would not be inconsistent with the equality principle. It would not, however, he rightly claims, be reverse discrimination, since this constitutes blanket treatment of whole groups. But if an invariable connection could be established between being black and having been harmed, then blanket treatment for the whole group of blacks would not be contrary to justice. The relevant criterion in such an instance would not be 'black' but 'having been harmed' (W. T. Blackstone 1977: 65 ff.). Blackstone argues that some might see in this a justicization of reverse discrimination, but he is right to question whether such procedures would in fact constitute reverse discrimination. The characterizing feature of positive discrimination, as has been indicated above, is not just the blanket treatment of groups but the use of morally irrelevant criteria to identify these groups. If *all* blacks have suffered harm, then, as Blackstone claims, the relevant criterion is 'harm' and not 'black'; programmes of compensation based on this predicate would simply be in fulfilment of the principle of compensation; they would not be positively discriminatory. However, argues Blackstone, in the absence of clear evidence of an invariable connection between ethnicity or sex on the one hand and harm on the other,[3] the use of ethnicity or sex as selection criteria for blanket-treatment positive discrimination remains prima facie morally unjustifiable and they remain morally irrelevant criteria.

This familiar critique of positive discrimination has been countered by two broad lines of argument, one of which we may call the 'orthodox' line and the other the more 'radical'. The orthodox line of defence has been put by, among others, Nickel and Silvestri during the course of a debate pursued in the pages of *Analysis* between 1972 and 1975. Nickel argues that the claim that morally irrelevant criteria operate both in primary negative discrimination (the original harm) *and* in positive discrimination programmes to compensate for that harm is mistaken; it is only apparently the case. The relevant criterion operating in positive discrimination policies is not 'black' but 'harm': 'if compensation . . . is extended to a black man on the basis of past discrimination against blacks, the basis for this compensation is not that he is a black man but that he was *previously subject to unfair treatment because he was black*' (Nickel 1972: 114, emphasis added). This formulation of the argument is at once confused and inadequate. Even if we take the argument at its face value (as relating to a 'black man'), the final clause ought to be otiose; the compensation is due *not* because he suffered unfair treatment 'because he was a black' but rather simply because he suffered unfair treatment. It is the unfair treatment (or harm) that justifies the compensation, not any particular reason for the unfair treatment. The equality principle enjoins the same compensation for the same harm irrespective of the ethnicity, sex, race, or religion of the victim. However, there is a more fundamental difficulty with Nickel's argument, and this is that it fails to address what must be at the heart of the problem. The issue is not as Nickel frames it, about the compensation due to a black man – there can be no quibble that someone harmed or whose rights have been overridden ought now to be compensated – but rather to the whole category 'black men' (or 'women' or 'Jews', etc.). The force of Nickel's argument – the substitutability of the morally relevant criterion 'harm' for the irrelevant one 'black' – must depend on an invariable conjunction of the two, and this he does not address. It is largely an empirical matter and ought therefore to be uncontestable, in the philosphical sense, although it is in practice highly contested.

Nickel does in fact clarify the issue in a later article in *Analysis* in which he defends his position against the intervening critiques. In this, he makes explicit what was left unsaid in his first paper, namely, his assumption that an almost invariable relation does exist between being black in the USA and having suffered harm: 'since *almost all* American blacks have been victimized by discrimination it would be justifiable to design and institute programmes of special benefit for blacks. Such programmes ... would be justified in terms of the injuries that *almost all* of the recipients have suffered – not in terms of the race of the recipients' (Nickel 1973: 155, emphasis added). Thus the missing link is added, and Nickel's defence of positive discrimination is seen to rest on an assumption of an almost complete correlation between 'harm' and 'black', so establishing the substitution of one for the other and salvaging the moral respectability of using ethnicity as the selection criterion for beneficiaries. In an attempt to push home the point, Nickel makes a distinction between the 'justifying' and 'administrative' bases of reverse discrimination programmes. The 'justifying' base is the harm or injuries 'that *many* blacks suffer', whilst the administrative base 'might be the presence in an *individual* of those needs and injuries, but it is more likely that it would be some other characteristics (such as race and *present income*) which were easier to detect and which were highly correlated with the justifying basis' (Nickel 1973: 155, emphasis added). The use of morally irrelevant criteria then becomes a matter of administrative efficiency and defensible on the grounds of their congruence with criteria that *are* morally relevant. The impression remains, none the less, as the emphasized words above show, that Nickel is less convinced of the ground he defends than he would like his readers to think. He again clouds the issue by referring to 'individuals'; he stops short of asserting a complete congruence of criteria ('many', but not 'all', blacks); and he throws in the irrelevancy 'present income', which is altogether a different issue from ethnicity, both empirically and morally.

An interesting twist is given to the same sort of defence of positive discrimination by Silvestri in the course of the same debate in *Analysis*. He goes the length where Nickel stops short, by asserting 'that Blacks have been discriminated against to such a degree that one is on fairly safe ground in assuming that in repaying *all* Blacks, we are, with few exceptions repaying fairly' (Silvestri 1973: 31, emphasis added). He then says, however, that such a defence of positive discrimination could be objected to on either or both of two grounds: that the extent of the alleged correlation could be questioned (an empirical objection), and that it is precisely the use of such correlations that is morally questionable (a moral objection). The latter, as Silvestri argues, is the more interesting of the two, and his defence against it is (as we saw, page 117) that it is more acceptable to run higher risks of unfairness when giving benefit than when meting out punishments. To punish the innocent is a far graver matter than to compensate the unharmed. Two consequences flow from this; Silvestri acknowledges the first and is silent on the other. The first consequence is the obverse side of the compensation coin. The costs of compensating the injured ought to fall on the harm-doers, but, to take Silvestri's own precept, it is a grave matter to visit the costs on the innocent. How then are we to ensure that the costs of compensating blacks (some of whom we accept will be unharmed) fall *only* on the harm-doers, which our moral sensitivities demand? Silvestri's answer – an unsatisfactory one from both a practical and a moral point of view – is that reparations by whites should be voluntary. The consequence is not hard to see; virtually no reparations would be made. A few East Coast liberals in an *Angst* of guilt might cough up, and every hard-hat, hard-nosed, red-necked, backwoodsman racist would pull another can of beer and pour a toast to Mr Silvestri.

The second consequence, to which Silvestri does not refer, is as follows. Whilst we may accept with few qualms the payment of compensation to unharmed blacks as a price to pay for ensuring that all the injured blacks are compensated, this hardly satisfies the demands of the equality principle. And this is simply because not all the injured are black. The equality principle, even if only to be approximated, demands that *all* those who have suffered harm be compensated and that the compensation be proportional to the injury. Our liberality with compensation would be acceptable only if and because it ensured that *all* those who had suffered injustice got reparation; so long as it failed to do that it would remain as a mockery to the uncompensated victims.

The second and more radical defence of positive discrimination has been argued by, among others, Bayles and Taylor. It is here that a direct challenge is made to the prima facie unjusticiability of positive discrimination. With varying degrees of emphasis, both Bayles and Taylor lay siege to the assumption that ethnicity is a morally irrelevant criterion for the purposes of positive discrimination.

In two articles published in 1973, Bayles spells out his claim that ethnicity (or sex) is not a morally irrelevant criterion for the purposes of reverse discrimination. The compensation principle involved, he claims, must be one where the wronged party is not an individual but rather a whole minority group that is identified by the characteristic that was the cause of the original negative discrimination (hence blacks, women, married women, etc.) Furthermore, because the defining characteristic is thus determined, *all* those defined by that characteristic are due compensation even though some of them will not, as individuals, have suffered harm. The composition of the group, in terms of its individual constituents, will change over time, although the defined *group* will persist and remain the subject of due compensation (Bayles 1973a: 305–06). These ideas are then developed at greater length in Bayles's contribution to the debate in *Analysis*. Here he claims that the solution proposed by Nickel and Cowan (see below), that the relevant criterion for positive discrimination is not 'black' but the morally relevant one 'harm', is a spurious one, and one that racists could adopt by analogous reasoning: that they had not discriminated on the irrelevant grounds of blackness but rather the functionally (if not morally) relevant one that all blacks are lazy, unintelligent and so on. (But, as we shall see, such a claim would represent only the delusory rationalizations of the racist.)

There is, says Bayles, no contradiction involved in claiming that 'black' is a morally irrelevant criterion when discriminating against people but a morally relevant one in selecting people for compensation: 'By using the characteristic of being black as an identifying characteristic to discriminate *against* people, a person has wronged the *group* blacks' (Bayles 1973b: 183, emphasis added). Furthermore, he argues that because the obligation to compensate is to the group, no single individual of the group has a right to reparation. But because the group so defined is an entity only by virtue of its constituent members (unlike an institution), the only way of paying compensation to the group is by paying it to individual members of the group. Thus, asserts Bayles, the criterion 'black' *actually becomes a morally relevant one* in identifying those to whom compensation is due. However, at this stage the argument becomes confused, for Bayles then claims that being black is 'only *derivatively* morally relevant' (emphasis added). By this he means that 'black' is not *inherently* morally relevant but only becomes so by virtue of having been the identifying characteristic of the group wronged. He continues:

> 'The way in which it is an identifying characteristic here differs from the way in which it is an identifying characteristic for the racist. Being black is an identifying characteristic for the racist only because he thinks it is contingently connected with other characteristics [see above]. But being black is not contingently connected with the group one has wronged. Rather it is logically connected as the defining characteristic of members of the group.'
>
> (Bayles 1973b: 184)

The substance of Bayles's claim is somewhat less than he asserts, and his argument is sophistic. He is correct in his assertion that the reasoning of the racist is different from that which makes of 'black' a relevant criterion, but for the wrong reasons. The racist does not use 'being black' as an identifying characteristic because he thinks it contingently connected to a variety of negatively valued characteristics (laziness, low intelligence, stupidity, etc.), even though this is what he may *claim*. To argue this is to pay to racism the compliment of a rationality it does not deserve. It is in the very nature of racism that it does *not* discriminate in so logical a fashion. Racists do *not* derogate *all* those whom they consider to be (or are) lazy, unintelligent, or stupid. They derogate blacks (and others) and if paid the flattery of being asked why they do so they may well rationalize their behaviour by attaching negative characteristics to those whom they irrationally discriminate against. But they do not discriminate, if they are whites, against lazy, unintelligent, or stupid whites. Conversely – and quite the reverse of what Bayles claims – the use of 'black' as a morally relevant criterion (if such could be sustained) *is* contingently connected with the criterion 'harm', and this is manifest in his own claim that 'black' is *derivatively* a morally relevant criterion. In other words, if 'black' can be sustained as a moral criterion it is just because it is contingently connected with 'having been harmed'.

More substantially, I do not believe that 'being black' *can* be sustained as a morally relevant criterion as Bayles asserts. For his claim that being black is derivatively a morally relevant criterion seems no more than a claim that, if all blacks have suffered harm, then 'black' can be an administratively convenient way of identifying those to whom compensation is due. The morally relevant criterion remains the harm done, and Bayles's claim turns out to be no different from those he began by criticizing. And like those, his claim must rest upon an assumption that *all* blacks have been harmed and that there is therefore a congruency between 'being black' and 'having been harmed'.

An alternative 'radical' defence of reverse discrimination, by way of a challenge to the prima facie assumption that it uses morally irrelevant criteria, has been made by Taylor. His argument takes the form of a defence of three views:

> '(1) With respect to the principle of compensatory justice, characteristic, "C", ["being black"] has been *made* a morally relevant characteristic by those who engaged in a social practice which discriminated against persons because they were C. (2) Since C is a morally relevant characteristic at time t2 with respect to the principle of compensatory justice, that principle requires reverse discrimination. (3) The reverse discrimination in question is aimed at correcting an injustice perpetrated at time t1 by a social practice of discriminating against C-persons because they were C. Given this aim, the reverse discrimination must be directed towards the class of C-persons as such.'
>
> (Taylor 1973: 178)

We shall not pursue Taylor's argument in all its detail but treat only of those parts that are germane to our present concern of the moral relevance or irrelevance of criterion 'C' ('being black'). Taylor formulates part of his defence by characterizing the discriminatory practice at time t1 'having C is a relevant reason or ground for performing a certain kind of action which is in fact unjust'. There is a subtle sleight of hand here, which enables Taylor to deduce that C is a relevant characteristic of a person. It lies in the apparent separation of 'C-ness' from the injustice. Formulated in a different way, what he is saying (or at least implying) is that C-persons are somehow picked out and *then* treated unjustly because they are C. But, in reality, the injustice lies in the moral irrelevance of C and is not consequent upon their having been picked out. Thus Taylor asserts: 'Within the framework of the social practice at tl, that someone is C is a ground for acting in a certain way toward him. Therefore C is a relevant characteristic of a person' (Taylor 1973: 178). Again there is an air of purposefulness about discriminatory practices in his formulation that does not ring true.

However, let us follow Taylor's argument a little further. Having asserted that C is a relevant characteristic of an individual, he then goes on to ask whether it is *morally* relevant. His answer is that whilst at time t1 it was *not* morally relevant, within the context of the principle of compensatory justice it is so at t2: 'Characteristic C, in other words, has become at time t2 a characteristic whose *moral* relevance is entailed by the principle of compensatory justice' (Taylor 1973: 179, emphasis in original). This being the case, argues Taylor, anyone with characteristic C has a right to compensation whether or not they as individuals have suffered harm or injustice in the past, because it is the category 'C-ness' that is now made morally relevant, because it was the grounds for past unjust behaviour. Furthermore, in response to the criticism that, since C was originally a morally irrelevant criterion, it cannot now become a morally relevant one (a fairly common ground for criticizing reverse discrimination), Taylor replies that in the past it was the requirements of *distributive* justice that were transgressed by the use of C in negative discrimination, whereas now the canons of *compensatory* justice require that C-persons be recompensed and that 'C-ness' be the relevant criterion for determining who the compensatees should be.

The rather tortuous logic involved here appears to be more a requirement of the exigencies of a defence of reverse discrimination than of a desire to see that the requirements of justice are fulfilled. Little is gained, other than a sophistic veracity, by the separation of distributive from compensatory justice and the assertion that what is morally irrelevant in the one becomes morally relevant in the other. The compensation that is due is for harm, injury, or injustice in the past, not for having been (and being) a 'C'. And the original injustice lay not in the C-ness itself or in C-persons having been picked out and then treated unjustly, but in C, an irrelevant criterion having been used in distributive processes. Thus neither distributive nor compensatory justice is now served by compensating all Cs. What justice requires is that those who have suffered harm now be compensated; and if all C-persons have been harmed, then they should all now be compensated in proportion to the harm they have suffered and to the same degree that all non-Cs who have been equally harmed ought now to be compensated. To use C as the criterion for selecting compensatees in circumstances where all Cs have been harmed is, however, as we have seen, not positive discrimination.

We now return, in our consideration of the debate about the moral relevance or irrelevance of ethnicity, sex, etc., to two critiques of reverse discrimination that take to task the view that prima facie morally irrelevant criteria can become morally relevant for the purposes of reverse discrimination. In a response to Nickel's first essay in *Analysis* (see above), Cowan has argued against reverse discrimination by concentrating on the question of the moral relevance of the groups identified. The kernel of his argument is that, since the original negative discrimination for which we wish to compensate was unjust precisely because it used a morally irrelevant criterion (such as 'black') to identify a group, that group cannot now be said to be a morally relevant group for the purposes of positive discrimination:

> '[A] fallacy arises when, rather than individuals, it is the group which is intended, and individuals are regarded merely as members of that group rather than in their individuality. This creates a contradiction since the original premise of the moral irrelevance of blackness, on the basis of which the original attribution of unjust discrimination rests, implies that there is and can be no morally relevant group which could have suffered or to which retribution [*sic*] could now be made.'
>
> (Cowan 1972: 11)

For Cowan, as for Blackstone, the only relevant criterion can be the original harm and injustice. Not only must a criterion such as ethnicity remain morally irrelevant, but nor can there be a morally relevant group (for purposes of compensation or distribution) identified by such a criterion.

In a response to Taylor (above, pages 135–37), Nunn considers the consequences of using, as morally relevant, criteria like 'black'. If a group of people identified by 'C' (e.g. 'black') are taken for the purposes of reverse discrimination to be a morally relevant group, who are thereby due compensation, then it must follow, he argues, that the compensators (the guilty) must be all other persons who are not C (or all non-blacks). We may call this second group of 'non-Cs' group C′. This second group, asserts Nunn, in being required *as a group* to make reparations will now be discriminated against: 'Thus, while certain C-persons are compensated for the wrongs done to them or other members of the C-group, the C′-group is unjustly discriminated against as a class' (Nunn 1973: 153).

This being the case, Nunn says, the unjust treatment accorded to C′ creates for them a right to compensation – or, as he calls it, to a form of reverse reverse discrimination. The iterative consequences are not hard to imagine. However, the argument is less compelling than Nunn asserts. It is true that if C can constitute a morally relevant group then group C′ must also be accorded a moral status. It does not follow however that, in making reparations to C, a moral right to recompense is created for C′. Because if C constitute a morally relevant group since they have suffered injustice *as a group* by C′, then a duty lies on C′ to make recompense, and no injustice is done them (for which compensation would be due) by requiring them to execute that duty. Nunn's case, it would seem, rests upon his accepting for the purposes of argument his opponents' logic but then changing the rules of the game half-way through. If we accept, even if only for argument's sake, the logic of the moral relevance of C and C′, then we must also accept that what is required of C′ does not establish for them any right to compensation. They are only fulfilling what is their duty.

We have spent some time examining the arguments about the moral relevance of ethnicity (and, by extension, sex and race). This has been occasioned in part by the fact that the dispute has constituted an important component of the United States debate on positive discrimination, but also because the assertion of the moral relevance of such criteria represents a direct challenge to our earlier assumption of the prima facie injusticiability of positive discrimination practices. Clearly, if ethnicity, sex, and so on can with reasonable plausibility be claimed to be morally relevant criteria, then our assertion about the injusticiability of positive discrimination must fall.

As the preceding pages have shown, of the two defences of reverse discrimination, only one asserts the moral relevance of the criteria, the use of which occasioned the original negative discrimination. The other claims that the relevant criterion for reverse discrimination is in fact 'harm' or 'injury'. Sustaining such a claim however requires that the criterion for the original discrimination – 'being black' – can be made congruent with the morally relevant criterion of 'harm', and this in turn depends on the (empirical) assertion that *all* members of the defined groups – blacks, women, etc. – have suffered harm. We shall examine this claim later on. Our immediate concern is with the more radical claim of the moral relevance of ethnicity and sex. Neither of the proponents of this case (Bayles and Taylor) has made out a convincing or conclusive argument. Bayles's assertion, that criteria such as skin colour *become* morally relevant by virtue of having been the grounds of unjust negative discrimination, is subsequently modified to a claim that such criteria are *derivatively* morally relevant, and this turns out really to be no more than what other defenders of positive discrimination have argued: that if all blacks have been harmed, then 'black' may be an administratively useful criterion for identifying compensatees, whose claim to reparations must remain the morally relevant one of 'having been harmed'. In like manner, Taylor's attempt to establish the moral relevance of ethnicity fails to convince, as does the means he adopts to achieve it. In particular, his separation of distributive from compensatory justice serves only to emphasize the flaw in his argument. The original injustice for which compensation is now due was indeed a transgression of distributive justice, in the use of a morally irrelevant criterion to distribute goods, services, and offices. But the injustice lay precisely in the *use of the criterion*, not in the criterion itself. The compensation now due must be for the harm, injury, and injustice incurred in the use of the criterion, not for mere possession of the characteristic.

Characteristics that are normally taken to be irrelevant from a moral point of view must remain so and cannot be made morally relevant by virtue of having been the cause of an injustice. If a case can be made that *all* blacks, women, Puerto Ricans, etc. have been harmed, then all are due compensation, and the criteria of ethnicity, sex, and race could justifiably be used as administratively convenient proxies to identify compensatees. This would not be positive discrimination, however, and would not therefore be a contentious practice.

2 The justiciability of positive discrimination as compensation

The claim that positive discrimination is not even prima facie unjust, because the selection criteria that it uses are actually morally relevant ones, does not stand up to scrutiny. We may therefore proceed to examine the two claims in defence of positive discrimination that we established earlier. It would be well to remind ourselves of the general context of such a discussion. If it could be shown that *all* members of a group had been harmed or suffered injustice, then all are due compensation, and the issue is not morally problematical – although it would pose many practical difficulties. If on the other hand it can be shown that only some, or a large proportion, have been harmed, then the issue reduces to a question of whether those who have actually suffered harm can be individually compensated or whether some blanket compensation for the whole, or parts, of the group of which they are members would remain the best way of meeting the requirements of justice in respect of compensation for harm. Our consideration of the two claims thus requires that we consider a number of issues that all revolve upon one broader issue: that of harm and compensation for groups as against for individuals. For the sake of our analysis, it will be expedient to divide this range of issues into two broad kinds (though with some overlap), that we may call 'theoretical' and 'practical'. The former relate to questions of the morality of group and individual compensation and the latter to questions about the practicality and effectiveness of administering whole-group compensation. Such a division, although far from perfect, will better enable us to marshal a fairly wide range of issues in a more comprehensible form.

2.1 The Theoretical Arguments

BENEFITS AND BENEFICIARIES

The first claim – that positive discrimination is justicized because *all* members of the preferred groups have suffered past harm – we have already in some measure covered in our discussion of morally relevant criteria. Claims to whole-group harm do not usually take the simplest and most obvious form – that is, an empirical claim that *every* black or *every* woman has suffered harm in the past and the present – although such claims *have* been made for example by Kilson (1983) in respect of Afro-Americans. More often the claim takes a more subtle form, as we saw in our earlier discussion of morally relevant criteria. The weaker claim here has been that positive discrimination is justicized because the criterion it uses is in fact 'harm' (Nickel 1972, Silvestri 1973) – a claim that requires an assumption of congruence between the selection criteria actually used (black, women) and the criterion of harm; the stronger claim has been that, because it has been used as the basis for past negative discrimination, a criterion such as 'being black' actually *becomes* a morally relevant one. The most forceful version of this argument has been put, we saw, by Taylor (1973), who contends on this basis that compensation must be paid to the whole group and not even to every member of the group *qua* harmed individuals but rather to all members *qua* members of the group. Institutionalized injustice, he claims, requires institutionalized compensation.

Another version of the 'whole group' argument asserts that it is the group (blacks, women, etc.) that has been harmed and that the group has a continuity of existence although its membership changes, with deaths and births. Thus it is to the group rather than its individual members that compensation is due (Bayles 1973b). More empirically, although no less tendentiously, there is the claim that although not every member of a group has suffered injustice or negative discrimination, all members of the group have none the less suffered vicarious psychological harm by virtue of being members of a group that has been held in low esteem or has not been accorded the respect due to all and any subsection of humanity. Thalberg (1973–74) has made psychological harm the basis of his claim for whole-group compensation. But, as Goldman notes, not only is such a claim empirically dubious, especially in the case of women, but even if true it provides little foundation for establishing the degree of harm and hence the quantity of compensation (Goldman 1979: 76–8). My own inclination is to discount psychological-harm arguments as a basis for compensation, although on rather less formal grounds than does Goldman. The claim itself seems empirically dubious – although with more veracity for some groups than others – but, to the extent that it does have substance, it is perhaps better used in consequentialist defences of positive discrimination rather than compensatory ones. Briefly to anticipate the subject-matter of a later chapter, the use of positive discrimination to provide role models for other members of disadvantaged groups would seem, potentially at least, to be a better response to the psychological-harm claim than a demand for compensation. Vicarious psychological harm may well be more effectively dealt with by vicarious role models than by attempts to reparate for it.[4] However, I remain wary of Goldman's argument that psychological harm provides no measure of the degree of harm and therefore of the extent of compensation due. The Aristotelian dictum that compensation be proportional to injury is a sound one and ought to be adhered to as far as possible, but the practical difficulty of assessing relative degrees of harm is not in itself a sufficient reason for making *no* compensation. To take that road is to court the possibility of leaving too much injustice unrighted.

The second claim – that, although not all members of a group have suffered harm, sufficient have done so to make positive discrimination the most effective and on balance most just way of making compensation – requires more lengthy consideration. Let us first examine the more theoretical issues raised by such a claim. At the risk of seeming repetitious, let us re-emphasize that *in theory* the practice we are dealing with is one in which the distinguishing characteristic that was the basis of past (and present) negative discrimination and injustice to a group is now used to identify the beneficiaries of compensation for that injustice. We are accepting for the sake of a greater justice that some injustice will be incurred in so far as some members of the group who had not suffered harm will now benefit. But on the whole we must require that like cases be treated alike and different cases differently in terms of the amount of harm suffered and the compensation paid, and that *all* who suffered harm now be compensated in proportion to the injury they suffered. Similarly, we must require as far as possible that the costs of compensation fall on those and *only* those who committed the injustice in proportion to the injury they inflicted. This is, as it were, the paradigm case against which we must test the practices of positive discrimination that we described earlier, which have already in some measure been tested in the courts of the USA in such cases as Bakke, De Funis, and Weber.

The most common and one of the most telling critiques of reverse discrimination programmes in the USA is that they simply do not approach anywhere near the paradigm case we have outlined. Whilst it is acknowledged that the language of whole-group compensation must in practice translate into benefits accruing to individual members of the group (since the group has no other existence than its component parts), our paradigm case does require that all individual members benefit, and in some rough proportion to the harm they have suffered. But the reality of preferential treatment in hiring for jobs, positions, or university places is that only *some* members of preferred groups benefit, and the manner in which beneficiaries are selected is arbitrary and quixotic (Goldman 1977: 205–06, Simon 1977: 43, Lustgarten 1980: 16). The main beneficiaries of preference programmes (leaving aside for the moment vicarious beneficiaries) will be women and members of minority groups who are in the job or education market – that is, applying for jobs, promotion, or places in universities – because it is in these areas that the programmes mainly operate (see Gross 1977: 387). Clearly, even if preferential hiring policies were extensive, and goals or quotas were achieved, the sum total of beneficiaries – women or minority group members who got positions they otherwise would not – would be very small compared with total group membership. It may well be argued that this would necessarily be the case in the early years of any preference programmes, and no one should look for nor expect rapid solutions. Generations of injustice will not be exculpated in a decade. This is an argument difficult to gainsay; after all, we have to begin somewhere.

A more fundamental problem with the sort of preference policy we are talking about is concerned less with the numbers who might initially benefit than with *who* they are.[5] Because preference policies operate at hiring and promotion levels within the job market and at the higher levels of education, and because merit rather than sponsorship will function to determine beneficiaries *within* minority groups and amongst women, it is most likely (as Simon 1977: 43, Goldman 1979: 88–92, and Greene 1977: 186 have pointed out) that those who *do* benefit from compensatory programmes will be those with qualifications (of whatever relevant sort) approximating the best at any given level among the group. ('Approximating' because we might assume that those with the very best qualifications would, on the whole, have got the job or position anyway without the preference policy. The beneficiaries are more likely to be those with relatively average-to-good qualifications who gain positions through a policy of preference but who would have failed to do so without.)

Recalling that the preference is being given as compensation for harm or injury (whether it be to individuals or notionally to whole groups does not matter here), is it likely that those most likely to receive the compensation, constitute those, or are even among those, who have suffered most harm? One does not have to subscribe to a view that present abilities and qualifications are solely or largely determined by the degree of past harm suffered to conclude that the answer is 'no'. Goldman goes too far in his assertion that

> 'Since hiring within the preferred group still depends on relative qualifications and hence upon past opportunities for acquiring qualifications, there is in fact an inverse ratio established between past discrimination and present benefits, so that those who benefit most from the programme . . . are those who deserve to least . . . those individuals will always be hired first who have suffered least from past discrimination.'
>
> (Goldman 1975: 169)

Such a claim for an almost invariable correlation between past harm and present qualifications is both patronizing and untrue. And even if it were true, the best qualified (and therefore the least harmed) would not need to benefit from preference policies, as we noted above. It is nevertheless reasonable to assume (notwithstanding the critique of libertarians such as Capaldi (1985),[6] that positive discrimination is founded on a belief in social determination), some sort of approximate association between present abilities and past harm such as would enable us to say that it is unlikely that those who receive the most compensation are among those most injured in the past.

Thus, although positive discrimination in the USA is notionally aimed at compensating whole groups, in practice it benefits individuals. These individual beneficiaries are chosen by a combination of the merit system and the wholly arbitrary allocation procedures of the market. Such allocatory mechanisms are wholly inappropriate as means of selecting the most harmed for compensation, and this deficiency is compounded by the disproportionate emphasis of preference policies at the university level in terms of both student enrolment and faculty employment. Indeed, it would be difficult to design a more inappropriate system of compensation for past harm than one in which the beneficiaries were selected by the market and where such an emphasis were placed on preference at university level.[7] There is precious little in such policies other than a slender assumption of a vicarious 'lift' for working-class blacks in the urban ghettos, or working-class women of any ethnicity anywhere.

If there is a mismatch between those who have suffered injury in the past and those who reap the benefits of present compensation programmes, how much more is there an inadequate correlation between the degree of injury and the amount of benefit?

We have seen that the equality principle (and the Aristotelian notion of proportionate justice) requires that compensation be proportional to harm suffered. Even given the virtual impossibility of estimating the degree of harm, it seems highly unlikely that to give preference in blue-collar skilled jobs, white-collar jobs, and university places and appointments will effect anything like a degree of compensation that is proportional to the degree of injury.[8]

Perhaps, however, we are requiring too much of positive discrimination and of the necessarily imperfect means for its implementation. Maybe we are falling into the trap against which we earlier cautioned, of doing nothing because we cannot do everything. We must weigh the injustices of doing something imperfectly against those of not doing anything. But before we can do this we need to look to the other side of compensation – to the compensators and the costs they incur in making due compensation.

COSTS AND COMPENSATORS

To parallel the claim that compensation is due to all women and all members of minority groups, it might be argued that the compensators – those guilty of past injustices – are *all* white males (or all whites, or all males, or all white Anglo-Saxon Protestants, or all male white Anglo-Saxon Protestants; the more precise the specification, the more likely it is that the guilty themselves become a minority). This is a claim that we shall examine later. Let us for the present adopt the more individualistic assertion that guilt is not equally attributable to all members of a group, be it a majority or a minority, but varies between individuals within the group. Let us also accept the Aristotelian assertion that compensation is *due from the guilty in proportion to their guilt*, just as it should be proportional to harm suffered. To what extent does the practice of positive discrimination in the USA approximate to this ideal?

We can disaggregate this question into two constituent parts, as we did with the issue of compensation. Firstly, is it the guilty who in practice bear the costs of compensation? Secondly, if it is, do they bear costs in proportion to their guilt? The answer to the first question is negative and *ipso facto* to the second also. The reasons are similar to those we have adduced for the failure of compensatory practices to meet the basic requirements of justice, namely, that the selection of compensators is both quixotic and arbitrary. The costs are borne by those (mainly white, and often but not always male) who do not obtain jobs, positions, promotions, or student places that they would otherwise have done had not policies of preference awarded them to compensatees. They are picked out to bear the costs not by any process of judicial selection but by the chances and happenstance of the merit system and the market. Far from falling on all white males – or any other sub-group – the costs fall disproportionately on the young and those who happen to be in the job or student market. As Gross (1977: 387) and Hoffman (1977: 367) point out, any potentially guilty party who happens not to be applying for a job or a university place will bear none of the costs of compensation. And if we make the not unreasonable assumption that injustices to blacks and women are more likely to have been committed by older males, then we are unjustly penalizing the younger generation for the faults of their fathers, grandfathers, and long-deceased ancestors. To visit the sins of the fathers on their children is, we saw, in general a practice that justice cannot sanction. Given, then, that the costs of compensation fall arbitrarily on the guiltless and guilty alike, probably more on the former than the latter, there is no possibility that the guilty bear costs in proportion to the injury they have caused. As with compensation, there can also be no way of apportioning guilt anyway, either in theory or in practice.

Distributively speaking, therefore, the practice of positive discrimination in pursuit of the principle of compensation for past harm serves only to compound the original injustices. It is unlikely, given the nature of positive discrimination practices, that those most harmed in the past *within* minority groups as well as *between* them (blacks, Puerto Ricans, Mexican-Americans, Amerindians, Appalachian whites, women, etc.) will be the ones to receive the greatest compensation. Contrarily, it is unlikely that the costs of compensation will fall largely on the guilty, more likely on the relatively innocent. Where an innocent white male loses a position or place to a relatively unharmed black (or any other sub-group member), then a double injustice is done.

We have noted that ascribing guilt to, and imposing the costs of compensation on, the innocent is generally considered to be a graver infraction of the principles of justice than to allow some of the uninjured to benefit from compensation. If, in the interests of a greater justice, some minor injustices such as compensating non-victims are incurred, then that perhaps is of little moment and a small price to pay. To exact reparations from the innocent in pursuit of the same greater justice, however, is itself a heavy price to pay and a grave injustice that ought not to be sanctioned. It may be argued that *all* white males (or whites) are guilty since all have benefited from the past negative discrimination to blacks and women. This raises the difficult concept of 'collective guilt' about which much has been written in other contexts. This is not the place to enter an extended discussion of the concept, and we must be satisfied with some brief comments.

There are two broad strands to the notion of collective guilt. The first concerns collective benefit from past harm; the second, collective responsibility, liability, fault, or guilt. Let us begin with the first and easier issue. The argument here is that even though not all white males (to use the paradigm example) can be held liable or responsible for past injustices, they are all a party to such injustices by virtue of having been beneficiaries of past (and present) discriminatory practices. There are two counters to this argument. The first is that benefit from past harm to others is an insufficient ground for exacting compensation. Benefit of itself does not imply guilt or responsibility for the acts from which the benefit derives. The second, related argument is one that has been put by both Hoffman (1977: 368) and W. T. Blackstone (1977: 68) and lays the emphasis on the inadvertency of the benefit derived by most white males. Most or many beneficiaries, so this argument goes, are inadvertent beneficiaries; they have not chosen – and could not choose – whether or not to benefit from the harm done to others. Not only can they not choose whether to benefit or not, they are probably unaware of the fact that they *are* benefiting. They cannot therefore be moral agents in this respect, and, as Hoffman says, 'there is something immoral in punishing someone for something that happens to him in contradistinction to something he has done . . . it is morally absurd to penalize him for an evil that he could not have prevented' (Hoffman 1977: 368). This is surely right.

However, such an approach can be countered on the grounds that it still fails to break out of the mental constraints of liberal individualism; it still assumes the ascription of guilt to individual and identifiable white males while what is really at issue is still the collective guilt of all white males. This is a counter-argument that has been put by Boxhill, and we must briefly examine it. It is Boxhill's assertion that 'it is the white community as a whole that prevents the descendants of slaves from exercising their rights of ownership and the white community as a whole that must bear the cost of reparation' (Boxhill 1977: 276). Within this general assertion Boxhill identifies two separate arguments: one, that each individual white owes reparation because membership of the white community identifies an individual as a recipient of benefits from past injustices to blacks (Boxhill confines his arguments to black reparations due to the descendants of slaves; they do not apply, for example, to the case of women of other groups). The other argument is that the white community as a whole 'considered as a kind of corporation or company' owes compensation to blacks. The first argument, Boxhill says, is one that individuals are to be held liable for reparations even if they have been only 'passive recipients of benefits'. To the rejoinder we have used above, that whites cannot choose whether or not to enjoy benefits and cannot therefore be morally responsible, he answers that the argument 'simply does not depend on or imply the claim that white people are culpable or blameable; the argument is that merely by being white, an individual receives benefits to which others have at least partial rights. In such cases, whatever one's choice or moral culpability, reparations must be made' (Boxhill 1977: 276–77). This answer it seems to me is morally inchoate. Stripped to its bare essentials it seems to be saying this:

(a) culpability or blame have nothing to do with it;
(b) whites are beneficiaries by virtue of being white;
(c) therefore whites (irrespective of culpability) must make reparations.

Thus no deductive logic is involved in the 'argument', which turns out to have no more substance than an assertion that beneficiaries, advertent or not, owe reparations. If we find ourselves the unwitting beneficiaries of a crime, with a tangible good and an assignable victim, then it must be our duty to return the good to its rightful owner and seek compensation from the criminal or with a sigh and good grace accept our loss. But this is clearly not the situation we are dealing with, and it is highly dubious whether unwitting beneficiaries of intangible goods at several generations' remove from the criminals and victims ought now to make reparation *solely* on the grounds of being beneficiaries. To impose upon the unwitting beneficiaries the same onus of compensation as ought to be laid upon the (now untouchable) guilty is both to stretch the web of justice too thin and to confuse guilt with liability. Nor is Boxhill consistent in this respect, because earlier in the same paper in making a distinction between compensation (which he treats as 'making up for' and thus in effect 'need') and reparation he claims that 'When reparation is due, it is not the case that no one is at fault, or that everyone is innocent; in such cases, *necessarily*, someone has infringed unjustly on another's right to pursue what he values' (Boxhill 1977: 273, emphasis added). Again, in respect of reparations: 'no supposition of prior commitment is necessary in order to be able to identify the parties who must bear the cost of reparation; it is simply and clearly the party who has acted unjustly' (Boxhill 1977: 273). In this formulation, if reparations are due, they are due from the guilty, of which there must necessarily be some (according to Boxhill's own logic) in order for the debt to exist at all. There is no mention here of reparations due from innocent but unwitting beneficiaries. The attempt to lay the costs of compensation on all individual whites, *qua* whites, does not stand up to scrutiny.

What then of Boxhill's second argument that all whites owe compensation not as individuals but as some form of corporation or company? The white community, he asserts – although with some acknowledged and obvious differences – does resemble a corporation or company in many ways in as much as it 'has interests distinct from, and opposed to, other groups in the same society, and joint action is often taken by members of the white community to protect and enhance their interests' (Boxhill 1977: 277). However in order to sustain his argument, Boxhill has had to caricature white America as being wholly in the mould of old-style southern white supremacists, and it simply does not ring true. This is what he has to say about group membership and culpability:

> 'What is important . . . is not how deliberately one chooses to become part of a community or company; what is relevant is that one chooses to continue to accept the benefits which circulate *exclusively* within the community, sees such benefits as belonging *exclusively* to the members of the community, identifies one's interests with those of the community, and finally, takes joint action with other members of the community to protect such interests'
>
> (Boxhill 1977: 277, emphasis added)

This might be a description of a sect, a closed community, or a club, but it hardly characterizes white America as a whole. There is no sense in which it can reasonably be said that all non-black Americans have a collective community of interest. Are Jews, Puerto Ricans, other Hispanics, and Appalachian whites included? They are all part of 'white' America. If the argument is that all these sub-groups that make up white America are united in interest against black Americans, it begins to sound a little like paranoia; it would certainly be contested by many other groups who remain deprived because of past injustices. Furthermore, even if white America could be so characterized, it remains difficult to see how *collective* reparations could be made or what form they would take. There just is no sense in which white America could or would act *in concert* to make reparations, and we are thus forced back to the problem of the distribution of the costs of compensation. The injustices of arbitrarily and quixotically allocated costs of compensation cannot be conjured away by assertions of group guilt. As Blackstone notes, ascribing guilt to the whole society, or the whole of white or male society, 'obviates the problem of holding individuals responsible for acts they did not commit . . . but it does not obviate the arbitrary distribution of the costs of compensation, nor the arbitrary distribution of benefits among the disadvantaged' (W. T. Blackstone 1977: 68–9).

The second dimension to what we have called 'collective guilt' is less concerned with who benefits from past harm but relates to the idea of guilt itself and the connected ideas of fault, liability, responsibility, and causation. Is there any sense in which we can reasonably say that *all* whites (or white males, etc.) are *collectively* guilty for the harm and injustices caused to blacks and women? Goldman (1979) notes that there is a wide range of degrees of guilt and of strict, vicarious, and collective liability, and that if we talk about the collective guilt of all whites we must be careful of our meaning. In fact there is little foundation for asserting that all *individual* whites are guilty of past harm at any point in the continuum of guilt from active commission to acquiescence and the guilt of omission. Even at the latter 'weak' end of the guilt continuum we can find, as Blackstone notes, white males who at cost to themselves were instrumental in promoting the rights and interests of blacks during the period of the civil rights movement. Are they to be counted guilty of the sin of omission or of acquiescence in negative discrimination?

There is nevertheless one way that Goldman identifies in which a form of guilt may be attributed to all white males collectively, and this is that they have shared (and continue to share) a set of *attitudes* that are conducive to the exercise of discrimination or to the maintenance of racist and sexist stereotypes – although even this sin could hardly be attributed to all white males. This is probably the only real sense in which we can speak of a genuinely *collective* guilt. However, as Goldman further notes, even if this *is* the case, such moral culpability is not a reasonable ground for establishing anything like a legal liability, and it would be a dangerous precedent therefore to hold people legally responsible for their attitudes. This would be doubly so where sets of attitudes are ascribed to groups by their adversaries. That is a very slippery slope to go down, for in reverse it opens the way for any unscrupulous and bigoted group to impute to others odious beliefs in the expectation of compensation.

On the question of collective guilt we may also note, with Blackstone, that if the view that white society as a whole owes compensation implies a collective responsibility, and if this implies (as it must) collective guilt, then the assertion is philosophically and morally unsound. Following Feinberg, he argues that whilst *liability* for compensation may transfer between agents, agency, causation, and fault (all components of 'contributory fault') certainly cannot, and neither can guilt itself. Although we may say that fault could *largely* be attributed, in the past, to white males, we cannot now attribute it to all white males collectively; nor can fault 'be transferred *simpliciter* across generations' (W. T. Blackstone 1977: 69).

There remains one aspect of group liability and compensation that we have not touched upon, which requires brief consideration here. Glazer describes how one of the common criticisms of the Civil Rights Act of 1964 was that it was unreasonable to expect that previously victimized groups could ever overcome a long heritage of discrimination and disadvantage by means of an instrument that allowed only individuals to seek recompense through the courts or to achieve jobs or equal education or political representation (Glazer 1978: 92). In short, could the language and law of individual rights ever be effective as a means of satisfying group wrongs? It is no doubt the strong tradition of liberal individualism in the USA (think, after all, of the nation's motto) that has prevented more than only a grudging acceptance of the idea of group compensation and liability (and that probably only by a minority).[9] It is not surprising therefore that the conflict of group rights versus individual rights should have played a part in the United States debate about positive discrimination. We have noted that, despite the rhetoric of whole-group compensation and whole-group liability (not to say guilt), it is not whole groups who reap the benefits or pay the costs of compensation but rather arbitrarily and quixotically selected individuals. We have argued further that this arbitrariness contravenes the requirements of distributive justice. The possibility of compounded injustice then arises when we introduce the idea of rights. To be sure, we began by asserting that compensation is itself a right – a right to have past injustices and rights transgressed amended – but is there a sense in which the process of putting right past injustices itself results in overriding the rights of others? If this is the case then the injustice of denying the rights of compensators is added to the distributive injustice of allocating benefits and costs arbitrarily. Much therefore revolves upon the question of whether those who pay compensation have their rights overridden, and if they do what these rights are. (It may be argued, as for example by Bayles (1973b: 308), that any principle of justice between groups will probably involve some injustice to some individuals and that this is simply a price that has to be paid.) This, it seems to me, is too bland an assertion. It surely must matter what the price is and whether it is worth it.

What rights then do potential compensators have that may be compromised by policies of preference? Two rights stand out for consideration. The first is the right to consideration as ends in themselves, which may be couched variously as the right to equal treatment or the right to treatment as equals; and the second is the right to positions based on hiring by competence or, more generally, the merit criterion. An adequate consideration of both of these rights and the part they play in the debate about positive discrimination takes us beyond the strict realm of compensation and requires discussion of the balance between rights and utility. That is the subject of Chapter 8, and we shall confine our remarks here to the collision between the demands of the justice of compensation and the integrity of rights.

The idea of a right to treatment as an individual or end in oneself is, as Dworkin has pointed out, a vague one, frequently elided with that of the right to consideration on one's merits. Certainly the two are close. The former usually, though not always, arises where individual rights come into conflict with broader societal ends, and the usual formulation is that an individual's rights ought not to be overridden in the service of greater welfare or utility, as would often be the case when individuals are treated as means to ends. In the situation we are considering, the 'end' that is being served is not a utilitarian nor even a consequentialist one, but a requirement of justice – that compensation is a right that those who have been injured possess. Clearly when guilty parties have duties of reparation it is nonsense to talk of *their* rights to consideration as individuals (all rights-talk carries this danger of degenerating into nonsense); but what if compensation is exacted from the non-guilty? We have already examined the possibility of holding all whites (or white males) guilty and have found it wanting, and the issue therefore is whether the rights of those white males who fail to obtain a position because of preference policies *in pursuit of compensation*, and who themselves cannot (at the least) be counted among the most guilty, are in fact overridden. Are they being used as proxy compensators and thus as means to a social or judicial end? I think they are, and I think this is a weighty argument in the balance of justice. As Lustgarten has argued:

> 'But where a white applicant has gained no wrongful advantage, to shunt him aside impersonally, due to the operation of a timetable or quota, is to use him as a means to a social end. The irony is that this end – the rectification of injustice – is in this instance carried out by fundamentally unjust means, since the person who suffers has neither contributed to nor been favoured by the injustice.'
>
> (Lustgarten 1980: 17)[10]

The second right that it has been argued might be compromised by positive discrimination policies is the right to be awarded positions on the basis of merit alone, or hiring by competence. The point at issue here is whether and to what extent the merit principle may be overridden in pursuit of the principle of compensation.

The defence of affirmative action or reverse discrimination against the charge that it involves overriding the merit principle takes two main forms both of which depend on the alleged inadequacies of the merit principle itself. The first emphasizes the 'impurity', inadequacy, and cultural bias of the merit principle, which both discriminates against and undervalues the abilities of ethnic minority members and women, and – more important from the point of view of a defence of positive discrimination – provides no solid moral foundation, departure from which would entail grave injustice. If the merit principle itself is flawed, overriding it need cause little difficulty. Varieties of this view have been put by Wasserstrom (1976) in respect of entry to the academic community; by Exum (1983), who maintains that the merit system is flawed, is in effect a patronage system of merit, and ill serves the advancement of minority group members; by Kilson (1983), who argues that the merit system must be seen in its historical context as having been moulded by past injustices; and by S. M. Miller (1973), who maintains that a 'pure' merit system has never operated in the USA, that other factors than merit are incorporated into the system, and that no great injustice is done in departing from such a system. A related argument is that made by Dworkin (1977b) and O'Neil (1975) among others that in practice what is called the merit system includes a number of criteria other than those that would strictly be accepted as indicative of merit. Some of these, it is argued, such as age (a ground on which Bakke was rejected by two medical schools), personability, and sporting ability (important for entry to some Ivy League colleges), are arbitrary; and no one ought to complain if race or sex is added to the list of criteria of 'merit'.

The second critique of the merit principle lays emphasis on its unjustness and moral arbitrariness. The strength of such a critique relies upon the distinction we made in Chapter 3 (see page 45) between merit and desert. It was argued there that, whilst desert most properly applies to people's actions, efforts, and sacrifices, merit applies to characteristics and traits that people possess; and that while the former may constitute legitimate material principles of distributive justice, the latter can carry no moral weight. Because people cannot 'deserve' their intelligence, quick-wittedness, manual dexterity, etc., such characteristics are arbitrary from a moral point of view. Even so, however, we are forced to concede that such morally arbitrary characteristics are in practice crucially important in the distribution of burdens and benefits in modern Western societies. As Nagel argues: 'In most societies reward is a function of demand and many of the human characteristics most in demand result largely from *gifts* or *talents*. The greatest injustice in this society, I believe, is neither racial nor sexual but intellectual' (Nagel 1977: 12, emphasis in original).

Whilst it may be argued that individuals may deserve the

benefits that flow from efforts and sacrifices involved in nurturing their talents, Nagel is surely correct in his assertion that they cannot deserve the latent talents that must be there to *be* nurtured. However, the connection between intelligence and rewards in capitalist societies is far from being as invariable as Nagel suggests. Indeed, the vagaries of the market-place result in quixotic distributions of burdens and benefits that often seem to bear little relationship even to utility let alone to distributive justice, especially where socially important functions (such as nursing and welfare) cannot reliably be provided by the private sector and have of necessity to be produced by an increasingly squeezed public sector. Given then that the merit system rewards characteristics that are morally arbitrary, and that even the gifts and talents usually associated with that system are only very imperfectly connected with rewards, there can be no injustice in overriding the system, especially if this is done to satisfy the requirements of justice. Affirmative action in these circumstances, it would seem, would not constitute a departure from justice.[11]

Why then does positive discrimination disconcert our intuitive notions of justice? There are probably two main reasons. The first is that most of us think the merit system is purer than in fact it is. There is a tendency in modern Western societies to believe that on the whole merit is rewarded and that the distribution of burdens and benefits more or less accords with people's talents and efforts. (There are occasional ritual outcries about the pay of nurses and teachers but these do little to dent the reputation of the accepted system of distributing burdens and benefits.) Even so, this still requires a belief in the justice of the merit system itself despite the fact that it rewards morally arbitrary characteristics. The second reason therefore is more fundamental and this is that the merit system is justified, not distributively, but in utilitarian terms. There is a strong belief in the 'justness' of functionally relevant criteria for distributing burdens and benefits. Goldman has put this case strongly, arguing that hiring by competence is the best and surest way of maximizing overall welfare (Goldman 1979: ch. 2). (In fact, Goldman's argument is a good deal more subtle than this, involving an argument about not only welfare maximization but also the maximization of liberty. Methodologically, his argument rests upon a form of Rawlsian contract theory. This is not the place to enter a discussion of his interpretation of what Rawlsian contractors would agree to, save to say that what contractors agree to is only *definitionally* just.) As the argument is framed here, positive discrimination *would* constitute an infraction of justice if the latter is taken to be the reward system that contractors in the original position would agree to in the interest of maximizing overall welfare. However, it is far from clear that the alternative to a merit system that Goldman attributes to egalitarians – a greater randomization of rewards – is the only or even the most likely alternative; nor is it a reflection of a truly egalitarian position. Furthermore, it seems unlikely that original-position contractors would contract to the particular imperfect merit system that holds today in modern Western societies even (or especially) if their main concern was welfare maximization.

There is a minor variation to the theme that the merit system itself is unjust. Rather than lay the emphasis on the morally arbitrary nature of the characteristics that the merit system rewards, Kilson argues that to accept the system at face value is to take an ahistorical view of the distribution of meritorious characteristics. The present distribution of these, he argues, is the result of past injustices to some groups and is itself therefore unjust (Kilson 1983: 467). No great injustice would therefore be incurred by positive discrimination practices which overrode a system that benefits people who gain rewards in virtue of abilities they possess only at the expense of others.

The question of positive discrimination practices overriding the merit principle is a particularly vexed one for our analysis. We have established that there must be a very good reason for preferring morally arbitrary criteria such as sex and race over morally relevant ones such as desert and need, and also a very good chance of achieving greater justice by so doing. Whether or not it is unjust to prefer one set of morally arbitrary criteria (again, sex and race) over another equally arbitrary set (which are only imperfectly effected anyway) is a much more difficult issue. My own view is that *if* positive discrimination were the only or best way of achieving compensation for past harm to particular groups then the problem of overriding the merit principle ought not to count heavily against it. I would be less sanguine if the merit principle was itself purer and more rigorously and universally applied. But because capitalist societies only imperfectly apply merit criteria, because these criteria are morally arbitrary, and because rewards do not on the whole go to those who undertake the socially most useful tasks, I see little harm and no injustice in adopting practices that cut across the merit system *provided such practices do in fact produce greater justice.* The conditional clause is important.

2.2 The practical arguments

We have examined some of the moral and theoretical issues surrounding the question of whether positive discrimination is the only, best, or on balance most just way of fulfilling the requirements of justice in respect of compensation for past harm. Practical issues ought ideally to be subordinate to moral ones (the mark of a good society is that it will accept the difficulties and costs involved in implementing moral imperatives) but they cannot be entirely ignored. We must now therefore weigh some of the practical problems and costs in the balance to establish whether positive discrimination could or would be the only or best means of compensating for past harm.

The most common administrative argument for positive discrimination complements one of the moral arguments we have already canvassed. This is that whilst the relevant criterion is harm or injustice, for practical or administrative purposes we may use proxy criteria that are immediately available, easy to measure, and clear-cut. Thus we might make a distinction between the justifying and the administrative criteria (Nickel 1973: 155) but one that would rely (as does Nickel's argument) on a virtual congruency between the two. The advantage of the proxy measure over the justifying criterion would simply be its ability readily to identify beneficiaries; that is, for administrative purposes, it would not be necessary to enter the debate about the moral relevance or otherwise of the proxy measures. It is on these grounds that Nickel argues that programmes of positive discrimination are probably the *only* effective and administratively feasible way of compensating blacks and other groups. Administrative efficiency justifies the use of criteria that would be unacceptable on grounds of justice alone. Furthermore, the use of such proxies, it is said, would in practice maximize the satisfaction of rights to compensation.

This is a strong practical reason in favour of positive discrimination; if such a practice in fact produced more *overall* justice than alternatives such as individual compensation or compensation for more narrowly defined groups, then this would be a persuasive argument in its favour. Whether or not positive discrimination *would* produce more overall justice is not a question to which an empirical answer can be given here, but the relevant entries on the balance sheet can easily be identified. Thus in calculating on-balance justice we should need to add in:

(a) whether positive discrimination would in practice lead to more of the harmed being compensated than alternative procedures;
(b) whether more of the *un*harmed would receive compensation than would be the case with alternative procedures;
(c) whether more of the guilt*less* would bear the costs of compensation than with alternatives;
(d) whether more of the guilty would be called to account than with alternatives.

If we were then to add to the balance sheet the administrative costs, efficiencies, and difficulties of positive discrimination as compared with alternatives, we would be on the way to producing a useful answer.

Specifying the relevant entries on the balance sheet is much easier than filling in the figures, as the foregoing analysis of the moral issues has shown. Goldman, for example, has raised the question of how high the correlation between injury or harm and the proxy measure must be before positive discrimination becomes an acceptable practice, and then argues that anything much short of 100 per cent would result in considerable injustices (Goldman 1975: 169–70). Because he is not convinced that the correlation does approach such a figure even for the most harmed groups, and because the correlation will vary a great deal as between different harmed groups, Goldman believes that compensation on an individual basis is the only acceptable method.

If a process of individual compensation were feasible and if it led to all, or almost all, of the harmed being compensated, and none of the unharmed, and if the costs did not fall on the innocent, then it would of course be vastly preferable to a programme of positive discrimination. However, it is just because compensation on an individual basis appears to be unfeasible and inadequate that the idea of whole-group compensation has been entertained. Goldman himself acknowledges that individual compensation would be difficult, uncertain, and costly, and would result in relatively few compensations, thus leaving much justice undone. He believes none the less that the moral costs of whole-group compensation are too high and that active programmes of individual compensation remain the only moral alternative. Likewise Glazer notes the pro-positive discrimination argument that individual compensation would be uncertain and wholly impractical on a large scale; but like Goldman he also thinks the costs of whole-group compensation too high (Glazer 1978: 94). Furthermore, he argues, we should not underestimate the progress that was made under the Civil Rights Act prior to the inception of affirmative action programmes, and which is still being made.[12] Glazer's view is an optimistic one. There is little reason to doubt that a process of individual compensation would be impractical, would lead to very little compensation being paid, would leave much justice undone, and would in any case be out of the question on grounds of administrative costs.

Having ruled out individual compensation, it has to be said that positive discrimination remains highly vulnerable to the charges made against it, outlined in earlier sections of this chapter; it is a very crude instrument, would deliver benefits to the unharmed, and would impose costs on the innocent. In recognition of this vulnerability some defenders of positive discrimination have proposed various ways of increasing the correlation between harm and the group characteristics, usually by selecting from within groups (blacks, women, etc.) those who are more likely to have suffered harm, and excluding other members of the group from the benefits of compensation. Such a process, it is believed, would result in greater on-balance justice. Thus, for example, Beauchamp proposes positive discrimination for 'narrowed' groups such as all blacks below a certain income level but not others (Beauchamp 1977: 107–08). Other supplementary criteria that have been proposed include those living in certain geographic areas (for example, southern states where black oppression was most widespread) and those in low status occupations. Such additional criteria are 'morally relevant' ones, being, it is assumed, clear indicators of past and continuing harm. By supplementing the morally irrelevant criteria (black, women) with morally relevant ones, it is assumed that the selected beneficiaries will more nearly approximate to those who have suffered injustice. (However, such arguments cannot easily be combined with those about psychological harm, since there is no necessary connection between the latter and such variables as low income and low status. In addition, relevant supplementary criteria would be hard to define in respect of some groups, particularly women.)

The use of supplementary morally relevant criteria represents, at first sight at least, a potentially viable and effective way of reducing the vulnerability of positive discrimination to the charge of moral coarseness. It is nevertheless subject to a number of flaws, some of which are fatal. Firstly, as Goldman points out, the more supplementary criteria you add in (in an effort to increase congruency) the higher become the administrative costs and the greater the loss in efficiency, both of which are reasons for adopting positive discrimination in the first instance (Goldman 1979: 97–8). Secondly, the social logic of adding in relevant criteria is at best an approximation. It rests upon an assumption that those members of minority groups (and women) who are currently the most economically and socially deprived are the ones who have suffered most harm. This may be approximately true, but it is not invariably so.

Less so is the correlative assumption that present low status is the result of past harm. There may be, and probably are, many contributory factors to present low status. In the case of women, as we noted above, it would be hard to identify relevant supplementary criteria, especially if we acknowledge that psychological harm is an important component (do we then give most compensation to those who are most sensitive to male chauvinism, and if so, how do we identify them?).

Thirdly, and most importantly, it is likely to be the case, ironically, that adding in supplementary criteria will in fact weaken the original case for compensation to ethnic minorities and women. Because once you acknowledge that blackness or being a woman is no longer *in itself* sufficient to justify compensation, the more difficult it becomes to sustain the view that blackness has *any* relevance: if compensation to (only) poor blacks, then why not compensation to all the poor? In a sense the addition of other criteria has the reverse effect from that intended, of making the original criterion (blacks, women) look even more morally arbitrary. Its susceptibility to such an attack has no doubt inhibited the adoption of the practice.

A further administrative cost, and difficulty, arises for positive discrimination programmes, especially in the USA (to a lesser extent in Britain), in the selection of beneficiary groups. We have so far, by way of shorthand, referred in this chapter mainly to blacks and women, but they are by no means the only affected groups. There are many others in the USA who are not black or female who would claim for their ethnic or nationality group the status of 'harmed'. Furthermore, we have assumed –

and for the sake of argument asserted – that affected groups are easily and unambiguously identifiable. This is far from always being the case, especially in such a polyglot society as the United States.

When affirmative action programmes were first introduced in the USA, the Department of Labor was charged with the task of identifying and defining 'affected groups'. As Glazer notes, the main intended beneficiary group was Negroes, but others were added. Thus Mexican–Americans and Puerto Ricans were grouped together as 'Hispanics' (a group that also included anyone with a Spanish surname); 'Asian' or 'Oriental' Americans represented a further affected group (predominantly composed of Chinese and Japanese). The remainder of the population was classified as 'white' or 'other' (Glazer 1978: 92–3). The problem with such classifications is both that they do not have unambiguous boundaries (and this is particularly the case for Hispanics) and that they do not obviously coincide with the category of 'harmed'. If we leave aside the case of blacks and Hispanics, for which groups there is evidence of *present* low socio-economic status (and at least prima facie of past harm), it is far from clear that the oriental groups in the USA suffered greater injury than many other early immigrant groups, and they are certainly not presently over-represented among the poor and deprived. By contrast, the 'other' or 'white' category contains a number of nationality groups such as Italians, Poles, and other Slavs that could lay claim to being currently over-represented among the low socio-economic groups. Also included in the 'other' category are Jews, who most certainly have suffered injury in the past but who are now over-represented among the socio-economically successful. Are the Jews to be excluded from compensation for past harm simply on the grounds that they have surmounted their hardships? Goldman (1979) sees no reason why presently affluent Jews should now be compensated, but it is far from clear that present success *of itself* wipes the slate clean of past injustice. As Gross puts it, the question is not 'who fails to do well' but rather 'who is discriminated against?' (Gross 1977: 380).

On the question of identifying beneficiary groups, Newton makes the somewhat exaggerated but still illustrative point that the USA does not consist of a small number of small 'minority groups' who have been harmed by the 'majority' but rather of a mass of 'minority groups' any number of which could claim discrimination at the hands of others (Newton 1977: 376–77).

Put in these terms, the notion of laying all the blame for past injuries on WASPs (themselves a minority group in the USA) takes on the aura of absurdity. The fact is, as both Bittker and Glazer note, that racial and ethnic classifications make poor categories for policy-making. Furthermore, such policies, where they exist, promote an exaggerated view of the homogeneity of ethnic, racial, and national groups (not to mention sex groupings).

We must add, then, to the administrative and practical costs of positive discrimination the difficulties, imprecisions, ambiguities, and occasional absurdities of identifying potential beneficiary groups. As Glazer remarks of such policies:

> 'they assume that these groups are so easily bounded and defined, and so uniform in the condition of those included in them, that a policy designed for the group can be applied equitably and may be assumed to provide benefits for those eligible. The fact is that, for many of the groups involved, the boundaries of membership are uncertain, and the conditions of those included in the groups are diverse.'
>
> (Glazer 1975: 202)

There is one further administrative cost to positive discrimination that we must take into account. We noted earlier that the principle of compensation requires not just restitution to the status quo ante but reinstatement to the position that those injured would hold today if the injustice had never occurred. In order to achieve this we shall require a process of counterfactual reasoning, and this will involve high administrative costs as well as formidable difficulties. Counterfactual reasoning is not however a peculiar requirement of positive discrimination but is common to any system of compensation that pretends to do more than reinstate the status quo ante;[13] it should not therefore be counted as a *particular* cost of positive discrimination. Before we comment on the feasibility or otherwise of counterfactual reasoning in positive discrimination we should note one variation of it. In his discussion of positive discrimination and meritocratic principles, Jones rejects what he calls the 'meritocracy of present qualifications' in favour of a 'counterfactual meritocracy' based upon the qualifications that ethnic minority members *would* now possess had they not be discriminated against in the past (Jones 1977: 350).

The first question that counterfactual reasoning – and in particular Jones's variation on it – raises is whether it is to apply to whole groups or to constituent members of them. Is it to be a group process or the individuation of a group process? The answer is important for a consideration of the costs involved. If we see counterfactual reasoning as a necessary component of positive discrimination (definitionally a group practice) then it would seem that it ought to be applied to whole groups. Thus the relevant question becomes 'What would be the current status (social, economic, cultural, psychological, physical, etc.) of blacks, women, Hispanics, etc. if no injustice had been done to them in the past?' Is this a meaningful question (quite apart from the logistics of providing an answer)? I suspect it is not, other than to invite the not altogether helpful answer of 'better'. Blacks, women, and others would certainly now be more generously represented among the ranks of the professions and higher business, but how many would there be, and in what professions, and which blacks or women? For again, we cannot ignore the heterogeneity of such groups, and simply to say that the whole group would now be better off does not provide a recipe for action; it is a rhetorical assertion. (The necessary corollary – if we are talking in relative terms – is equally problematical. What groups would now be worse off, by how much, and in which areas, had they not benefited from past injustices?) It is not enough to say that the whole group should benefit from compensation, because compensation must entail the distribution of benefits within the group, even if it is whole-group compensation. Even at the most basic level of, say, a lump-sum payment to all members of a group, it is still a particular distribution within the group, although in such an instance, given that harm has been unequally distributed, an inequitable one.

Thus if positive discrimination were to be more systematically implemented than it has been in the past – and such an improvement would be a necessary condition of its acceptability – it would require counterfactual reasoning on an individual, or at least sub-group, basis within the affected groups. Counterfactual reasoning on a whole-group basis does not make sense.[14] The problems involved in counterfactual calculations on an individual basis require no emphasis and would, I suggest, be insurmountable. Jones's own answer to this criticism is informative if only to reinforce the critique it attempts to turn aside. It is threefold. Firstly, he argues, because counterfactual reasoning is complex and an uncertain art, we should accept only minor differences between the qualifications of a preferred applicant and those of the white (male) who is supplanted. A black woman should be given a white man's job only if her qualifications are just slightly less good than his. Secondly, he argues, we *do* have some information about individuals to enable us to make the counterfactual calculations; and thirdly, we should be prepared to take some risks that our calculations might be inaccurate – risks that are accepted every day in the judicial system. There are two replies to his defence. The first, and practical, one is that his second and third answers, far from reassuring us about the magnitude and complexity of the task, serve only to emphasize it. The second is that to allow only minor differences in qualifications to count for compensatory purposes is hardly a design for ensuring that the most harmed receive the greater compensation. In fact, it turns out that his 'counterfactual meritocracy' is no such thing; it is simply a slightly displaced shadow of the real thing.

The administrative costs (in terms of difficulty, complexity, scale, and finance) of positive discrimination would seem, on the basis of the foregoing analysis, to be enormous. Positive discrimination programmes in the USA have been sustainable only because they have been piecemeal, small in scale, arbitrary, and quixotic in their application and results. But despite all this, does positive discrimination remain the only or best way of fulfilling the requirements of justice in respect of compensation? We know what is required – compensation proportional to harm on a case-by-case basis using counterfactual calculations, where the costs fall only on the guilty in proportion to their guilt. And we know that this is unattainable. So is what we have – a system of positive discrimination that in the arbitrariness of its application is a travesty of compensatory justice – better than nothing? My view is that it is not. A system of compensation that is so far removed from producing anything like the minimal requirements of the equality principle in respect of compensation and in the course of its application creates so much injustice (to compensatees as well as compensators) is not a system worth having. Current practices of affirmative action (or reverse discrimination, as it has become) just do not atone for the past. I suspect that no administratively or politically or ethically acceptable system of compensation for past harm other than in clear and measurable instances (such as property loss) could be devised.

3 The British experience

There are two components to the issue of positive discrimination as compensation for harm in Britain. The first is whether a case can be made for the necessity for or desirability of compensating some groups for harm done to them. Are there groups in Britain who have been and are being harmed to an extent that justice will not be done unless they are compensated in some way? The second question is whether, if this turned out to be the case, positive discrimination would be the only, best, or most efficient way of doing the compensating. We have already given an answer to the second question in the foregoing arguments. It need come as no surprise in the light of what has been said about the moral and practical arguments for and against positive discrimination as compensation that there is little or nothing to sustain a view that positive discrimination could be the only, best, or on balance most just way of compensating for harm, were that deemed to be necessary. True, most of these arguments have been developed in the context of the United States experience, which we have seen to be fundamentally flawed, in particular, in relation to who gets the most compensation and who ends up paying the costs. Certainly, a better system of positive discrimination could be devised – one not so perversely designed to compensate those least harmed. But the preceding arguments also surely show why a better system would still not be anything like satisfactory or morally acceptable.

Because our concern is with positive discrimination and not primarily with the condition of ethnic minorities or women in Britain, these conclusions about positive discrimination leave the first issue disconnected. However, the question of compensation for harm in the British context is a matter of importance, and we must for the sake of completeness briefly consider it. Indeed, if the case for compensation turned out to be a pressing one and if no other means of satisfactorily fulfilling it could be found, then the case for using positive discrimination would have to be re-examined.

We have seen in earlier chapters that arguments for positive discrimination in Britain are virtually all couched in terms of need, even when they use the term 'compensation'. No one has seriously argued that positive discrimination should be implemented in Britain in order to meet the just claims to compensation for harm of any particular group. Nevertheless, racial discrimination does occur and has been widespread and probably systematic in the past (Daniel 1968, Jowell and Prescott-Clarke 1970, McIntosh and Smith 1974, D. J. Smith and Whalley 1975, Firth 1981, M. Cross 1982). Negative discrimination does cause harm; it is unjust treatment; it does deny people's rights. There must therefore exist some grounds for compensation to those discriminated against, and this would include women as well as members of ethnic minority groups, although our remarks will be confined to the latter. Our besetting problem is that we just do not know the magnitude of present and of past racial discrimination. We do know from our own history that discrimination against blacks and Asians is not so long-standing nor so systematic as in the USA. At the most basic we know that ethnic minorities in Britain, unlike those in the US, came out of choice, or at least the majority did so. (Conjecturally, it could be argued that the circumstances from which they came and that contributed in large measure to their coming were a creation of Britain's exploitation of its colonies, and this in itself might provide grounds for compensation. The precedent exists in the claims of the Sioux and Inuit Indians in the USA and Canada. However, this takes us beyond the scope of the present work.) Unlike the guest-workers in West Germany and France, they came as British citizens with all the rights and obligations that go with citizenship. There may be many whites who now regret this and who wish we had imported guest-workers to do the menial jobs in the health service and elsewhere in the public sector, but that is now beside the point. We *did* invite people from the Commonwealth; we *did* invite them as cheap labour; they *are* British. These factors, taken together, along with the treatment the minorities have received since, mean that we must at least entertain the possibility of compensation for harm.

The question then is whether the harm has been so great, so systematic, and so widespread that only group compensation will right the balance of justice. My own view is that, so far as the history of immigration from the Commonwealth is concerned, it would be impossible to apply counterfactual reasoning to calculate what the situation would now be had minority group members not been invited to this country – and if Britain had not exploited theirs – or if they had not been invited to fill the role of cheap labour. It may be argued that this is not a sufficient reason for not acting justly, but the problem is then who to compensate, and by how much.

As to compensation for discrimination and harm since the arrival of minority group members in any numbers, there is of course the alternative of individual recompense through the courts under the 1976 Race Relations Act. But few would seriously argue, other than on grounds of political expediency, that this is adequate machinery. However the alternative of whole-group compensation would, on grounds of justice, be hardly any better. Indeed, if justice to minority groups and to whites is our prime concern, it most certainly would not be, for *any* ethnic minority group we might choose.

We are left then with a wholly unsatisfactory situation. We know that harm has been (and is being) done. We know the existing machinery to compensate for it is inadequate, and we know that the alternative would create even greater injustices – for the reasons argued throughout this chapter. There is no easy answer. It seems platitudinous to say so, but it may well be that there is no really effective alternative to improved and more effective machinery for individual compensation for discrimination through the courts. Other than that, to the extent that the present relatively deprived condition of some minority groups in Britain is the result of past discrimination, then the best way of atoning for the past is to ensure, through the more rigorous and less vindictive use of the needs principle, that minority groups are no longer over-represented among the least well off.

Chapter 8
Consequentialism, justice, and positive discrimination

Justice is a harsh but compelling test for positive discrimination; harsh, because the prerequisite conditions for positive discrimination to be a justiciable practice are hard to fulfil (as we saw in the case of need in the UK and of compensation in the USA); compelling, because if the preconditions are fulfilled, positive discrimination becomes a *requirement* of justice and ought to be implemented if we wish to act justly. There would have to be very strong overriding reasons for *not* putting positive discrimination into practice.

It would seem, however, as preceding chapters have argued, that positive discrimination fails the test of justice. (This is not to say that this will always be the case. If the relative condition of some minority groups in the UK deteriorates, it is possible that positive discrimination could become the only or the best way of meeting their greater needs.) It would be hard to sustain an argument that justice requires us to implement positive discrimination on grounds of either need or compensation. There is at present no compelling argument for positive discrimination either in Britain or the USA on the grounds of justice.

There are nevertheless 'softer' arguments for (and against) positive discrimination, which appear in a variety of forms but are all broadly consequentialist. Sometimes they manifest specifically as such. At other times they masquerade as justice-regarding reasons.

We noted in Chapter 3 the broad division in ethics between deontic and teleologic arguments, between 'duty-regarding' and 'consequence-regarding' claims. The preceding five chapters have examined deontic arguments for and against positive discrimination, and we must now look to 'softer' teleologic or consequential arguments. Positive discrimination has been found wanting when measured against deontic (in this case, justice-regarding) principles, but justice is not the whole of morality and does not have to be the only test of the acceptability or desirability of positive discrimination (although, as I have argued, it is the most rigorous). To revert to the important distinction referred to earlier (see page 36), we have thus far examined the *justicizing* grounds for positive discrimination and now require to look at the broadly *justifying* grounds: the teleologic as against the deontic.

Although many of the calls for or defences of positive discrimination in Britain have been broadly consequentialist in nature, they have varied, and continue to vary, greatly not only in the desired consequences adduced, but also in their moral status, from the morally 'respectable' and defensible to the purely politically expedient and the ritual post-riot incantations. Since our concern in this book is with the morality of positive discrimination as a policy practice, part of our task in this chapter must be to clarify the varieties of consequence (and consequentialism) invoked by calls for positive discrimination and to attempt to sift those claims that might be sustainable on broadly moral grounds from those that are no more than expedient, rhetoric, and cant.

More significantly, the present chapter will attempt to compare and assess the variety of consequential arguments (utilitarian, 'ideal'-regarding, functional, and so on), consider the balance of utilities in particular examples of the proposed use of positive discrimination, and, solely as it applies to positive discrimination, examine whether and under what circumstances utility may override justice or rights. As before, our concern is with the situation in Britain, but our arguments must necessarily be illumined by the US debate. Our ultimate goal is to see whether a sound case for the use of positive discrimination in Britain can be made on consequence-regarding grounds.

1 Teleology, consequentialism, and utility

We need say no more about teleologic ethics, consequentialism, and utility than is absolutely necessary to enable us to distinguish between the varieties of claims for positive discrimination and to assess the morality of its application in pursuit of any given set of ends. Chapter 3 considered briefly the characteristics of a teleologic ethic (in contradistinction to a deontic one) and its relationship to utilitarianism and consequentialism more generally. We must briefly elaborate on this, but without entering on an arid terminological dispute. This may involve taking a few liberties with conventional usage but only in the interest of providing a clearer framework for our analysis of positive discrimination. We shall need to distinguish between varieties of generally consequentialist argument in order to be able to identify arguments for or defences of positive discrimination that fall into one or more of the following:

- strictly consequentialist;
- teleologic;
- utilitarian;[1]
- ideal-end-regarding;
- functional;

I take all these to fall under the more general heading of broad consequentialism.

Strict consequentialism I take to refer to that mode of ethical thinking in which the rightness of a course of action is determined by the balance of goods and evils not only of the consequences but also of the action itself. As noted earlier (Chapter 3, note 2), this is a broader usage than that originally attached to the word by Anscombe (1958), but it is in broad agreement with Mackie's characterization of consequentialism (Mackie 1977: 159) as an ethic that does *not* justify any means as the servant of a given end, but rather makes no moral distinction between means and ends, and balances the goods and evils of both. The significance of this for our present purposes is that the *practice* of positive discrimination and the nature of positive discrimination as a means must be weighed in the balance with the goods and evils it produces. This is different from simply weighing in the balance the utilities and disutilities of the *results* of applying positive discrimination. The nature of positive discrimination as a *means* must also weigh in the balance, and if positive discrimination is an unjust practice (as measured, for example, against the formal and material principles of justice) then this must weigh as a cost along with the costs and benefits of the outcomes.

A *teleologic* ethic is a sub-group of broad consequentialism wherein right action is always determined as that which on balance maximizes the good.[2] It is distinguished from consequentialism in its broad sense by always being good-maximizing (as opposed only to being ends-regarding) and in using only *ends* in the calculus of costs and benefits.

Frankena (1963) has remarked that there are a variety of teleological theories depending on the stipulation of *whose* good is to be maximized. At the extremes are ethical egoism and ethical universalism (maximizing one's own personal good, and maximizing the good of humanity as a whole); in between are theories that stipulate the good of a nation, a state, a society, an ethnic group, and so on.

Such variations are not so esoteric as they may seem. Appeals to the 'common good' or the 'public interest' are often, as we shall see, merely forms of political flatulence. What is really at issue (positive discrimination is no exception here) is *whose* good is being served by any particular policy or set of policies.

Where a teleologic ethic purports to promote the maximum on-balance good of a society or nation or nations, it may be equated with the various forms of *utilitarianism*. Clearly, ethical egoism as a form of teleology is not utilitarianism, but it is probably of little value to try to decide at what point on an ascending scale of population group size we may equate teleology with utilitarianism. We need only mention that, just as a teleologic ethic is a sub-category of broad consequentialism, so utilitarianism is a sub-category of teleology.

There are a variety of schools of thought under the utilitarian umbrella. For present purposes we need note only those that might affect our judgements about the claimed justifications for positive discrimination when these are alleged to be or appear to be utilitarian in some form or another.

The distinction between act and rule utilitarianism (see Bayles 1968, Smart and Williams 1973) is one that, although it seems to have an air of philosophical expediency, may help illuminate the nature of some claims for the use of positive discrimination. If positive discrimination were to be defended on utilitarian grounds (of some sort), would it be as act utilitarian (i.e. in these particular circumstances and with these particular costs and benefits it is the right thing to do), or in accordance with following some rule or rules that on the whole conduced to the greatest overall benefit? If the latter, could we identify the rules, and what would they be? Are there any such set of rules following which would lead us to promote positive discrimination as a consistent action or policy given certain circumstances, or is positive discrimination on the other hand an expediency, inconsistent with usual practice but welfare-maximizing in this peculiar set of circumstances?

An alternative to classical Benthamite psychological utility is the idea of preference utility.[3] In preference to a scheme whereby quanta of pleasures and pains, burdens and benefits can be only inadequately measured and summed, utility ought, it is argued, to be seen in terms of maximizing the preferences people have for one course of action over another. We need elaborate no further on this here but we shall subsequently see the complications that arise in the case of a practice like positive discrimination of counting and balancing personal, external, and political preferences.

We shall be less concerned with the other major distinction in utilitarianism, between collective and average utility, but it is noted here for its relevance to our later discussion about the distribution of welfare maximization.[4]

Not all broadly consequentialist action is utility-maximizing or balances the goods and evils of means and ends. Some actions are undertaken or policies pursued because the end they are designed to achieve is thought to be good in itself (although it might not represent maximal utility) or because under a given set of circumstances it is deemed necessary. These we may call *ideal-end-regarding* and *functional* actions. Among the first we may include such actions as may be thought to promote, say, greater justice, a more equal society, or more racial justice. The second would include acts of expediency such as curbing football or racial rioting, politically damaging demonstrations, and so forth.

The dividing line between ideal-end-regarding actions on the one hand and deontic or apodictic action on the other is a narrow one but exists none the less. Deontic action is distinguished by its relative blindness to ends; ideal-end-regarding action, as its name dictates, is thoroughly determined by the ends it is thought it will bring about. Similarly, functional actions will often appear indistinguishable from welfare- or common-good-maximizing actions, but again a real distinction remains. I take functional actions to be those dictated by the necessities of the moment and not to be based upon a calculus of harm and benefit. Such actions will often, however, be explained or defended in the rhetoric of utilitarianism. We are all – except, it would seem, politicians – familiar with political expediency dolled up in the finery of 'the common good' or the 'benefit of society as a whole'.

2 Consequentialist arguments for positive discrimination

Although deontic principles of needs and rights claims constitute the most common bases of claims for or defences of positive discrimination in both Britain and the USA, a variety of generally consequentialist arguments have also been made. We shall first examine such claims in terms of the ends that they adduce; in a later section the balance of utilities and the weighting of deontic with teleologic arguments will be discussed. For this reason, we shall not at present attempt to distinguish between strictly consequentialist claims, which weigh both ends and means in the balance, and utilitarian claims, which pay regard only to the balance of ends. However, from an examination of the ends adduced in any particular claim for positive discrimination, we can identify at this stage three of the types of consequentialism we have listed above – namely, utilitarian (with a variety of subjects whose utility is to be maximized), ideal-end-regarding, and functional.

We remarked above that utilitarian arguments vary according to the stipulation of the groups whose utility is to be maximized. We tend to think in terms of overall utility – of the people of the UK or the USA, say – but this is by no means always the relevant group for any particular policy. If, for example, we were to use some form of preference utility calculus to determine which to adopt of two alternative ways of paying old age pensions, we would not think it necessarily relevant to canvass the preferences of the entire population. A similar argument may be put in respect of student grants or loans. And so it is with positive discrimination. Some arguments for and against positive discrimination consider the balance of utilities over the whole population; some confine the calculus to particular minority groups or women; and yet others to such groups as university students as a whole, where preferential university admissions policies are being considered. What is important about this is that the calculus of utilities may well produce different results depending on the defined group.

The first set of utilitarian arguments for positive discrimination that can be identified are those that take the target populations (ethnic or racial minorities or women) as the group whose good is to be maximized. Both Dworkin (1977b) and Nagel (1977) have argued, for example, that some form of positive discrimination in medical or law school admissions procedures would be justified on the grounds that the health and legal needs of black communities would be better served by having more black doctors and lawyers.[5] At a more general level, Thalberg has argued for positive discrimination as a means of producing 'an improvement in the conditions of ethnic minorities' (Thalberg 1973–4: 302), and Bayles (1973b) and O'Neil (1975) have promoted preferential admissions treatment to the professions on the grounds that an increase in the number of ethnic minority professionals will both raise the status of such groups and contribute to shaping their self-respect. In the UK as well positive discrimination (and positive action) has been promoted on similar grounds. Lord Scarman called for more positive action (although he later called it positive discrimination) in order to redress the balance of racial disadvantage (Scarman 1981: 109), and the London Borough of Hackney has promoted twenty-eight traineeships for professional and managerial jobs exclusively for Asians and Afro-Caribbeans on the grounds of providing a 'better, more sensitive service in an area that has many people from the ethnic minorities' (*The Times*, 11 December 1982). Indeed, many of the calls for positive discrimination in the British policy and academic literature could be interpreted in a similar manner; the boundary between calls for positive discrimination on the (apodictic) grounds of need and on grounds of minority-group utility is largely a matter of nuances of interpretation, which it would be purposeless to pursue.

Closely related to arguments for the use of positive discrimination to accelerate ethnic minority membership of the professions, so as to enhance the status and self-respect of members of such minorities, are claims that its practice will produce role models or exemplars for others to follow. Such claims are frequent in the United States literature (O'Neil 1975: 97, Dworkin 1977b: 11, Jones 1977: 349, Nagel 1977: 16, Goldman 1979: 142–43). Goldman has perhaps best argued the case for role models even though he is in the end doubtful of their efficacy and wisdom:

> 'the idea is that minority group members and women are given jobs and seen to function in them as well as white males . . . this will enable more members of minorities to obtain jobs on their own . . . Second, individuals who initially acquire jobs through the policy can serve as models for younger members of their group, creating motivation formerly lacking.'
>
> (Goldman 1977: 142–43)

As a utilitarian argument for positive discrimination, the production of role models is but a means to a further end the like of which is usually to be found among those listed above: the enhanced status of the group, greater representation among the status professions, and so on. Whether or not positive discrimination does or could produce role models, and whether, if it does, they serve the purpose intended, we shall examine below when we evaluate utilitarian arguments for the practice.

Groups other than the ethnic minorities or women themselves have on occasions been identified as beneficiaries from positive discrimination. Thus in the decision in the Bakke case Justice Powell argued that race might be a relevant factor to be taken into account in university admissions for the purpose of achieving a greater racial diversity among the students (see Dworkin 1978: 20). Goldman has argued a similar case – that university students as a whole would benefit from a greater racial diversity of classmates, although in what particular ways this is thought to be beneficial is not stated. One must assume that the benefits would be thought to lie in the development of greater understanding, tolerance, sensitivity, and mutual respect. It may be true, but there is an uneasy element of paternalism in the argument.

The second type of utilitarian argument is that which takes the population as a whole (of a country) as the group whose 'welfare' is to be maximized. Claims to the general utility of positive discrimination are relatively common both in the USA and Britain, although they frequently take the form of insubstantial platitudes.

The general utility claimed to derive from positive discrimination is 'greater social harmony' or some variant of it. Goldman, for example, describes the line of argument often adopted in the USA in defence of positive discrimination as that it will gradually reduce tensions among races and between the sexes, integrate minority group members into the mainstream of US life more quickly, and hence reduce racial antagonisms (Goldman 1977: 141–42).[6] Similar arguments have been put by Dworkin – that in the longer term, positive discrimination may reduce the extent to which the USA is a racially conscious society (Dworkin 1977b: 11). Blackstone has claimed that the whole population of the USA would benefit from the reduction in racial frictions that would be a longer-term consequence of positive discrimination (W. T. Blackstone 1977: 73).

General utility arguments lend themselves easily to the requirements of ponderous leader writers in the 'quality' press and to the platitudes that politicians need when addressing grave matters. So we find in a *Times* leader, pompously entitled 'One Nation', that '*for the health of society as a whole*, there must be a loading in favour of a minority racial group' (*The Times*, 30 March 1982, emphasis added). The costs of not taking positive action (called 'reverse discrimination' in the same context elsewhere in the editorial) will be 'a further polarization of black and white, less mutual understanding and confidence, more racialism, a two-tier society with blacks at the bottom, the perpetuation of injustice, and, not least, the great danger of violence and rioting on a scale far in excess of Brixton and Toxteth' (*The Times*, 30 March 1982).[7] This is a formidable catalogue of calamities leaving no doubt about the general utility of positive discrimination. Later in the same year, *The Times* was to adopt a similar stance in respect of a proposal to provide additional training for Asians and blacks who wished to join the police force, to bring them up to entry standard qualifications. The plan was, like many similar ones, more like positive action than 'hard' positive discrimination, but still borderline in so far as it promoted preferential treatment for aspiring police entrants from minority groups. On this occasion *The Times* asserted the need for a greater ethnic minority representation in the police force on the grounds of 'the harmony of a multi-racial society' (*The Times*, 19 May 1982).

An easing of racial tensions, a more integrated society, and general social harmony may therefore be counted as the general utilities, beneficial to *all* members of society, that are claimed as the consequences of practising positive discrimination.

The second of the three broadly consequentialist arguments for positive discrimination that can be identified is one that is ideal-end-regarding rather than utility-maximizing. Such arguments are distinguished by their reference to some good to be achieved that is regarded as a good in itself and not subject to utility calculations.[8] Dworkin has most clearly presented the distinction between ideal and utilitarian arguments for positive discrimination in his comparison of the arguments adduced in the De Funis case with those in the case of *Sweatt* v. *Painter* in 1945. Sweatt, a black, applied for entry to the University of Texas Law School but was refused admission because state law permitted only whites to attend. Both cases were fought on the grounds of rights violation under the Fourteenth Amendment. Dworkin (1977a: ch. 9) sets out to show why the two cases are different, that Sweatt had a case but De Funis did not. His argument, briefly, is that the claims of the University of Texas that segregating was better for the community as a whole were at odds with Sweatt's right to equal treatment under the Equal Protection Clause because the claims were all utilitarian and, furthermore, based on both personal and external preferences. The University of Washington Law School on the other hand could defend its preferential admissions policy (under which De Funis failed to gain entry) both on utilitarian *and* ideal-end grounds – namely, that the long-term aims of its policies were to produce a more just and more equal society. Such a claim, argues Dworkin, is not incompatible with De Funis's rights to treatment as an equal. For Dworkin, therefore, ideal-end arguments for positive discrimination are stronger and more telling than utilitarian arguments. The calculus of utility can be turned on the defenders of positive discrimination, whereas ideal-end arguments may not be dragooned into the service of racists, sexists, or segregationists. In this way Dworkin tries to have his consequentialist cake and eat it. The difficulty comes in trying to swallow the claim that positive discrimination will conduce to such grandiose ends as a more equal and just society.

The third of our consequentialist arguments we have called functional; that is, they are neither necessarily utility-maximizing nor ideal-end-regarding (although they may be decked out as either or both), but rather actions to achieve a given end or ends that may be, and often are, expedient.[9] Perhaps what makes functional arguments functional and expedient is not so much their content as the manner and timing of their utterance. Certainly, many such claims are not dissimilar to general utility claims we noted above about social harmony and reducing racial tensions. But the coincidence in the timing of arguments for positive discrimination on grounds of preventing social unrest and civil disorder with actual episodes of unrest makes their expedient nature inescapable. Indeed, although arguments in favour of positive discrimination in the USA on the grounds of preventing social unrest are fairly common in the literature (see, for example, O'Neil 1975: 97, W. T. Blackstone 1977: 73, Goldman 1979: 142), they did not appear in Britain until after the riots of 1981.

Thus Lord Scarman twice hints at the danger of civil strife, once in direct reference to positive discrimination as being 'a price worth paying if it accelerates the elimination of the unsettling factor of racial disadvantage from the social fabric of the

United Kingdom' (Scarman 1981: 135), and again in arguing for more black policemen (Scarman 1981: 77). We have already noted the call in *The Times* for positive discrimination (or positive action – the terms are confused) to (among other things) stave off the potential for unrest. This call was repeated more explicitly later the same year by Lord Beloff, writing in the same newspaper:

> 'It is wrong, so Conservatives believe, to lower standards of entry to the police or other professions to assist in recruitment from the ethnic minorities; but it may be possible to convince the white majority that some "positive discrimination" in respect of schooling and training is an acceptable price to pay for social peace.'
>
> (Beloff 1982)

It may well be that the prevention of riots is to everyone's benefit – or at least, if you believe in the rioting-for-fun-and-profit thesis, to the benefit of the majority. But there does seem to be an important moral distinction between general utility arguments for positive discrimination and those that see in positive discrimination the means for preventing or reducing the likelihood of civil unrest. For this reason we can make a distinction between utilitarian arguments for positive discrimination and functional or expedient ones.

There is, then, not only a broad spectrum of ends that, it has been claimed, positive discrimination might achieve, but also a variety of *kinds* of end within the broad rubric of general consequentialism. Some of these are subject to balance-of-utility calculations; others, and in particular ideal-end-regarding arguments, less so. Our main concern in the next few pages must be to examine the likely balance of utilities of positive discrimination. We shall see subsequently how positive discrimination fares when we pit utility against justice.

3 The calculus of utilities

For present purposes we can assume that ideal-end-regarding arguments are not as negotiable in terms of a balance between good and evil outcomes as are utilitarian and functional arguments. (This is not to say that all costs are to be ignored, however.) Similarly, strictly consequentialist arguments raise issues beyond the balance of outcomes, and we shall consider these when we compare utility with the demands of justice. Our concern here is with utilitarian and functional arguments for positive discrimination. The latter, as the former, are subject to the calculus of utility, though the ends to be achieved may well be more limited and short-term. We may assume that even for reasons of expediency we would not wish to proceed at *any* cost.

The purpose of our exegesis here is to examine the balance of utilities likely to result from the implementation of positive discrimination procedures. Would the balance of outcomes, however measured, be such as to justify the practice of positive discrimination in Britain? This is a very difficult question, one to which we shall not be able to give an unequivocal answer. However, if we are to treat utilitarian arguments seriously, we shall need to provide more than just a few speculative assertions; in particular, if we want to treat such arguments as articles of *practical* policy evaluation, we must acknowledge and explore some of the difficulties involved.[10] What follows is therefore an attempt to lay out some of the necessary questions that would have to be asked, and answered, in order to fill out the parameters of a utilitarian calculus of positive discrimination.

3.1 Specifying ends

Consequential arguments for positive discrimination necessarily require a specification of desired or expected ends, and we have noted above the kinds of consequence that have been adduced for the practice. These range from the relatively particular to the very general. It is in the nature of arguments to general utility that the ends to be achieved are couched in very broad and non-specific terms of the 'general good' or 'public interest' kind. In the case of positive discrimination, as we have seen, the particular variety that 'general utility' takes is 'social harmony', 'the health of society as a whole', or 'racial integration'. The problem with such grandiose formulations, as Benn and Peters (1959: 229 ff.) have pointed out, is that not only do they lack the specificity required for them to be measured, they also assume a unitary value system – that there can in fact be a *common* good.[11] In practice there are a variety of common goods; and other than in certain exceptional circumstances, such as a threat to the whole nation by an outside aggressor, there will not be a unitary common interest. In such circumstances the 'common good' may well turn out to be what the majority wants (if there is one) at the expense of all other minority interests. This is especially the case where positive discrimination for ethnic minorities is concerned. Indeed, the very juxtaposition of 'the interests of minorities' with 'the common interest' immediately points up the contradiction. The response might be that there is no conflict, that ethnic minorities and the white ethnic majority do share a common interest – to exist in integrated harmony as the British nation. Such a view, I believe, is little more than pious platitude and flies in the face of the facts of present-day British society. Perhaps in the longer term this is what we would all wish for, but it is hardly realistic to assert that the interests of minority groups and the ethnic majority are coterminous.

The more practical problem with arguments to general utility – if such were to be the benchmark of the acceptability of positive discrimination – is specifying what they mean and how they are to be measured. 'The common good' or 'the health of society as a whole' or 'social harmony' do not lend themselves to calibration. How are we to know whether or not (let alone by how much) the health of society is improved or the common good increased by any particular policy practice? (There are two problems involved here: measuring changes in 'social health' and, assuming this, ascribing such change to the policy under evaluation. There were several assertions in early 1985 of the efficacy of new community policing practices at preventing riots.) It is for these reasons that asseverations about 'the common good' or 'the health of society' are likely to be a political pretence.

When we come to consider the evaluation of positive discrimination programmes, to think in terms of what success would look like, the ambiguity of the ends to be achieved becomes most evident, Nowhere is this more so than where there is a hierarchy of ends some of which may be implicit or assumed, or for expediency's sake just not stated. Such was the case with the preferential treatment programme of the University of California Medical School, which Bakke challenged. Dworkin has said that the *immediate* goal of the programme was to increase the number of people with certain ethnic backgrounds in the medical profession. This however was a means to a further goal – the more effective satisfaction of the health needs in black communities. But this in turn, claims Dworkin, was but a step on the road to the ultimate goal, of a less racially conscious society (Dworkin 1977b: 11). A similar sequence is apparent in the arguments in favour of, and attempts towards, increasing the number of blacks and Asians in the police force in Britain.[12] The immediate goal is to increase ethnic minority representation; the second aim is more sensitive or effective policing of areas with high ethnic minority populations; this in turn is a means to better community relations and racial harmony in the area, which in turn (although this need not be read into the sequence) is a step on the road to more social harmony and a peaceful society.

It is usually the aim or goal at the end of the sequence that is left implicit or, if articulated, is couched in flaccid terms. Thus no politician (or any others in the policy-making process) will be heard aloud saying that we must increase black representation in the police force in order to prevent more riots. That, however, as we all know, *is* just the expedient reason behind such attempts.

When there is a hierachy of goals, some of which remain implicit or tacit, there is a corresponding difficulty attached to measuring success. Some of the lower-level ends – which are really means to further ends – are measurable. It is easy (given goodwill and co-operation) to see whether ethnic minority representation in the police or medical or legal profession has increased. But the more grandiose the goal, the less easy this becomes.

One further point in respect of sequence of ends (we shall touch upon it at greater length subsequently): this concerns whether and to what extent the goal sequence of a policy of positive discrimination is a rational, socially coherent, and plausible one. It does appear, at least in some instances, that the assumption that achievement of one goal will facilitate success in subsequent ones is more of a hope than a reasonable expectation. The sequence identified by Dworkin (see page 180) is just such a case.

3.2 Estimating consequences

It is surprising how unreticent most writers and commentators on positive discrimination (both proponents and opponents) are about the actual or likely consequences of its implementation.[13] There are two points to be made about this. Firstly, if positive discrimination were always implemented only on a small scale (as is the case in Britain today), the consequences can safely be predicted as minimal; and grandiose if tacit goals such as greater social harmony can be dismissed as nonsense. Secondly, if positive discrimination is implemented on a large scale, the multifarious consequences, unintended as well as intended, cannot all be predicted, let alone measured.[14] This is not sufficient reason for not proceeding with a policy; but neither can it be ignored by those whose defence of, or opposition to, positive discrimination is wholly utilitarian.

A further point, related to the estimation of consequences and of direct relevance to calculating the balance of utilities resulting from a given course of action, is that, as Finnis (1983: 86 ff.) points out, consequences are rarely, if ever, simply additive. Although ideal utilitarianism posits calculus along some monotonic scale of a unitary variable (such as human happiness, satisfaction, or well-being), this is not reflected in the real world. Indeed, preference utility has been advanced as an alternative to the impossibility of measuring quanta of happiness or well-being, but this also has its drawbacks especially in so far as policies designed to benefit only small proportions of the population are concerned.[15] More realistically, balancing the good and evil consequences of an action or a policy does require that non-additive outcomes be weighed in the same balance, and this must necessarily involve *qualitative* judgements about the relative importance of different results. So far as positive discrimination is concerned, this implies weighing against each other such dissimilar variables as the increase in welfare of a minority group, the enhanced status of the group, improved race relations, reductions in dependency on the Welfare State (hence the Exchequer), more social peace and harmony, on the one hand, with 'white backlash', general resentment, worsened race relations, increased inefficiency, lowered status of the group, greater racial separation, and so on, on the other. It is hardly any wonder, then, that in the face of such an impossible task either we are selective of those items that bolster our own feelings or prejudices about positive discrimination or we revert to intuitive apodictic notions of 'fairness' or justice.

3.3 Means and ends

A part of the calculus of utilities must be an estimation of the likelihood of the policy or action proposed achieving the ends it is designed to meet. This is common to all consequentialist arguments but so far as utilitarianism is concerned it must be weighed in the balance. We may, for example, decide that although the balance of utilities – supposing such could ever be calculated – favours the implementation of positive discrimination practices, *if those practices were to work* (i.e. achieve their desired aims) the evidence suggests that this would not be the case and that the policy ought not, in consequence, be introduced.

Assessing the likelihood of success may seem an obvious preparatory exercise, but not all those who have proposed positive discrimination appear to have been particularly vigilant in pursuing it. Dworkin, for example, in his various commentaries on Bakke and De Funis, has argued (as we saw above) that whilst the short-term aim of preferential admissions policies was to increase minority-group representation in the professions, the long-term aim was to make the USA a less racially conscious society. Similarly, the longer-term consequence of increasing the numbers of blacks and Asians in Britain's police force is posited as greater social and racial harmony. Whilst both of these *may* be the longer-term results of positive discrimination, an equally strong case could be made out that just the opposite would be the case. Certainly, if positive discrimination is to be promoted on these grounds, a much more convincing case is required than has yet been advanced.

3.4 Utility for who?

We remarked earlier that the results of a calculus of utilities will vary with the size and identity of the group whose welfare is being assessed. (This applies to both psychological and preference utility.) Should we, in counting the balance of utilities, confine the assessment to the 'beneficiary' group? Normal practice would dictate otherwise, and circumstances would anyway preclude such a limitation. Practices of positive discrimination would have extensive knock-on effects beyond the group in question; phenomena such as 'white backlash' would force themselves into the calculation; and if a generalized goal is adduced such as 'racial harmony' or 'the health of society as a whole' then the calculus cannot but include all those who might be affected.

3.5 What to calculate?

We have already, in passing, answered this question, but it is worth posing in more direct form. There are three broad categories of item that might be included in a calculus of utility.

Firstly, we may be concerned with tangible indicators of welfare or well-being. Thus we may ask, would positive discrimination on balance result in better education, housing, and health provisions, higher incomes, and greater representation in the professions for members of minority groups or women? Secondly, we might ask whether positive discrimination would on the whole result in greater overall satisfaction (which would include social and racial harmony). And thirdly, we may adopt a preference utility and assess whether, on balance, most people would prefer a policy of positive discrimination to some other policy or no policy.

The answer is that we must perforce include both of the first two types, as we noted above; indeed, given present social circumstances they are inextricably linked. The third is more problematical. Apart from the difficulties of counting both personal and external preferences, mentioned earlier, there is the problem of accepting a result that we knew to be based on attitudes and beliefs that were ill-informed, ignorant of the likely outcome of the policy (since everyone, including policy-makers, would initially be ignorant), and possibly based in prejudice. A strict utilitarian would argue that none of this mattered – if that is what people wanted. But this raises again the fundamental conflict between a deontic justice and utilitarianism, which we cannot pursue here, although we shall have some comments to make about it subsequently.

3.6 Balancing utilities

In the foregoing pages we have attempted to specify some of the problems and requirements of a utilitarian calculus of positive discrimination. When these are spelled out they look formidable. They cannot, however, be wished away and they must, as is intended, put a question mark over some of the more facile consequentialist claims for positive discrimination. But we cannot likewise brush aside all consequentialist arguments for the practice on the grounds of the difficulties involved in calculating the balance of advantages. What is required therefore is a realistic appraisal of the feasibility of assessing consequentialist arguments, and this must include accepting that such an assessment must necessarily be imperfect, dependent on partial calculations, and based on best estimates. The answers must always be provisional.

It is not the intention to attempt a particular and specific calculation of the balance of consequences of the application of positive discrimination in any given set of circumstances. Our present purpose will be better served by noting the *claimed* utilities and disutilities of positive discrimination (including those that have been adduced in both Britain and the United States). Many of these have already been mentioned in the preceding discussion; they are simply brought together here in a more concise form.

The utilities largely coincide with the aims that have been adduced for positive discrimination. The practice of positive discrimination will conduce to, or achieve, the following (utilities):[16]

- produce more ethnic minority doctors and lawyers, so better to meet the health and legal needs of minority communities;
- improve the social and environmental conditions of ethnic minorities;
- by increasing minority recruitment to the high-status professions, improve the status of minority groups in society;
- by increasing minority recruitment to welfare bureaucracies, increase the sensitivity of welfare provision in ethnic minority areas;
- help to redress the balance of racial disadvantage;
- by providing more role models, help to raise the self-respect, self-image, and expectations of minority group members;
- by increasing minority enrolment in universities, produce a greater racial diversity in university classes and thus promote better understanding and sensitivity;
- promote social and racial harmony, which is beneficial to the health of society as a whole;
- prevent civil unrest.

The most frequently claimed benefits of positive discrimination from the above list are the more generalized ones: improvements in social and racial harmony, and increases in the status of minority groups – both self-perceived by members of the group and as perceived by the majority. There are of course a variety of practices that are positively discriminatory as we have defined it, and their application in particular circumstances will be in pursuit of different aims. Not all will be directed at achieving all the benefits listed above, and for this reason a calculation of utilities in any given set of circumstances would not put all of these benefits in the scales at the same time. Hence the importance of stipulating, for any given application of a positive discrimination policy, what the intended and likely benefits would be. The same naturally holds for the alleged disutilities of any particular application.

The most commonly cited disutilities of positive discrimination are:

- a loss in efficiency or a drop in standards in those institutions that use positive discrimination in recruitment;
- a loss of self-esteem on the part of minority group members;
- lowering in status of the minority group in the eyes of the majority;
- resentment and the danger of a backlash from the majority (white ethnic) group.

Of these, potential white backlash and reduced efficiency are the consequences most usually adduced.

Such are the utilities and disutilities that would have to be weighed in the balance in a calculus of the utilities of positive discrimination. Which ones would require to be weighed in any particular circumstance would depend upon the nature of the positive discrimination practice used and its aims or purposes.

Any calculation of the balance of utilities of positive discrimination must, we saw, include an estimation of the likelihood of the practice yielding the predicted results – and of precipitating the anticipated disutilties. For if it is unlikely that the hoped-for consequences of an action would actually flow from it, then there is little point weighing them in the balance. Whether or not this would be the case would depend on particular circumstances and on the nature of particular positive discrimination practices; for that reason we shall not pursue the matter in detail here but rather confine ourselves to some general comments about the alleged utilities and disutilities and about the *general* likelihood of their being brought about by the implementation of positive discrimination.

The use of positive discrimination to increase the number of black doctors and lawyers has hardly surfaced at all as an issue in Britain, although it has been central to the debate in the USA. There, given the appropriate form of positive discrimination (or, in its milder version, affirmative action), it has been and could continue to be effective. That the same would be true in Britain is more doubtful, although this would differ significantly as between Afro-Caribbean and Asian ethnics. So far as the former are concerned, the paucity of black doctors (and lawyers) is as much a matter of motivation as of qualifications. Positive discrimination at medical-school-entry level may well produce only limited results. In the case of Asian ethnics the situation is more complex. There are large variations between Asian sub-groups in the proportions of population with first and higher degrees and in professional occupations; the closest it is possible to come to a measure of the number of Asian doctors (see C. Brown 1984: chs. 4, 5, 7). (There are of course substantial numbers who qualified abroad.) Overall, however, there is little indication of a massive shortfall in either qualifications or motivation such as would justify the use of positive discrimination.

The consequential aim of increasing the numbers of minority doctors is better to serve the health needs of minority communities (page 185). If it is the case that minority communities have special health needs (and greater health needs) than the rest of society, and if some form of positive discrimination were the only or best way of meeting these, then this would be a matter of justice rather than utility and would have to be considered in the light of the needs principle (see Chapters 4 and 5).[17] If, on the other hand, it were a matter of minority group members preferring doctors of their own ethnicity, this would be a less compelling reason to practise positive discrimination.[18] It might also be argued that doctors recruited through positive discrimination might be less good doctors and that if they were to practise largely in minority-group areas then the health needs of such areas would in consequence be less well served. But since there is no evidence to suggest that if, say, blacks were motivated, if they could entertain a reasonable expectation of entering the profession, if they were better educated, and if they were as well trained as whites, they would still make less good doctors, the argument is unfounded. The issue is about entering the profession, not about doctoring skills.

There are more substantial grounds for doubt about another anticipated consequence of increasing minority representation in the professions. We have seen (page 183) that Dworkin has argued that the longer-term aim of so doing is to make the USA a less racially conscious society (which I take to mean less racially divided, more socially harmonious, and less subject to racialism). It is, however, far from evident that this latter condition would flow from the former, especially if, as Dworkin anticipates, the larger numbers of black doctors worked predominantly in the black ghettos. A more likely consequence of this would be increased racial separatism. One has only to speculate on the ensuing situation in Britain – black doctors, lawyers, social workers, and teachers for blacks, Asian professionals for Asians, and white for whites – to be easily persuaded of the disutility of such an outcome for racial integration, mutual understanding, trust, and awareness. There may well be utilities arising from increasing minority-group representation in the professions by means of positive discrimination, but a less racially divided society is certainly not one of them. This is an issue of crucial importance for the next twenty or so years in Britain. The relation between positive discrimination and racial separateness in Britain is considered in Chapter 9.

Whether positive discrimination would in practice improve the social and environmental conditions of ethnic minorities (the second utility we listed above) will depend on the particular condition in question, the extent of the current deprivation, the type of positive discrimination practice used, and the resources committed to it. In Chapter 5 we noted that it would be hard to *justicize* positive discrimination in pursuit of the needs principle in Britain. The greater deprivations of some minority groups call for greater resources under the needs principle but not for positive discrimination. The question here then is whether we can *justify* positive discrimination on grounds of utility. Since we have already established positive discrimination as prima facie unjust, what is now at issue is whether, and under what circumstances, utility can override justice. We shall leave this broader consideration until later in the chapter. We need comment only on the likelihood of positive discrimination producing the result claimed for it, and this, as we said above, will depend on the circumstances. But there is no reason why, given the political will, adequate resources, and the right kind of positive discrimination practice, social and environmental conditions could not be markedly improved.

There are many components to the status ascription of groups (not the least for minority groups being ethnicity itself), but when it is alleged that increasing minority representation in the professions by means of positive discrimination will conduce to an improvement in their status, it is normally social status or repute that is meant. Whilst white racists are not prone to making fine distinctions between black navvy or black doctor, or between Asian road-sweeper and Asian solicitor, it remains open to investigation whether white non-racists share this facility for blurring social status divisions.[19] The essence of the claim is that the status enhancement of black or Asian doctors, solicitors, accountants, teachers, and so on will rub off on other members of their ethnic group in the eyes of the white majority.

However, the claim makes a bigger demand on whites than is usually acknowledged. It requires of them not only that they become less racially aware but less *socially* aware too, and this is probably too much to ask. And even if the claim were true, it is a sad reflection on our society that a group within it can gain respect only in proportion to its representation in the upper socio-economic classes.

There are many good reasons for having more minority group members in the high-status professions, but enhancing the status of the group as a whole is not, I suspect, one of them.

Whether or not increased minority recruitment to welfare bureaucracies will lead to more sensitized welfare provision to areas of ethnic minority concentration will depend upon both their position in the bureaucracy (social workers may be more effective than supplementary benefit officers) and the relative weight of the bureaucracy itself and its constituent personnel in decisions about welfare allocation. This is too big and too complex an issue to enter into here; but it would seem at a first glance that the potential for individual employees to bend welfare provision to the benefit of their ethnic compatriots is very limited. Discretion has its limits.

The use of positive discrimination as a means of providing more role models for other members of the same ethnic group has frequently been suggested in the USA (see, for example, O'Neil 1975, H. E. Jones 1977, Nagel 1977, Goldman 1979) but less so in Britain. The idea is simple: that if you can demonstrate people coming out of the ghettos and, with the help of positive discrimination, into professional training and thence into high-status professions, this will act as an exemplar to others to follow the same course. The production of role models is a means to the broader end of enhanced minority-group status.

Although role-model provision has often been cited in the USA as an important function of positive discrimination, there is virtually no evidence that it works (although it must be acknowledged that it would be difficult to test). It may well be that some individuals have been inspired by the achievements of others, but this hardly amounts to a significant shift in the socio-economic profile of blacks in the USA. Indeed, it would seem wholly unrealistic to claim anything other than marginal benefits from the provision of role models. (Moreover, the logic behind role models has a patronizing flavour about it.) As Goldman (1979) has noted, it could be that individuals who have been seen to achieve high-status positions only by virtue of being the beneficiaries of positive discrimination would make poor exemplars. Certainly it is unlikely that people whose success apparently comes only as a result of a hefty shove from below will epitomize the strong American ethic of individualism and success through effort and merit.

As to enhancing minority enrolment in universities by means of positive discrimination so as to produce a greater diversity of students and thus promote better understanding and sensitivity, this may also be the case, but it does appear to be a 'well, if nothing else it will at least . . .' kind of argument. And as we mentioned in respect of the compensation principle, universities are not the most obvious place to begin.

The most frequently asserted utility of positive discrimination in Britain at least is, as we have seen, that it will promote greater social and racial harmony and be beneficial to the health of society as a whole. This is the general utility argument. Were it to be true (that is, if positive discrimination could and would produce a more racially harmonious society) it would count very heavily in the balance of utilities. Unfortunately, as we have indicated, the claim bears a closer relation to rhetoric than to reality. It has yet to be spelled out how positive discrimination could achieve such an elevated result, but one must assume that it would be by a combination of some or all of the preceding utilities. Yet, as we have argued, most of these must be treated with a degree of scepticism. Apart from the disutilities – and one in particular, as we shall see – it does not seem to be a reasonable expectation that positive discrimination by itself would significantly alter the socio-economic profile of ethnic minority groups (and particularly of Afro-Caribbeans) in Britain, or enhance their status in the estimation of the white majority, or lead to a radical change in social, economic, and environmental conditions, or significantly reduce racialism and discrimination. Much would of course depend on the scale with which it was implemented. There is no indication that any government in Britain would entertain the idea of large-scale positive discrimination, largely because, although the more ambitious the scale the greater the chances of real change, so also would be the chances of white resentment and backlash, which would be counter-productive to racial harmony.

The final goal or 'utility' that we identified above is that of preventing civil unrest. We have characterized this as not so much a utilitarian claim as a functional or expedient one and thus not utility-maximizing. The immediate and particular goal, although never stated so boldly, is to prevent more riots. This is not the place to enter a discussion of the aetiology of riots save to say that, if conventional orthodoxy is correct, that the seed-bed for riots lies in social and economic deprivation and unemployment, that this combines with friction between youth and police, and that only a flashpoint is then required for a riot to occur, then alleviation of deprivation and reduced friction between minority youth and the police ought to reduce the likelihood of rioting. But whether this can be achieved by positive discrimination is a very different matter. We shall return to this in Chapter 9.

We have so far considered the utilities of positive discrimination and the likelihood, in general terms, of their coming about. Clearly, if these gains from positive discrimination *were* to eventuate they would weigh very heavily in favour of the practice. However, our brief dicussion does not provide significant grounds for optimism. Some of the claims made for positive discrimination are too grandiose; others have yet to be demonstrated. But what of the disutilities? We identified four of these; one is more significant and far-reaching than the others, and most of our remarks will be addressed to this.

The first three disutilities concern the loss of efficiency, reduction in self-esteem, and lowering of status of minority groups in the eyes of the ethnic majority. Whilst all three are possible consequences of positive discrimination, none seem very significant. The first assumes that personnel hired by a process of positive discrimination will be less able (or in the case of university students, that, to increase minority intake, entry standards must be lowered). There are no grounds for assuming either; positive discrimination – even hard-case reverse discrimination – does not require that unqualified or underqualified students be taken, and there is no reason to think that personnel hired by positive discrimination would be underqualified either. Indeed, the purpose of positive discrimination is to hire qualified personnel who because of discrimination or lack of opportunity would not have been accepted.[20] Furthermore, there is a host of factors affecting the efficiency of organizations, of which the quality of personnel is but a minor component.

Again, it may be that some ethnic minority members may suffer some self-doubt as a result of achieving a position by virtue of positive discrimination, but this is a minor factor; it could be argued that they might work all the harder to prove themselves. More significantly, as Goldman (1979: 144–45) has pointed out, there is no large-scale rejection of positive discrimination by ethnic minorities in the United States on the grounds that it causes loss of self-esteem.

Whether or not positive discrimination would result in a loss of status of minority groups in the eyes of the majority is probably more a function of the attidues of the majority than of the practice itself. Racists need no such excuse to fire their prejudice; the effect on non-racists would probably be negligible; but for the mass of the population, the reaction (if there were one) would probably manifest itself in ways other than a diminution of minority-group status.

The most common, and the most significant, alleged disutility of positive discrimination is the likelihood of resentment on the part of the majority ethnic population, which may turn into a white backlash. This, it is argued, could take a number of forms, not the least of which, as Glazer (1975) maintains, would be a political reaction against the political party or parties held responsible for instituting the positive discrimination. Whether or not this is a widespread sentiment, it is one that politicians, especially those who think they have a racially sensitive electorate, go in fear of. This is manifest in another, related context, that of immigration control. Thus every amendment to immigration law and regulations is accompanied by the ritual incantation by the Home Secretary of the day (especially Conservative ones) of 'firm but fair'. There is a wealth of meaning in that little phrase; 'fair' satisfies the English sense of fair play; 'firm' mollifies the white constituents who might abstain at the ballot box at the first hint of 'wetness' over immigration. Unfortunately (or fortunately) for such politicians, positive discrimination might, at a push, be construed as 'fair', but never as 'firm'.

It is difficult to say how real is the threat of a white backlash (other than to electorally sensitive politicians); we have lived with the contested belief for so long that it has taken on a life of its own. We can only speculate that if positive discrimination were extensively used and if it included not only preferential admissions and hiring policies, but also the sort of hard-case positive discrimination in the allocation of welfare benefits outlined in Chapter 5, then the likelihood of some form of white resentment would be high. Certainly, the political fear of it would be almost paralytic – to such a degree that it would not be implemented in the first place.[21]

The potential of a white backlash is a disutility of a rather different kind than the others. It raises two important issues that, because they have broader implications, require further consideration. One we shall examine here; the other will be postponed to a subsequent section.

We saw earlier that strict consequentialism will weigh in the balance not only the consequences of an action or policy, but the goods and evils of the policy itself. This may in effect become a balancing of utility versus justice (as we shall see), or it may entail weighing the knock-on effects ensuing from the nature of the policy (i.e. the means) itself. Such is the case with the real or threatened white backlash to positive discrimination. We may treat the backlash simply as another consequence (with negative utility) of positive discrimination, but it would be a mistake so to do. The anticipated white backlash has a number of components, but two in particular may be identified. One is simply a resentment that 'blacks' are getting more attention, more resources, more concern, when there are plenty of whites in just as bad a condition. The other is fuelled by a belief that positive discrimination is simply unfair and unjust. It hardly matters in this context whether it is or not; it is the perception that is the potent disutility. (The backlash to the *perceived* injustice of positive discrimination is the relevant factor here, not its actual justice or injustice.) 'White backlash' therefore presents us with a situation in which the *nature of the means* (or policy) becomes a potent factor in itself in the balance of utilities; and once the *means* to an end become a function of the calculus, we cannot confine our balancing of utilities to the consequences themselves. Policy-makers (and we ourselves) may share the view that positive discrimination is unjust or unfair, but it remains important none the less to distinguish between counter-arguments to positive discrimination based on a conviction of its unfairness and those based upon a fear of a reaction to this unfairness. The former is a moral argument, the latter an expedient one.

Any attempt to balance the utilities and disutilities of positive discrimination must, as we have argued, give very heavy weight to the likelihood of it achieving its alleged goals. This, I believe, will ultimately determine the answer. If a convincing case could be made that any particular application of positive discrimination in any particular set of circumstances would produce the intended and hoped-for results, then the disutilities are sufficiently insubstantial to justify proceeding with it. The most serious disutility is the potential of a white backlash, but if on other grounds positive discrimination is thought to be justified (by what it would achieve) or justicized (deontically) then these considerations ought to override what must then in consequence be seen as the unjustifiable resentment of white non-beneficiaries. To act otherwise is to allow expediency to override justice.

However, as we have argued, there must be severe reservations about the likelihood of positive discrimination achieving its ends; in *practice* the utilities may be scant.[22] If this is the case, then it is probably not worth the candle, but it would be premature now to close off all applications of positive discrimination on such grounds. It *may* work in some circumstances and in certain types of application (in particular, some of the milder forms of positive action and, if policed, contract compliance programmes) and is worth continuing on its present limited scale for that reason. The balance of utilities is nevertheless not such as to provide an unconditional go-ahead for positive discrimination.

4 Utility jousts with justice

Any utilitarian defence of social policies, especially (as is usually the case) those concerned with distributive principles as applied to welfare, must at some stage face up to social justice. For most defences of most policies, this does not prove to be particularly problematic; few social policies are *manifestly* unjust (which is not to say that there are no unjust social policies). This is not the case with positive discrimination where we may well encounter utilitarian defences or promotion of policies and practices that are prima facie and, some would argue, manifestly unjust. Indeed, when the delicacy of positive discrimination combines with the sensitivities involved in race and ethnic relations, we are treading a minefield. When utility jousts with justice here we must tread very warily. We shall examine firstly some arguments against utiliarian defences of positive discrimination and then go on to pit utility against justice.

The principal problem of defending positive discrimination on grounds of utility – apart, that is, from the particular result of the calculus of utilities and disutilities – is that you may find yourself on weak moral ground. On the principle of 'what's sauce for the goose', utilitarian defences of prima facie unjust practices may open the way to defences of practices that we would on other grounds, but mainly grounds of social justice, wish to eschew. Thus, if positive discrimination is justified (but not justicized) on grounds of racial or social harmony, then why not *negative* discrimination on the same grounds? What if a managing director argued that, on the grounds of harmony on the shop-floor, he was not going to employ any blacks or Asians? He would be acting illegally, but then so would hard-case positive discrimination be illegal. He could well argue that the legal proscription was merely an artificial constraint on his action that, if pursued, would produce greater on-balance satisfaction.[23] And what if a referendum in Britain were to find that a large majority of the population would support a policy of repatriation for minorities, supposing there were somewhere to be repatriated to? In both such instances it would not be too difficult to construct a counter-argument to the effect that such actions would not be utility-maximizing. But equally the arguments themselves have some plausibility, and what these examples demonstrate is the utterly unsatisfactory nature of trying to settle delicate moral issues in terms of a calculus of utilities. Such an approach leaves a bad taste in the mouth; and I for one would prefer to argue from firmer moral ground such as would enable one to say 'this is the right thing to do, and it cannot be open to balancing utilities'. For this reason any arguments for or against positive discrimination on utilitarian grounds must always be underpinned by some deontic principles (again, usually concerning justice), which arm us against the possibility of utilitarian defences of morally odious practices.

Less seriously perhaps, utilitarian arguments seem to breed mendacious claims. Many of the 'white backlash' and 'social harmony' arguments are of this kind – rationalizations for less than worthy ideas. A familiar argument against positive discrimination and even more frequently against more (or any) immigration is that not to practise positive discrimination and to restrict or stop immigration is 'in the interests of good race relations'. What this really means is 'in the interests of pacifying racially prejudiced whites generally (and my constituents in particular)'. Such arguments in their coded form are specious but mendacious and pusillanimous.

When positive discrimination is considered in the context of utility and justice, it is usually in terms of the question of when and under what circumstances the utilities of positive discrimination may override the demands of justice, as is the case for example in the treatments by W. T. Blackstone 1977, Nagel 1977, and Goldman 1979. This must also be our main concern, but it is also worth mentioning the (hypothetical) reverse situation, which would be a consequence of our earlier reservations about utilitarian arguments. Suppose, contrary to what we have argued earlier, that positive discrimination, though prima facie unjust, did turn out to be the only or most effective or efficient means of fulfilling the requirements of justice in respect of needs or compensation. (We argued in Chapter 5 that this is probably not the case in Britain at the present time; we have not precluded the possibility that it might become so.) Would it then be right, or just, or both, or neither, *not* to implement it on either consequentialist or utilitarian grounds? The most likely reason for abstaining from its use would be the real or imagined fear of white backlash, ranging from mild political embarrassment for some politicians to outright civil unrest and racial harassment. (Whilst positive discrimination is an important issue, I do not think it so important that the latter situation would result; but let us for the moment assume it.) Much of the answer then hangs on the likelihood and degree of the expected disutilities. *If* extensive racial harassment by outraged whites were to be a consequence, then the balance of utilities would certainly be against implementing it. It would be *right* not to implement it. It would not however be just. It cannot be just to allow utility – even less, simple consequence – to override justice, but justice is not the whole of morality, and morality is not always best served by *fiat justitia, ruat caelum*. However, the disutilities must be very considerable and real, and not just such as might discomfort some politicians, before we allow utility to override justice. In the absence of such disutilities we must pursue positive discrimination if that is the best way of fulfilling the requirements of justice.

What, then, of positive discrimination as utility challenging justice (usually manifest in this context as the merit principle and as rights to positions)? We shall assume for the sake of this discussion that positive discrimination is prima facie unjust, as we have done in preceding chapters. (It is necessary to re-emphasize however that positive discrimination comes in a variety of manifestations from the 'hard' variety of which we gave examples in an earlier chapter to 'softer' forms, which are usually called positive or affirmative action. These will vary in the extent to which they are deemed unjust, the former being more so, the latter less.) The question that faces us here is whether, if positive discrimination were to be utility-maximizing or ideal-end-regarding, it ought to be implemented even though it would override justice in the form of merit or rights to positions.

We have already examined whether positive discrimination in fulfilment of justice as compensation may override merit. Here we have the weaker case of positive discrimination as utility-maximizing, overriding merit. Suppose that, although we accept that positive discrimination is an unjust practice, there is good reason to believe that if implemented it would, on a balance of utilities, produce more good than harm. Suppose too, for the sake of argument, that it would improve the socio-economic and social status position of minority groups (and, although the calculus would be different, of women), would increase self-esteem among such groups, and would improve race relations and social harmony. Ought we then to implement it even though it would override the rights to positions and employments of the most meritorious and the best qualified? To answer this, we may duplicate our argument above where positive discrimination was on the other side of the fence. We said there that the disutilities must be very considerable before they could be allowed to override justice. So too with the present question; the utilities of positive discrimination must be real and considerable before we allow them to take precedence over the claims of justice. If the situation we hypothesize above were real, this would surely be sufficient benefit to allow us to override merit, especially given our earlier strictures about the merit system. However, as will by now be clear, I do not believe the likelihood of positive discrimination achieving such benefits to be high, and as so often in the real world of policy, the right moral road to take is not clearly signposted. To make navigation more difficult, we have to recogize that the justice we are putting on one side of the joust – like the utilities on the other – is not a fixed and invariable quantity. Nagel, among others, argues that we need not be too squeamish about overriding the merit principle since it too is impure and imperfect (see above, pages 153–56). If this is true – and it certainly is in Britain and the USA today – then the utilities required on the one side, to enable us to feel comfortable overriding merit on the other, will be so much less; a relatively small positive balance will do. Furthermore, given this situation, we would require a much smaller positive balance of utilities than we would a negative balance of disutilities to override the use of positive discrimination in pursuit of justice, since the claims of need and rights of compensation (which, in the former case, positive discrimination is used to fulfil) must represent stronger claims of justice than an imperfect merit principle.

Whilst I believe this is the case, it does not accord with common practice (nor, very likely, with intuitive thinking). The merit principle and the right to positions of the best qualified are dignified with greater importance and weight than rights to have needs met and rights to compensation outside the criminal arena. This is because whilst merit and being best qualified *are* dignified as rights – because of habitual practice and the principle of 'reasonable expectations' – having one's needs met and claiming compensation for being demeaned (an habitual practice as well) are not.

It is to fly in the face of customary moral beliefs to argue that we ought more readily to allow positive discrimination as a utilitarian practice to override justice as merit than we permit disutilities to confound positive discrimination when it is justly practised in fulfilment of the requirements of justice, but that, I believe, is so.

Chapter 9
Thinking morally about social policy

It has been our purpose to put the practice of positive discrimination to the test of social justice. Our conclusion has been that in the circumstances in which it might be applied, and for the purposes (need and compensation) for which it might be applied in Britain today, it must fail the test.

Not only is positive discrimination – or, to be more precise, those practices that have become known as positively discriminatory as opposed to those more generally known as positive action – prima facie unjust in so far as it uses morally irrelevant criteria; it must also be counted unjust when practised for the same purposes, when set against our secondary criteria. Thus we have found that the first claim for positive discrimination – that it is not unjust because all members of the beneficiary group can also be described by the morally relevant criterion (most in need, most harmed) – is manifestly empirically false; and if it were true, the practice would no longer be a distinctly peculiar one that could be called positive discrimination. The second claim, that there is a sufficiently high correlation between need or harm on the one hand, and the distinguishing characteristic of the beneficiary group on the other, to make the latter a reasonable proxy for the former, and that positive discrimination might therefore be the only, best, most effective, efficient, or on-balance just way of meeting the requirements of justice, we have also found to be empirically unsubstantiated in the present circumstances of Britain. In respect neither of meeting needs nor of compensating for harm done could positive discrimination in favour of ethnic minorities or women in Britain today be a just practice. The required correlations are too low to prevent too many of the needy remaining without benefit, too many of the non-needy benefiting, and the costs of meeting need and compensating for harm falling too heavily on the innocent. In short, too much injustice would be done.

There was a third claim for or defence of positive discrimination in respect of the needs principle. This was that positive discrimination is really about giving 'additional' resources, or possibly 'more than due' (the specification is never precise), to the most needy. This claim fell on the grounds of logic rather than empirical circumstances. It was found to be logically inchoate, a sleight of hand.

Our conclusion must therefore be that the practices we call positive discrimination, when pursued in fulfilment of the principles of need and compensation for harm, would be unjust and ought not in consequence to be implemented in the present circumstances in Britain. This does not rule out the possibility that circumstances will alter and that positive discrimination might, in respect of the needs principle at least, become a just practice. If the *relative* position of some ethnic minorities were significantly to worsen as a whole, then positive discrimination might turn out to be the best or most efficient means of meeting their needs. This is less likely in respect of the compensation principle. There is no currently sound argument for whole-group compensation for ethnic minorities. Future mistreatment (in its broadest sense) of such groups would have to be systematic and significant for one to become so. The same arguments apply to women as a needy or a harmed group, but the circumstances in which positive discrimination in their favour would become a justicized practice are more remote.

Our rejection of positive discrimination is on moral grounds. We have made no claim, other than in passing, about its actual or potential effectiveness. In particular, we are not rejecting positive discrimination on the grounds that it would not work, although it has been necessary in places to express reservations about this. One of the main difficulties that must be faced in assessing the likely effectiveness of positive discrimination is that of knowing what it is supposed to achieve. We have already touched on this in respect of the problems of counterfactual reasoning in connection with compensation for past harm, and calculations of equality of welfare in relation to need-meeting, but we must return to the problem in subsequent pages. While the injustices that would accrue from the implementation of positive discrimination could be minimized by using it sparingly and on a small scale, to do this would also minimize its likely effectiveness. To be effective in bringing *all* members of minority groups out of poverty, and to compensate all members for past harm, positive discrimination would have to be implemented on a vast scale and with a vast amount of injustice in consequence.

We have expressed grave moral and practical doubts about the 'solution'; but what about the problem? We shall confine our remarks to the situation of the ethnic minority groups in Britain. The problem in respect of the relative position of women is both different and in some respects more complicated – although not, I think, more pressing.

What then is the nature of the problem as a solution of which we might want to marshal the forces of positive discrimination were it a just practice? We illustrated aspects of the problem in Chapter 5 (the most recent data available), and further evidence can be found in D. J. Smith and Whalley 1975, CRE 1977, D. J. Smith 1977, *Social Trends*, the House of Commons Home Affairs Committee report on *Racial Disadvantage* (1981), and the 1981 Census. These sources demonstrate that in many, though not all, aspects of welfare – in its widest sense, including housing, employment, and socio-economic status, as well as health, education, income, an vulnerability to social problems – some ethnic minority groups and in particular the West Indian and the sub-groups that go to make up the Asian population are relatively worse off than the white majority *taken as a whole.* In some areas of welfare minority groups are not worse off, but in many they are more highly represented among the deprived than would be expected from their representation in the population as a whole. None the less, the majority of the most deprived people in Britain are white ethnics, and it is this single fact more than any other that makes positive discrimination in favour of ethnic minorities in pursuit of the needs principle unjust.

The fact still remains nonetheless that members of ethnic minority groups (but varying between groups) suffer higher levels of deprivation than white ethnics relative to their representation in the population. More disconcerting is the fact that the relative position of minority groups in Britain is not improving – and has not improved over the past twenty years. To be added to their relatively higher levels of deprivation is the unabating problem of racial discrimination and racial harassment. Whilst the degree of these inequalities is not such, as we have seen, as to justicize positive discrimination, they are significant and they are not getting better. This is the problem we face. The problem is not riots or civil unrest or any other calamity that we fear may spring from the relative deprivation of minority groups. It is one of justice itself. So long as this situation continues, Britain is not a just society, and we ought to be concerned about that.

What then should be done? Should we abandon positive discrimination or any pretence to it and look to other solutions, and if so what? Or can we, ought we to, salvage positive discrimination on other grounds? Will utility grant what liberal justice appears to deny: a justification, although not a justicization, of positive discrimination? Or will some milder form of positive discrimination, nearer to the anodyne 'positive action' end of the continuum, pass the tests of justice that harder-case positive discrimination has failed? To answer these questions we need to be able to specify why the problem persists and what we wish to achieve in solving it (assuming it to be solvable). This is not the artful suggestion it looks. All too seldom in social policy do we specify what success would look like, and unless we do have some picture of it we can never know whether our policies have worked. This is perhaps true above all in a field such as race. Assertions that what we want is a more equal or more just or more racially just society, or that a reduction in racial inequality, or a more (or less) racially aware society, or more harmonious race relations are our goal, do not stand up to scrutiny under the harsh light of proper policy analysis and evaluation. Perhaps more importantly, such assertions are inadequate in the face of the vicissitudes of popular opinion and instant punditry, where the evils of the day are always worse than they ever were before, and the historical perspective is never deeper than the last round of riots.[1]

The problem is only partly one of race. The same forces that impoverish and demean blacks also produce the white poor. Britain is a capitalist society. Capitalism will always create its own victims, for whom welfare provision will probably never be wholly adequate. But here is not the place to enter a critique of capitalism. We live with it and we must, if we are to provide any solution at all, provide one within its framework. This is just the job that we expect the needs principle itself to do – to make provision in proportion to their needs for the deprived and dependent, irrespective of their race or ethnicity. The problem then is that servicing the needs principle to any level of equality of welfare that would leave no one in poverty (given some generally agreed specification of this) costs more than most governments wish to spend or claim they can afford, and probably more than most taxpayers would willingly bear. But this takes us to a broader realm of argument about welfare provision that we cannot enter into here.

Overlaying the general problem of deprivation there is the racial component, which for present purposes we may divide into two. Firstly, as we have seen, although ethnic minorities share their deprivations with whites, they are, to varying degrees, more strongly represented amongst the deprived. Secondly, for ethnic minority members, social, physical, and economic deprivation is compounded by varying degrees of racial discrimination and racial harassment. The solutions to the two parts of the problem are probably not the same. The latter will prove more intractable than the former, will not be susceptible to treatment by positive discrimination in any form, and may be exacerbated by it. It is to the first problem, of racial inequalities, that positive discrimination is relevant. Before we can know whether positive discrimination could be an effective (if unjust) strategy, we need to know why racial inequalities persist in Britain. Again, an adequate analysis is beyond the scope of this book, and a few remarks must suffice.[2]

Although the reasons for continuing disadvantage will vary between the main dimensions of welfare, we can advance five possible general candidates. Firstly, it may be argued, blacks fall behind in the education and employment stakes simply because they are less able. No doubt this view has currency among some sections of the white majority (and among some ethnic minority members) but it is not one that can be entertained by anyone who has taken even a cursory look at the evidence. Secondly, and with good reason, the argument has been advanced that it is the 'newness' of the 'immigrants' to a strange culture that has accounted for their disadvantage.[3] This argument assumed that with the passage of time the 'immigrant community' would 'take its place in British society'. Sadly, it has proved to be too sanguine a view. More than a half of all the West Indians in the UK today were born here, as were 40 per cent of the Asians. The 'newcomers' argument is no longer tenable. The remaining three reasons have more substance and together provide a good deal of the explanation for the continuing disadvantage of minority groups. Firstly, there are in some areas of welfare structural reasons why ethnic minority members appear deprived. For example, the greater presence of ethnic minorities in poor quality public housing is partly accounted for by the fact that a greater proportion of them enter it as a result of homelessness than is the case for white tenants. They therefore fall foul of the frequent practice of local housing authorities of putting homeless families in the poorer quality parts of their stock while reserving the better quality and more popular stock for waiting-list tenants. Such practices are often called indirect or inadvertent racial discrimination, but this is misleading because the implication of 'unjustness' or 'wrongness' that thereby attaches to it is unwarranted. Provided that practices adhere to rule conformity and provided that the rules themselves are not *intentionally* discriminatory, then the fact that the consequences differentiate between groups is not necessarily unjust.[4]

This example amply illustrates the implications of structural or institutional practice explanations. For what are the consequences that follow in this case? There are two courses of action if we wish to reduce the proportion of ethnic minority members entering poorer quality stock under the 1977 Housing (Homeless Persons) Act. Firstly, we may change the rules that many local authorities use so as not to put the homeless in the worst stock. But then you have to explain to those who have been on the waiting-list for ten years or more why they should not have priority.[5] Secondly, we could house ethnic minority homeless in good quality stock and white ethnic homeless in poorer stock. That would be positive discrimination, and we have already canvassed the arguments for and against just such a practice.

The second explanation of continuing racial inequalities holds that straightforward racial discrimination in varying degrees of intention must account for much of the disadvantage suffered by ethnic minorities. To the extent that this occurs in the public sector in the allocation of welfare goods and results in just need claims not being met, positive action is proving a useful means of weeding it out.

In the immediate term, however, policy practice may be confined to dealing with the consequences of racial discrimination. As we noted above, the problem itself will be more intractable. (It will also become more complex as divisions between minority groups harden into prejudice and mistrust.)

The third and final reason for continuing disadvantage is more difficult to identify and characterize. It seems likely that some disadvantage must result from the relative isolation and self-containment of some minority groups. In some measure this is a defence against real and perceived discrimination and hostility on the part of the white majority and other minority groups. The Pakistani and Bangladeshi communities are clear examples of 'communities on the defence' both from intangible hostility and real physical violence from white and West Indian youth (see, for example, Edwards, Oakley, and Carey 1987). But self-containment is not only a defence mechanism; it can be, and sometimes is, a positive desire on the part of some communities. This is not to say that such communities will always remain isolated.

It is in the light of these explanations that solutions to the problem of continuing racial inequalities must be canvassed. And although positive discrimination (which theoretically at least must be among these 'solutions') cannot itself be an instrument for dealing with racial discrimination, the latter must be seen as at least a contributory component of the problem to which positive discrimination may be canvassed as a possible solution. The manifestations of and the explanations for the problem that we seek to solve – which is the reason for our discussing positive discrimination at all – are many and various. We cannot hope for simple, single, or easy solutions. We ought none the less to have some vision of the situation that successful solutions would bring about.

What would success look like? What is the goal we seek? As ever, the answer is not simple – certainly not as simple as the high-minded but vacuous nostrums we cited earlier. Most importantly, the 'we' in the question are not undivided. There is no general consensus; there is not even a consensus within different ethnic groups, whites included. It would be a rash person indeed who conjured a universal prescription. At the most superficial, most of us might hope for and work towards less racial strife, and in particular less civil unrest. We have already noted however that that is not really the problem. Or, we may think the measure of success is to be found in proportionalism as in some of the more simplistic arguments for positive discrimination as compensation for harm in the USA in the 1970s. Thus the related notions of 'under-utilization' (as defined in Office of Federal Contract Compliance guidelines) and 'proportionality' argued that where a given ethnic or nationality group was under-represented in a given profession or occupation, compared with its representation in the population as a whole, this constituted prima facie evidence of past discrimination.[6] Translated to the British scene, we could analogously argue that racial inequalities would have been eliminated only when statistical parity of all racial groups over all occupational groups and statuses had been achieved.

Whilst it is almost certainly true that the under-representation of some ethnic groups in some occupations and professions is a result in part of discrimination and in part of unmet social need (in particular educational need), it cannot be the case that the 'natural' result of eliminating all unjust practices (including discrimination and the non-fulfilment of the needs principle) would be statistical parity of all groups over all occupations and statuses. To expect this is to deny all cultural and social preferences and propensities.[7]

A different vision of success is what has become known as 'multi-culturalism', which is itself a reaction to another such vision – 'integration', which was the orthodoxy of the 1960s and early 1970s but is now rejected (at least, by the more fundamentalist factions of the race relations industry). Multi-culturalism suffers from having to share company with a good deal of obfuscating progressive liberal education jargon, but it seems to mean promoting in all children (and, where possible, adults) an awareness and appreciation of all the cultures and cultural manifestations that now exhibit themselves in Britain. The dominant white cultures ought no longer to be dominant; all cultures now represented ought to be of equal status – and, some would say, of equal importance. And this means in Saffron Walden as well as in Southall.

That children in Britain today should learn about the variety of Asian, Caribbean, and African cultures whatever their own ethnicity seems unexceptional. It is, however, a limited goal, and one with costs and in its more extreme manifestations with dangers. The costs lie on the children and teachers. It is a tall order to require children to absorb the rudiments of other cultures including, in addition to those mentioned, Chinese, Jewish, Greek, Turkish, Welsh, Irish, and Scottish, unless it is to be at the expense of other areas of learning. It is limited in two respects. Firstly, it may do a disservice to ethnic minority young people in encouraging them to believe that their own culture *is* considered generally to be as important and useful as the dominant white cultures when in fact it is not. Ideology and liberal sentiments apart, Britain is predominantly white, has a broadly Anglo-Saxon culture, legal system, and religion, and is part of the European Community, towards which its centre of gravity is moving as fast as it moves away from allegiance to the old Commonwealth and colonies.

Secondly, if the assumption behind multi-culturalism is that learning about other cultures will make us more tolerant of their practitioners, then it is a naïve one. Familiarity with and understanding of other peoples and practices are not the same as tolerance of, agreement with, or even sympathy towards them – although this may be a first step. At best, then, a limited goal, multi-culturalism may also be a misconceived one.

A fifth view of success and one, I suspect, that *force majeure* we shall increasingly have to pay obeisance to is that of 'separatism'. Indeed, this may turn out to be one of the consequences of multi-culturalism. By separatism I mean a turning inwards by ethnic minority groups to seek fulfilment, progress, and satisfaction within the ethnic community rather than compete in what is increasingly seen as a hostile and rejecting white society. However, if such a process is to be seen at all as a goal or as success (by anyone), it must include material progress at the least. Separatism may involve rejecting any status attribution in white society, but it will not accept continued deprivation and low economic status. If separate but equal development could go hand in hand with 'peaceful coexistence' then it may be a goal that many would (or could bring themselves to) accept, inimical though it is to older notions of integration. If it could not, then it might be a recipe for disaster. Either way, we may not have much choice in the matter. If this is the 'success' that circumstances force upon us, then, ironically, positive discrimination may well be rejected as the means of getting there – not by the English 'sense of fair play' but by the ethnic minorities themselves.

Despite our dour conclusions above, suppose for the moment that the future is still ours (social policy-makers') to influence. We have sketched the problem and canvassed some pictures of success. We have lacked the courage (or the means, or both) properly to implement the needs principle. The conclusion of this essay is that in present circumstances in Britain the strategy of positive discrimination would not be justicized. Is this a judgement we wish to hold to or should we have some second thoughts? That there is a little ground as yet uncovered in respect of the British situation, in particular, prompts us to pursue the latter. There are two considerations about positive discrimination in Britain with which we shall conclude.

It was argued in conclusion to Chapter 8 that if positive discrimination were the only, best, most efficient, or on-balance just way of fulfilling the needs or compensation principles – that is, if it were a justicized practice – then the disutilities of implementing it (such as the danger of white backlash) would have to be very great before we should allow them to override its use. However, we have also shown that in respect neither of meeting needs nor of compensating for harm *is* positive discrimination justicized in the present circumstances in Britain. It just is not the only, best, or most efficient way of allocating goods and services only to the most needy and in proportion to their need, or of compensating only the harmed in proportion to their injury. It ought not for these reasons to be implemented; and the dangers of white backlash, chimerical or not, or any other disutilities, need not come into play.

The parallel conclusion in Chapter 8 was that if positive discrimination could be shown in any given set of circumstances to be utility-maximizing then we ought not to be too squeamish about its implementation overriding justice where this is represented by an impure merit system. However, grave reservations were expressed there about utilitarian justifications for social policies in general and positive discrimination in particular. Furthermore, we argued that, in any balancing of utilities and disutilities, the likelihood of positive discrimination achieving its goals (whatever they might be) must weigh very heavily. So, we may now ask, even though positive discrimination is unjusticized, does it none the less present us with a way of dealing with the problems we have outlined and bringing us to some version of the success we have envisaged? If it does, and if it were likely to succeed, it may well be utility-maximizing (even counting in white backlash and other disutilities), and as such we may be justified in using it (even though it may override merit). Will utility allow what liberal justice has refused us – a justification if not a justicization of positive discrimination?

The answer I fear is the same as the conclusion we reached in Chapter 8. The likelihood of positive discrimination even achieving limited goals, such as better police/ethnic community relations by preferential minority police recruitment, is very remote given our experience so far, let alone its potential for realizing any of the other more grandiose goals we have outlined. No doubt positive discrimination *could* be made to work to some end – by, for example, massive preferential hiring into professions, preferential treatment in housing, and so on – but the costs in terms of injustice and white backlash (at this scale a real possibility) would be far too great. And no doubt some forms of positive discrimination will be implemented sporadically in response to immediate crises but they will be small scale, short lived, and futile. Our conclusion must be that positive discrimination in Britain at the present time can be neither justicized in terms of need or compensation nor justified in terms of utility.

Our discussion has been about a practice that we characterized in Chapter 2 to which the name 'positive discrimination' has been given. There are other, related practices to which reference has occasionally been made in the course of the discussion and that are known collectively as 'positive action'. Might it be the case that, although we have found positive discrimination wanting in terms of both justice and utility, positive action provides an alternative road to some kind of success? The answer is 'yes, to a very limited extent'. The potential of such practices is limited for two reasons. Firstly, they are limited in what they can achieve in a purely practical sense. They will not in themselves bring about any of the kinds of success outlined above. The second reason is a moral one. The wider acceptability of positive action compared with the unacceptability of positive discrimination rests upon the assumption that they are two different and easily distinguishable animals. This is mistaken. Positive discrimination and positive action lie, as we have noted, on a continuum where anodyne positive action merges into 'soft' positive discrimination and the latter into 'hard' positive discrimination. None of the boundaries is clear. However, this does not mean that we cannot make any distinctions. There are some clearly identifiable practices that do pass the test of justice and, because they are more 'acceptable', could be widely implemented to some effect. All the practices that fall into this category are ones called positive action, although not all so called practices fall into this category. We shall first identify some such practices and then some others that are more marginal to positive discrimination.

At the 'soft' end of our continuum we may identify policies that would include the weeding out of discriminatory practices or any practices that, whilst not discriminatory in themselves, have that *de facto* consequence. They may on the one hand amount to ensuring strict rule conformity in the allocation of welfare, and on the other the questioning of rules that have discriminatory effects. Again, positive action of this kind will sometimes involve the reassessment of long-held assumptions about the qualities and qualifications necessary for the performance of particular tasks. Where, for example, the criteria used for selecting people to fill positions are found not to be strictly relevant to task performance and at the same time debar disproportionate numbers of one section of the population (for whatever reason), then these criteria can be replaced by others that do not have the debarring effect. The essence of this sort of positive action is to monitor policies and practices (usually in the public sector) to ensure that they are not discriminatory by intent or default. More controversial is the policing of such monitoring to ensure that it does take place. One example of policing is the idea of contract compliance whereby firms with government (or state or federal) contracts are at risk of having the contracts rescinded or not renewed if compliance with equal opportunities legislation or monitoring of the ethnic and sex composition of the workforce is not fulfilled. Contract compliance procedures have met with much success in the United States, though they are in only a rudimentary stage in Britain.[8]

When positive action takes these forms, the potential effect may be considerable if they are implemented on a large scale. Neither would they contravene the canons of justice; indeed such practices may be seen as a way of ensuring the implementation of the principle of equal treatment. They will not reach a solution but they are a necessary step in its direction.

Other forms of positive action, nearer to the 'hard' end of the continuum, are morally marginal because virtually indistinguishable from positive discrimination. If the practices we have just discussed have largely a monitoring role, these more marginal ones may be called broadly 'promotional' in so far as their purpose is to increase the benefits (of whatever kind) that go to ethnic minorities and women. Some practices of this kind are uncontentious – advertising jobs in the ethnic minority press, printing official forms in all appropriate languages, and so on. More controversial would be the practice of advertising jobs *only* in the ethnic minority press, or precepting a part of inner area programme funds for use by ethnic minority groups, or (as Scarman proposed) giving young blacks additional tuition to bring them up to qualifying standard for entry to the police force. Such practices have been called positive action but in reality, certainly in moral terms, they are indistinguishable from the practice we have characterized as positive discrimination. There can be no *moral* difference, for example, between allowing blacks into the police force with lower qualifications than whites and giving additional tuition to reach a given entry standard to blacks but not to whites.

Whether or not therefore we see such practices as viable means to our chosen goal, and whether or not we would want to implement them, they must be subjected to the same tests of justice that we have applied to positive discrimination. Because they are virtually indistinguishable from positive discrimination, the results would be the same.

This has been an essay in applying moral thought to social policy practice. Moral thought – be it about justice or utility – cannot provide definitive answers to often complex problems in social policy, but nor can it do any harm. The study of social policy and social administration in Britain has been heavily descriptive, with occasional excursions into ideology. The reality of social policy practice has too often been expediency dressed up in the finery of political conviction. To the extent that social policy is made and effected in the political market-place this is inevitable; and a value-free analysis of policy, by means of moral thought or any other medium, is a chimera. Indeed the foregoing analysis is 'ideological' in that it is founded on liberal-democratic notions of social justice. Nevertheless, to subject social policy thinking to the test of social justice is to provide a valuable alternative critique to those based on expediency and political ideology. Morality and political ideology are not at all the same thing, and just as social policy does not exist in a political vacuum, neither does it exist in a moral one. It only seems as though it does.

Notes

1 Introduction

1 The use of this term needs to be qualified for service in later arguments.

2 Positive discrimination in Britain: the idea and its practice

1 'Seemingly' because in essence they do not differ from earlier priority area designations such as post-war regional development policies writ small, or the 'areas of special control' proposed by the Milner Holland Report (Milner Holland Report 1965: 122).
2 This important point will be elaborated in a later chapter. The 1977 White Paper on *Policy for the Inner Cities* firmly ruled out the possibility of paying higher scales of benefit (an individual good) to people living in inner-city areas (Department of the Environment 1977: 3).
3 This Bill was overtaken by the change of government in 1979.
4 For details of Section 11 grants see Hall 1981: 91, Edwards 1984.
5 In most cases the resource allocation is the direct injection of funds for establishing projects to counter or alleviate deprivation. In others (Designated Authorities, Enterprise Zones, Urban Development Corporations, Freeports) the benefit takes the form of incentives or hidden subsidies usually for industry (Edwards 1984). Both direct allocation and preference by the use of incentives are counted by S. M. Miller (1973) as varieties of positive discrimination.
6 Practices of both kinds are rejected by Cullingworth's committee so long as the selection criterion was ethnicity rather than need.
7 Interestingly, an almost identical passage but without any reference to positive discrimination occurs in a piece that Titmuss published in the *New Statesman* in September 1967. It is worth quoting the relevant parts for the context it provides. 'The challenge that faces us is not the choice between universalist and selective services. The real challenge resides in the question: "what particular infrastructure of universalist services is needed in order to provide a framework of values and opportunity bases within and around which can be de-

veloped acceptable selective services provided as social rights on criteria of the *needs* of specific categories, groups and territorial areas and not dependent on *individual tests of means*?"' (published as 'Universal and Selective Social Services' in Titmuss 1968: 122, emphasis in original).

8 Titmuss's rhetorical question is more illuminating in the version without mention of positive discrimination than with it.

9 Corbett has argued that priority area schemes may stigmatize recipient *areas*: see Corbett 1968, 1969.

10 For a discussion of the rationale behind area-based concepts of deprivation and their shortcomings, see Hamnett 1979, Higgins *et al.* 1983: ch. 6.

11 The idea of equality of welfare is discussed in Chapter 4.

12 Liverpool, for example, was excluded from eligibility for Section 11 grant because most of its ethnic minority members were not new arrivals.

13 Although the debate was marked by expressed hostility to positive discrimination, the Bill passed its second reading, only to fall with the change of government later in the year.

14 Despite his enthusiasm for positive discrimination, Pinker noted in 1971 that some positive discrimination programmes were likely to invoke public hostility.

3 Positive discriminaton and social justice

1 To avoid semantic gymnastics, the term 'positive discrimination' is for the present used to cover practices that are given this label in Britain, and practices of affirmative action or reverse discrimination in the USA.

2 I use the term 'consequentialist' in a general sense of 'having regard to consequences' rather than in its more strict and original usage by Anscombe (1958) of 'consequentialism', the purpose of which was to place more emphasis on the *process* of maximizing (or optimizing) and less on the nature of the maximand, which heretofore had characterized utilitarian theory.

3 I do not believe with Benn and Peters, however, that 'to seek the common good' can be interpreted as 'to try to act justly' (Benn and Peters 1959: 273). As Barry points out in this respect, notions of justice, fairness, equity, and so on are analytically quite different from such as public interest, common good, general welfare, all of which are aggregative concepts; to claim a congruence of the two types of concept is 'to make nonsense of the subtle and complex way in which we go about criticising political programmes' (Barry 1967b: 193).

4 As we shall see later, however, simple restoration of the status quo

ante is not what is required in those circumstances where positive discrimination might be seen to be relevant.

5 See also Hart 1961: 154–55, where questions of compensation are treated as distributive issues.

6 Honoré (1968) argues that it is the like treatment principle that yields the *suum cuique* principle; the reverse seems more logical.

7 Perelman (1963) argues that it is no more than a statement of rationality.

8 Ake (1975: 78) makes this point in his discussion of self-induced need.

9 Probably the best known discussion of the prioritization of principles is Rawls's treatment of lexicographic ordering (Rawls 1972: 42 ff.).

10 Two writers give 'desert or merit', which, given our separation of the two principles, is unallocatable. For the sake of counting, one has been allocated to 'desert' and the other to 'merit'.

11 For useful discussions of the shortcomings of the categorical imperatives as ultimate foundations of material principles of justice see Raphael 1955, Williams 1969. See also Finnis 1983: ch. 5, for a discussion of Kantian principles.

12 For further discussion of intuitionism see Nowell-Smith 1954: ch. 3, Warnock 1967: ch. 2, Williams 1972: chs. 2, 4.

13 There is a useful series of exchanges on this issue to be found in *Analysis* over the period 1972–75. See, in chronological order, Nickel 1972, Cowan 1972, Taylor 1973, Bayles 1973a, Shiner 1973, Silvestri 1973, Nunn 1973, Nickel 1973, Goldman 1975. We return to this debate in subsequent chapters.

4 Social justice and the needs principle

1 Arguments against social rights are less common, but see Lucas 1966, Cranston's (1967) penetrating critique, and Campbell 1974.

2 The division is admittedly a rough and ready one. Some functional needs are acknowledged in the public domain especially in the area of taxation policies, where for example clothing, tools, books, or cars necessary for the pursuit of individuals' occupations can be set against tax liability. For further discussion of this see Edwards 1983, 1985.

3 To treat it as a continuum is only an approximation; we do not always want what we need nor need what we want. This construction suffices for present purposes however.

4 Braybrooke's (1968) pleas for a restriction on needs to enable a greater satisfaction of wants and preferences fails to gain much purchase precisely because he pays little heed to the distinction between public obligation and private desires.

5 For further discussion of Miller's concept (and the need to add to it a

moral dimension) see Edwards 1985: 35 ff.

6 Fried (1978: 120) argues against objective as well as subjective measures but in respect of the former his arguments are less than convincing.

7 In the USA the agency charged with responsibility for affirmative action programmes is called the Equal Employment Opportunities Commission – despite the fact that, as is argued in Chapter 6, the most common justification for such programmes is compensation for past harm.

8 There is a teleologic basis for equality of opportunity; a meritocratic system that does not ensure that *all* the best abilities are exploited to the full is operating less than efficiently and is not therefore maximizing utility.

9 However, much discourse on equality of opportunity places excessive weight on (and hence over-emphasizes) the value of a limited range of professional or commercial occupations. The rapid growth of self-employment in Britain since 1979 (largely a response to high levels of unemployment) indicates an important alternative means of achieving rewards and one, it might be argued, that opens up opportunities previously denied to many along the more usual paths to career advancement. The risks of failure are also high, as the figures on bankruptcy show.

10 For versions of such an ordering see also Benn and Peters 1959: 118, Raphael 1976: 187 ff., Goldman 1979: 170–74.

11 Some such characteristics, as we noted in Chapter 3, such as efforts, sacrifices, and contributions, may be acceptable as material principles of justice (under the general rubric of 'desert') and as such would not be morally arbitrary. Others, such as intelligence, clearly are.

5 The needs principle and positive discrimination

1 A modest trawl through the books on my shelves produced such references in the context of positive discrimination by fifteen authors.

2 This prescription could not be derived from the equality of welfare principle when benefit was *subjectively* measured (see pages 72–5). Prioritization and allocation in such a case would be hostage to the quixotic nature of private satisfactions and dissatisfactions. And utility maximization may well give priority and more resources to the non-handicapped in such circumstances.

3 Section 11 grants under the Local Government Act 1966 are made on the basis of the needs generated by concentrations of ethnic minorities; but until 1982 this was a very small-scale programme, and only since 1982 has ethnicity been an explicit criterion for the selection of projects to fund under the Inner Area Programmes of the Partnership and Programme Authorities (see Higgins *et al.* 1983,

Edwards 1984). It might also be argued that both Section 11 and the Inner Area Programmes are essentially *area* based but with an ethnicity bias.

4 For details of each of these programmes see Edwards 1984, There are also some non-resourced initiatives such as City Action Teams but these are administrative and implementary devices rather than programmes.

5 S. M. Miller (1973) has identified 'allocational priorities' and 'incentives' as two of the three main types of positive discrimination. The third, he maintains, is preference policies.

6 The growing emphasis on economic infrastructure regeneration, and employment creation, reflects a changed conception of the nature and causes of inner-city problems. For a discussion of this see Edwards 1984.

7 There is little evidence to show that immigrant industry and commerce increase the employment available to the labour force in the recipient area. Most migrating firms are involved in high-technology enterprise and often bring their labour forces with them. Nor will employment incentives help to meet the needs of the majority of inner-city residents who are not in the labour force, in the absence of separate strategies to use the increased rates base for redistributive purposes.

8 In most cases relevant analyses are confined to such deprivation-relevant data as are available from the Census, which has the singular advantage of nationwide coverage at enumeration district level. The most recent analysis is that carried out by the Department of the Environment on the 1981 Census (Department of the Environment 1983). Useful earlier examples are to be found in Hatch and Sherrott 1973, Holtermann 1975, Alnutt and Gelardi 1980, MacLaran 1981. Non-census data have the advantage that they may more specifically relate to measures of need, including income measures, referrals to social services departments, morbidity measures, housing benefits and rate rebates, and so on, but the (for present purposes fatal) disadvantage of only local and non-systematic coverage. Although now out of date, the most comprehensive and thorough example of morbidity data analysis remains that carried out in Liverpool in the early 1970s (Liverpool Corporation 1971).

9 A comparable analysis using 1981 Census data has not yet been produced.

10 Rural enumeration districts were excluded from the analysis.

11 I do not mean by this that all area-collective benefits are (or might be thought to be) less important than individualized benefits. Employment generation is a collective benefit and meets a very important need. Territorial justice would require that the resources and energy devoted to real job creation ought to be in proportion to levels of unemployment.

12 The Urban Programme was in part a response to 'the immigrant problem' and was intended to bring some assistance to ethnic minorities, but this was never said explicitly (see Edwards and Batley 1978: ch. 3).

13 Some practices, such as additional training for certain jobs and positions being reserved for ethnic minority members, do come close to being hard-case even though they are (for safety's sake) called positive action. They are few in number. The relation between positive action and positive discrimination is discussed in Chapter 9.

14 This was *not* true, however, for Bangladeshis and Pakistanis on some dimensions of deprivation, where they remained significantly worse off than all other groups.

15 For the reasons given in Chapter 2, I wish to avoid the term 'compensate'.

6 Positive discrimination and rights to compensation

1 For the present we shall group these terms together. Later in the chapter we shall need to distinguish their meaning.

2 We shall examine Dworkin's essentially consequentialist view of positive discrimination in a subsequent chapter.

3 Whilst the US experience is relevant to our consideration of the moral justifiability of positive discrimination, our practical and empirical concern is with the UK.

4 One writer does make a distinction between compensation and reparation but this derives in large measure from an interpretation of compensation as 'making up for' a deficiency, which, as we have noted, is really a formulation of the needs principle (see Boxhill 1977: 271).

5 Bittker (1973) probably comes closest to such an approach in his argument for black reparations.

6 The distinction between legal and moral rights is in some measure misleading. They are not mutually exclusive. Most legal rights are also moral rights, although not all moral rights are legal ones.

7 For further discussion of the relationship between compensation and *distributive* justice, see Hart 1961: 160 ff.

8 There are, as Fried notes, degrees of 'intentionality'. Unintended but foreseeable or unintended but foreseen consequences may be deemed by degrees to be more culpable than purely accidental ones.

9 On De Funis see W. T. Blackstone 1977, Dworkin 1977a: ch. 9. The greatest volume of literature has been generated by the Bakke case; the most exhaustive treatments are to be found in Dreyfuss and Lawrence 1979, Eastland and Bennett 1979: chs. 1, 9. Another useful discussion is to be found in the first two of three articles by

Dworkin in the *New York Review of Books* (Dworkin 1977b, 1978). Analysis of some of the issues involved in the Weber case can be found in Eastland and Bennett 1979: ch. 1, and in Dworkin's third article for the *New York Review of Books* (Dworkin 1979).

7 The justiciability of positive discrimination as compensation for harm

1 A third argument was adduced in respect of needs but this is irrelevant to our consideration of compensation.

2 As we noted earlier, US terminology is far from value-neutral. Some proponents of affirmative action assert its distinction from reverse discrimination; others do not shy away from applying the latter to programmes of which they approve. Some opponents of affirmative action are concerned to stick the label 'reverse discrimination' on it as a malediction. Proponents of affirmative action claim that it is not at all the same as reverse discrimination; opponents say the one must necessarily entail the other. Many claim that the difference between the two is that affirmative action uses goals, while reverse discrimination implies quotas. We have remarked that the distinction between goals and quotas is a tenuous one (at least in moral terms). 'Affirmative action', 'reverse discrimination', and 'positive discrimination' will all be used synonymously here except where a distinction is necessary and stated.

3 This assertion is contestable. Blackstone's precise formulation is: 'What I deny is that any given black or any given female in the here and now necessarily suffers from past injustice' (W. T. Blackstone 1977: 67).

4 Although, as we shall show in Chapter 8, the efficacy of role models is far from certain.

5 This is not a problem for utilitarian or consequentialist arguments for positive discrimination.

6 Capaldi's critique of affirmative action is conducted for the most part in terms quite different to others presented here. He makes no mention of justice and the burden of his argument is that doctrinaire liberals (a term with varying degrees of inclusion but consisting it would seem of a hard-core of academic social scientists) are, by the use of affirmative action, attempting to change the face of American society by creating a pool of debtors (blacks, etc.). In payment they will owe permanent allegiance to the Democratic Party and thus effect a permanent majority, so bringing about a fascist state. The language is Capaldi's not mine.

7 On the inappropriateness of markets as allocators of compensation see Hoffman 1977: 369, Simon 1977: 43, Goldman 1979: 88–92.

8 This is a point that has been made by, among others, W. T. Blackstone 1977: 67–8, Goldman 1977: 206, Hoffman 1977: 368–70.

9 Group-based practices seem often to engender occasional dissent, unrest, and even riots, but the *principle* of group rights seems to have a stronger hold in countries such as Belgium, India, and Canada, with large and distinct sub-groups within the population. (I hesitate to dilate on this matter in respect of Northern Ireland.)
10 Dworkin (1977b: 13) disputes that in these circumstances the white applicant is used as a means to a social end.
11 It may be argued that a merit system establishes sets of legitimate expectations which would be disappointed by positive discrimination practices. Habituation, however, is not the same as justice.
12 See also Bittker (1973: ch. 9) for a discussion of the problems involved in individual compensation for blacks. The results, he rightly claims, would be capricious, and the costs enormous.
13 For example, Nozick's principle of 'rectification of injustice in holdings' would also, as he admits, require complex counterfactual reasoning (Nozick 1974: 152–53).
14 The same would hold *pari passu* of Nozickian rectification.

8 Consequentialism, justice, and positive discrimination

1 Although, as we saw (page 35), there can be a difference between teleologic and utilitarian arguments, we shall not in practice need to treat them separately.
2 As was explained on page 35, I use Frankena's (1963) distinction between teleologic and deontic ethics as the clearest and most practical statement. This classic dichotomy in ethics will not be elaborated further here; but for useful discussions that could have a bearing on public policy see Downie and Telfer 1976: 163 ff. (in which utilitarian arguments are brought to bear in a critique of extreme deontism or 'rule-worship'), Melden 1977: 129 ff., W. T. Blackstone 1967: 242, Finnis 1983: ch. IV.
3 For a good though critical treatment of preference utility see Dworkin 1977a: 233 ff. Elster (1982) provides a valuable analysis of the problems that preference formation provides for the utilitarian.
4 For a useful discussion of, and comparison between, collective and average utility see Rawls 1972: 161–75, 183–92.
5 However, Dworkin identifies this as a short-term aim of positive discrimination, the longer-term purpose being to produce a less racially divided society.
6 It says something about the inadequacy with which the social mechanics of positive discrimination and its effects have been thought out, that race and sex can be lumped together here. Why should it be assumed that if positive discrimination worked it would have the same results in both cases?
7 When subsequent riots did occur in 1985, editorial policy on *The Times* had changed, and the leader writer's response was very

different – hard policing and the full rigours of the law were by then the answer.

8 It may well be argued that, if it is a good, then we shall want to maximize it, but I take 'good' in this context to be of a deontic nature. Hence the close association between deontic arguments for positive discrimination and such ideal-end-regarding arguments that we have noted.

9 This is not to say that actions taken for functional reasons might not also turn out to be utility-maximal.

10 I take it as axiomatic that policy evaluation ought not to be a merely technical exercise. It must also include judgements about the morality of policies and their likely consequences.

11 For other excursions into the realms of 'the general interest', 'the common good', and 'the public interest' see Barry 1967a: 112 ff., 1967b: 192 ff., Hare 1978.

12 Particular attempts to do this hover at the margins of positive discrimination and positive action, or midway on the continuum of which they constitute the ends. Most involve some form of preferential treatment; only blacks and Asians, but not whites, get additional training, although the actual qualifying criteria remain inviolate. The most ambitious though still small-scale scheme has been that operated by the Derbyshire police force.

13 Some of the briefs *amicus curiae* submitted in the Bakke and De Funis cases are an exception to this.

14 Mackie (1977: 154–55) makes this point in respect of consequentialism more generally.

15 Dworkin (1977a: 234 ff.) has pointed out the possible double-counting that may occur (and hence bias the result) from including both personal and external preferences in the calculus. For a counter to Dworkin see Ware 1983.

16 The lists refer to the utilities and disutilities in respect of ethnic minority groups. Different, but in some respects similar, lists would be required in respect of women.

17 Any discussion about positive discrimination seduces us into thinking and generalizing in group terms. It is worth reminding ourselves periodically that all ethnic groups are heterogeneous, as are their needs. The ranges of health needs of blacks and Asians are as wide as those of whites; particular parts of the range may have greater urgency or frequency.

18 This argument has been more commonly put in respect of women.

19 I presume to assert what some would deny – that not all whites are racist.

20 It *would* be the case that some of the best qualified might not get the job, but the differences would probably be marginal and not such as to affect efficiency. This is separate however from the issue of justice involved in preferential hiring.

21 It would be interesting to speculate what the reaction would be if such positive discrimination were in respect of women rather than ethnic minorities.

22 This is apart from, and additional to, the arguments about the potentially unjust outcomes of applying positive discrimination that we canvassed in earlier chapters. These may also, however, be seen as examples of positive discrimination not achieving its aims.

23 Nagel (1977: 15 ff.) has examined this issue and concludes that negative discrimination cannot be utility-maximizing. Dworkin (1977c) has done the same (in respect of Sweatt and the University of Texas) and found that it can.

9 Thinking morally about social policy

1 A useful example of this is the work of Dunning *et al.* (1987) on the history of violent crowd behaviour in Leicester since the beginning of the century. The idea that we are an increasingly violent society must, at the least, be qualified in the light of their findings.

2 Some useful analyses of the reasons for continuing racial inequalities in Britain can be found in C. Cross 1978, Daniel 1968, Rex and Tomlinson 1979, Banton 1983, Cashmore and Troyna 1983, Glazer and Young 1983, Pilkington 1984.

3 This argument was frequently put in evidence to the Home Affairs Committee investigation of racial disadvantage during its sessions in 1979–82.

4 We are not here concerned with the discrimination that may exist in the exercise of discretion in implementing a rule. This would clearly be unjust and ought to be remedied.

5 We are not talking here about individual housing need assessment but about *general rules* from which there ought to be departure in special or great-need cases.

6 Hoffman 1977 among others has argued that mere statistical disparity does not constitute prima facie evidence. The Civil Rights Act does not accept it either.

7 To achieve it would involve reducing the number of Australian dentists, Jewish accountants, Irish builders, and Italian waiters among thousands of other 'adjustments'.

8 They are also disliked by the hard right. An announcement by a Home Office minister that the government was moving towards contract compliance met with a good deal of opposition from his back-bench colleagues who saw the spectre of more government meddling in the affairs of the private sector. (Reported in *The Times*, 14 October, 15 October, and 17 October 1985.)

References

Ackerman, B. (1980) *Social Justice in the Liberal State*. New Haven: Yale University Press.

Acton, H. B. (1971) *The Morals of Markets*. London: Longman.

Ake, C. (1975) Justice as Equality. *Philosophy and Public Affairs* 5 (1): 69–89.

Aldridge, M. (1979) Urban Planning and Social Policy. In D. Marsh (ed.) *Introducing Social Policy*. London: Routledge & Kegan Paul.

Alnutt, D. and Gelardi, A. (1980) Inner Cities in England. *Social Trends* 10.

Anscombe, G. E. M. (1958) Modern Moral Philosophy. *Philosophy* 33: 1–19.

Aristotle (1925) *The Nicomachean Ethics*. Oxford: Oxford University Press (25th edition).

Banner, W. A. (1977) Compensatory Justice and the Meaning of Equity. In W. T. Blackstone and R. D. Heslep (eds.) *Social Justice and Preferential Treatment*. Athens: University of Georgia Press.

Banton, M. (1983) *Racial and Ethnic Competition*. Cambridge: Cambridge University Press.

Barlow Report (1940) *Report of the Royal Commission on the Distribution of the Industrial Population*. London: HMSO, cmnd 6153.

Barnes, J. (1974) A Solution to Whose Problem? In H. Glennerster and S. Hatch (eds.) *Positive Discrimination and Inequality*. London: Fabian Society.

Barry, B. (1965) *Political Argument*. London: Routledge & Kegan Paul.

—— (1967a) The Public Interest. In A. Quinton (ed.) *Political Philosophy*. Oxford: Oxford University Press.

—— (1967b) Justice and the Common Good. In A. Quinton (ed.) *Political Philosophy*. Oxford: Oxford University Press.

Batley, R. (1978) From Poor Law to Positive Discrimination.

Journal of Social Policy 7 (3): 305–28.
Bayles, M. D. (ed.) (1968) *Contemporary Utilitarianism.* New York: Doubleday.
—— (1973a) Reparations for Wronged Groups. *Analysis* 33 (6): 182–84.
—— (1973b) Compensatory Reverse Discrimination in Hiring. *Social Theory and Practice* 2 (3): 301–12.
Beauchamp, T. (1977) The Justification of Reverse Discrimination. In W. T. Blackstone and R. D. Heslep (eds.) *Social Justice and Preferential Treatment.* Athens: University of Georgia Press.
Beloff, M. (1982) What's the Price of Racial Harmony? *The Times,* 15 November 1982.
Benn, S. I. and Peters, R. S. (1959) *Social Principles and the Democratic State.* London: Allen & Unwin.
Bindman, G. (1980) The Law, Equal Opportunity and Affirmative Action. *New Community* VIII (3): 248–60.
Bindman, G. and Carrier, J. (1983) A Multi-Racial Society. In H. Glennerster (ed.) *The Future of the Welfare State.* London: Heinemann.
Bittker, B. (1973) *The Case for Black Reparations.* New York: Random House.
Black Report (1980) *Inequalities in Health.* London: Department of Health and Social Security.
Black, V. (1974) The Erosion of Legal Principles in the Creation of Legal Policies. *Ethics* 84 (2): 93–115.
Blackstone, T. (1980) Education. In N. Bosanquet and P. Townsend (eds.) *Labour and Inequality.* London: Heinemann.
Blackstone, W. T. (1967) On the Meaning and Justification of the Equality Principle. *Ethics* 77 (4): 239–53.
—— (1977) Reverse Discrimination and Compensatory Justice. In W. T. Blackstone and R. D. Heslep (eds.) *Social Justice and Preferential Treatment.* Athens: University of Georgia Press.
Blackstone, W. T. and Heslep, R. D. (eds.) (1977) *Social Justice and Preferential Treatment.* Athens: University of Georgia Press.
Bosanquet, N. and Townsend, P. (eds.) (1980) *Labour and Inequality: A Fabian Study of Labour in Power 1974–79.* London: Heinemann.
Bowie, N. E. (1970) Equality and Distributive Justice. *Philosophy* 45 (142): 140–48.
Boxhill, B. (1977) The Morality of Reparation. In B. R. Gross (ed.) *Reverse Discrimination.* Buffalo: Prometheus.
Brandt, R. B. (ed.) (1962) *Social Justice.* Englewood Cliffs:

Prentice-Hall.

Brandt, R. B. (1979) *A Theory of the Good and the Right*. Oxford: Oxford University Press.

Braybrooke, D. (1968) Let Needs Diminish that Preferences May Prosper. *American Philosophical Quarterly Monograph Series* 1: 86–107.

Brown, C. (1984) *Black and White Britain: The Third Policy Studies Institute Survey*. London: Hutchinson.

Brown, M. (1977) *Introduction to Social Administration in Britain*. London: Hutchinson.

Brown, M. and Madge, N. (1982) *Despite the Welfare State*. London: Heinemann.

Buxton, M. J. and Klein, R. (1978) *Allocating Health Resources: A Commentary on the Report of the Resource Allocation Working Party*. London: HMSO.

Campbell, T. D. (1974) Humanity Before Justice. *British Journal of Political Science* 4: 1–16.

Capaldi, N. (1985) *Out of Order: Affirmative Action and the Crisis of Doctrinaire Liberalism*. Buffalo: Prometheus.

Cashmore, B. and Troyna, B. (1983) *Introduction to Race Relations*. London: Routledge & Kegan Paul.

Cheetham, J. (1982) Positive Discrimination in Social Work: Negotiating the Opposition. *New Community* 10 (1): 27–37.

Cherry, G. (1982) *The Politics of Town Planning*. London: Longman.

Coates, B., Johnston, R., and Knox, P. (1977) *Geography and Inequality*. Oxford: Oxford University Press.

Coates, K. and Silburn, R. (1970) *Poverty: The Forgotten Englishmen*. Harmondsworth: Penguin.

Cohen, G. A. (1978) Robert Nozick and Walt Chamberlain: How Patterns Preserve Liberty. In J. Arthur and W. H. Shaw (eds.) *Justice and Economic Distribution*. Englewood Cliffs: Prentice-Hall.

Cohen, M., Nagel, T., and Scanlon, T. (eds.) (1977) *Equality and Preferential Treatment*. Princeton: Princeton University Press.

Commission for Racial Equality (1977) *Urban Deprivation, Racial Equality and Social Policy: A Report*. London: Commission for Racial Equality.

—— (1978) *Multi-Racial Britain: The Social Services Response*. London: Commission for Racial Equality.

Community Relations Commission (1974) *Community Relations 1973–74: Annual Report*. London: HMSO.

Corbett, A. (1968) The New Priority Schools. *New Society*, 30 May: 785–87.

—— (1969) Are Educational Priority Areas Working? *New Society*, 15 November: 763–67.

Cowan, J. L. (1972) Inverse Discrimination. *Analysis* 33 (1): 10–12.

Cranston, M. (1967) Human Rights Real and Supposed. In D. D. Raphael (ed.) *Political Theory and the Rights of Man*. London: Macmillan.

Cross, C. (1978) *Ethnic Minorities in the Inner City*. London: Commission for Racial Equality.

Cross, M. (1982) Racial Equality and Social Policy: Omission or Commission? In C. Jones, and J. Stevenson (eds.) *The Yearbook of Social Policy in Britain 1980–81*. London: Routledge & Kegan Paul.

Cullingworth Report (1969) *Council Housing: Purposes, Procedures and Priorities* (Ninth Report of the Housing Management Sub-Committee of the Central Housing Advisory Committee). London: HMSO.

Cullingworth, J. B. (1973) *Problems of an Urban Society, Vol. II: The Social Content of Planning*. London: Allen & Unwin.

—— (1976) *Town and Country Planning in Britain* (6th edition). London: Allen & Unwin.

Daniel, W. W. (1968) *Racial Discrimination in England*. Harmondsworth: Penguin.

Daniels, N. (1981) Health Care Needs and Distributive Justice. *Philosophy and Public Affairs* 10 (2): 146–79.

Danto, A. (1984) Constructing an Epistemology of Human Rights: A Pseudo Problem? *Social Philosophy and Policy* 1 (2): 25–30.

Davies, B. (1968) *Social Needs and Resources in Local Services*. London: Michael Joseph.

Day, J. P. (1981) Compensatory Discrimination. *Philosophy* 56 (1): 55–72.

Department of the Environment (1977) *Policy for the Inner Cities* London: HMSO, cmnd 6845.

—— (1983) *Information Note No. 2: Urban Deprivation*. London: Department of the Environment.

Department of Health and Social Security (1976) *Sharing Resources for Health in England: Report of the Resource Allocation Working Party*. London: HMSO.

Donnison, D. (1974) Policies for Priority Areas. *Journal of Social*

Policy 3 (2): 127–35.

Downie, R. S. and Telfer, E. (1976) Respect for Persons and Public Morality. In N. Timms and D. Watson (eds.) *Talking About Welfare*. London: Routledge & Kegan Paul.

Dreyfuss, J. and Lawrence, C. (1979) *The Bakke Case*. New York: Harcourt Brace Jovanovich.

Dunning, E., Murphy, P., Newburn, T., and Waddington, I. (1987) Violent Disorders in Twentieth Century Britain. In G. Gaskell (ed.) *The Crowd in Contemporary Britain*. Manchester: Manchester University Press.

Dworkin, R. (1977a) *Taking Rights Seriously*. London: Duckworth.

—— (1977b) Why Bakke Has No Case. *New York Review of Books*, 10 November: 11–15.

—— (1977c) De Funis vs Sweatt. In M. Cohen, T. Nagel, and T. Scanlon (eds.) *Equality and Preferential Treatment*. Princeton: Princeton University Press.

—— (1978) The Bakke Decision: Did it Decide Anything ? *New York Review of Books*, 17 August: 20–25.

—— (1979) How to Read the Civil Rights Act. *New York Review of Books*, 20 December: 37–43.

—— (1981a) What is Equality? Part 1 Equality of Welfare. *Philosophy and Public Affairs* 10 (3): 185–246.

—— (1981b) What is Equality? Part 2 Equality of Resources. *Philosophy and Public Affairs* 10 (4): 283–345.

—— (1983) In Defence of Equality. *Social Philosophy and Policy* 1 (1): 24–40.

Eastland, T. and Bennett, W. (1979) *Counting by Race: Equality from the Founding Fathers to Bakke and Weber*. New York: Basic Books.

Edel, A. (1977) Preferential Consideration and Justice. In W. T. Blackstone and R. D. Heslep (eds.) *Social Justice and Preferential Treatment*. Athens: University of Georgia Press.

Edwards, J. (1975) Social Indicators, Urban Deprivation and Positive Discrimination. *Journal of Social Policy* 4 (3): 275–87.

—— (1983) L'Analisi della Qualità della Vita. Paper presented at Scuola Superiore di Servizio Sociale, Venice, September.

—— (1984) UK Inner Cities: Problem Construction and Policy Response. *Cities* 1 (6): 592–604.

—— (1985) Social Indicators and the Concept of Quality of Life. In A. Robertson and A. Osborn (eds.) *Planning to Care: Social Policy and the Quality of Life*. Aldershot: Gower.

Edwards, J. and Batley, R. (1978) *The Politics of Positive Discrimination: An Evaluation of the Urban Programme 1967–77*. London: Tavistock.
Edwards, J., Oakley, R., and Carey, S. (1987) Street Life, Ethnic Minorities and Social Policy. In G. Gaskell (ed.) *The Crowd in Contemporary Britain*. Manchester: Manchester University Press.
Elster, J. (1982) Sour Grapes – Utilitarianism and the Genesis of Wants. In A. Sen and B. Williams (eds.) *Utilitarianism and Beyond*. Cambridge: Cambridge University Press.
Exum, W. H. (1983) Climbing the Crystal Stair: Values, Affirmative Action, and Minority Faculty. *Social Problems* 30 (4): 383–99.
Feinberg, J. (ed.) (1969) *Moral Concepts*. Oxford: Oxford University Press.
—— (1973) *Social Philosophy*. Englewood Cliffs: Prentice-Hall.
Finnis, J. (1983) *Fundamentals of Ethics*. Oxford: Clarendon Press.
Firth, M. (1981) Racial Discrimination in the British Labour Market. *Industrial and Labour Relations Review* 34 (2): 265–72.
Flathman, R. E. (1967) Equality and Generalisation: A Formal Analysis. In J. R. Pennock and J. W. Chapman (eds.) *Equality* (Nomos IX). New York: Atherton.
Foster, P. (1983) *Access to Welfare*. London: Macmillan.
Frankena, W. K. (1962) The Concept of Social Justice. In R. B. Brandt (ed.) *Social Justice*. Englewood Cliffs: Prentice-Hall.
—— (1963) *Ethics*. Englewood Cliffs: Prentice-Hall.
Fried, C. (1978) *Right and Wrong*. Cambridge, Mass.: Harvard University Press.
—— (1983) Distributive Justice. *Social Philosophy and Policy* 1 (1): 45–59.
Gewirth, A. (1984) The Epistemology of Human Rights. *Social Philosophy and Policy* 1 (2): 1–24.
Ginsberg, M. (1965) *On Justice in Society*. Harmondsworth: Penguin.
Ginsburg, R. (1977) Realising the Equality Principle. In W. T. Blackstone and R. D. Heslep (eds.) *Social Justice and Preferential Treatment*. Athens: University of Georgia Press.
Glazer, N. (1975) *Affirmative Discrimination, Ethnic Inequality and Public Policy*. New York: Basic Books.
—— (1978) Individual Rights Against Group Rights. In E. Kamenka and E. S. Tay (eds.) *Human Rights*. London: Edward Arnold.
Glazer, N. and Young, K. (eds.) (1983) *Ethnic Pluralism and*

Public Policy. London: Heinemann.

Glennerster, H. (ed.) (1983) *The Future of the Welfare State: Remaking Social Policy*. London: Heinemann.

Glennerster, H. and Hatch, S. (eds.) (1974a) *Positive Discrimination and Inequality* (Fabian Research Series No. 34). London: Fabian Society.

—— and —— (1974b) Strategy Against Inequality? In H. Glennerster and S. Hatch (eds.) *Positive Discrimination and Inequality* (Fabian Research Series No. 34). London: Fabian Society.

Goldman, A. (1975) Reparations to Individuals or Groups? *Analysis* 35: 168–70.

—— (1977) Affirmative Action. In M., Cohen, T. Nagel, and T. Scanlon (eds.) *Equality and Preferential Treatment*. Princeton: Princeton University Press.

—— (1979) *Justice and Reverse Discrimination*. Princeton: Princeton University Press.

Goodin, R. (1975) How to Determine Who Should Get What. *Ethics* 85 (4): 310–21.

Greene, M. (1977) Equality and Inviolability. An Approach to Compensatory Justice. In W. T. Blackstone and R. D. Heslep (eds.) *Social Justice and Preferential Treatment*. Athens: University of Georgia Press.

Gross, B. R. (ed.) (1977) *Reverse Discrimination*. Buffalo: Prometheus.

—— (1978) *Discrimination in Reverse*. New York: New York University Press.

Guttman, A. (1980) *Liberal Equality*. Cambridge: Cambridge University Press.

Hall, P. (1980) Two Nations or One? The Geography of Deprivation. *New Society* 51 (906): 331–33.

—— (ed.) (1981) *The Inner City in Context*. London: Heinemann.

Hall, P., Land, H., Parker, R., and Webb, A. (1975) *Change, Choice and Conflict in Social Policy*. London: Heinemann.

Halsey, A. H. (ed.) (1972) *Educational Priority*. London: HMSO.

Ham, C. and Hill, M. (1984) *The Policy Process in the Modern Capitalist State*. Brighton: Wheatsheaf.

Hamnett, C. (1979) Area-Based Explanations: A Critical Appraisal. In D. T. Herbert and D. M. Smith (eds.) *Social Problems and the City: Geographical Perspectives*. Oxford: Oxford University Press.

Hansard (1967) House of Lords, 14 February: col. 209.

—— (1967) House of Lords, 14 March: cols. 177–78, 208, 209,

214, 737–38.

—— (1967) House of Commons, 16 March: cols. 737–38, 789, 824.

—— (1979) House of Commons, 12 March: cols. 78, 100, 101, 166.

Hare, R. M. (1978) Justice and Equality. In J. Arthur and W. H. Shaw (eds.) *Justice and Economic Distribution*. Englewood Cliffs: Prentice-Hall.

Hart, H. L. A. (1961) *The Concept of Law*. Oxford: Clarendon Press.

—— (1967) Are There Any Natural Rights? In A. Quinton (ed.) *Political Philosophy*. Oxford: Oxford University Press.

Harvey, D. (1973) *Social Justice and the City*. London: Edward Arnold.

Hatch, S., Fox, E., and Legg, C. (1977) *Research and Reform: Southwark Community Development Project 1969–72*. London: Home Office.

Hatch, S. and Sherrott, R. (1973) Positive Discrimination and the Distribution of Deprivations. *Policy and Politics* 1 (3): 223–40.

Haworth, L. (1968) *Utility and Rights*. American Philosophical Quarterly Monograph Series No. 1. Oxford: Blackwell.

Hayek, F. (1976) *Law, Legislation and Liberty, Vol. II: The Mirage of Social Justice*. London: Routledge & Kegan Paul.

Heslep, R. D. (1977) Preferential Treatment in Admitting Racial Minority Students. In W. T. Blackstone and R. D. Heslep (eds.) *Social Justice and Preferential Treatment*. Athens: University of Georgia Press.

Hewitt, P. (1980) Sex Equality. In N. Bosanquet and P. Townsend (eds.) *Labour and Inequality: A Fabian Study of Labour in Power 1974–79*. London: Heinemann.

Higgins, J. (1978) *The Poverty Business: Britain and America*. Oxford: Blackwell.

Higgins, J., Deakin, N., Edwards, J., and Wicks, M. (1983) *Government and Urban Poverty*. Oxford: Blackwell.

Hoffman, R. (1977) Justice, Merit, and the Good. In B. R. Gross (ed.) *Reverse Discrimination*. Buffalo: Prometheus.

Hohfeld, W. (1923) *Fundamental Legal Conceptions*. New Haven: Yale University Press.

Holtermann, S. (1975) Areas of Urban Deprivation in Great Britain: An Analysis of the 1971 Census Data. *Social Trends* 6: 33–47.

Honoré, A. M. (1968) Social Justice. In R. S. Summers (ed.) *Essays in Legal Philosophy*. Oxford: Blackwell.

House of Commons (1980) Home Affairs Committee: Race Relations and Immigration Sub-Committee: Session 1979–80. *Racial Disadvantage*. Minutes of Evidence, Association of Metropolitan Authorities: HC 610 1X. London: HMSO.

—— (1981) Home Affairs Committee: Race Relations and Immigration Sub-Committee: Session 1980–81. Fifth Report. *Racial Disadvantage*. HC 424 IV. London: HMSO.

Jones, H. E. (1977) On the Justifiability of Reverse Discrimination. In B. R. Gross (ed.) *Reverse Discrimination*. Buffalo: Prometheus.

Jones, P. (1980) Rights, Welfare and Stigma, In N. Timms (ed.) *Social Welfare, Why and How?* London: Routledge & Kegan Paul.

Jowell, R. and Prescott-Clarke, P. (1970) Racial Discrimination and White Collar Workers in Britain. *Race* 11 (4): 397–417.

Kilson, M. L. (1983) In Defence of Affirmative Action: The American Case. *New Community* 10 (3): 464–69.

Kogan, M. (1978) *The Politics of Educational Change*. London: Fontana.

La Follette, H. (1978) Why Libertarianism is Mistaken. In J. Arthur and W. H. Shaw (eds.) *Justice and Economic Distribution*. Englewood Cliffs: Prentice-Hall.

Lessnoff, M. H. (1978) Capitalism, Socialism and Justice. In J. Arthur and W. H. Shaw (eds.) *Justice and Economic Distribution*. Englewood Cliffs: Prentice-Hall.

Little, A. (1974) Schools: Targets and Methods. In H. Glennerster and S. Hatch (eds.) *Positive Discrimination and Inequality*. London: Fabian Society.

Little, A. and Robbins, D. (1982) *Loading the Law: A Study of Transmitted Deprivation, Ethnic Minorities and Affirmative Action*. London: Commission for Racial Equality.

Liverpool Corporation (1971) *Social Malaise in Liverpool*. Liverpool: Liverpool Corporation.

Loney, M. (1983) *Community Against Government*. London: Heinemann.

Lucas, J. R. (1965) Against Equality. *Philosphy* 40: 296–307.

—— (1966) *The Principles of Politics*. Oxford: Clarendon Press.

—— (1972) Justice. *Philosophy* 47: 229–48.

—— (1980) *On Justice*. Oxford: Clarendon Press.

Lustgarten, L. (1980) *Legal Control of Racial Discrimination*.

London: Macmillan.

Mack, E. (1978) Liberty and Justice. In J. Arthur and W. H. Shaw (eds.) *Justice and Economic Distribution*. Englewood Cliffs: Prentice-Hall.

Mackie, J. L. (1977) *Ethics: Inventing Right and Wrong*. Harmondsworth: Penguin.

MacLaran, A. (1981) Area-Based Positive Discrimination and the Distribution of Well-Being. *Institute of British Geographers Transactions* 6 (1): 53–67.

Marshall, T. H. (1950) *Citizenship and Social Class*. Cambridge: Cambridge University Press.

—— (1975) *Social Policy* (4th edition). London: Hutchinson.

McIntosh, N. and Smith, D. J. (1974) *The Extent of Racial Discrimination*. Political and Economic Planning Report No. 547. London: Political and Economic Planning.

McLeay, E. (1982) 'Affirmative Action', 'Positive Discrimination' and Democracy. Paper presented to the SSRC Workshop on Political Theory and Social Policy, University of York: January.

Melden, A. I. (1977) *Rights and Persons*. Oxford: Blackwell.

Miller, D. (1976) *Social Justice*. Oxford: Clarendon Press.

—— (1978) Democracy and Social Justice. *British Journal of Political Science* 8 (1): 1–19.

Miller, S. M. (1973) The Case for Positive Discrimination. *Social Policy* 4 (3): 65–71.

Miller, S. M. and Rein, M. (1966) Poverty, Inequality and Policy. In H. Becker (ed.) *Social Problems: A Modern Approach*. New York: Wiley.

Milner Holland Report (1965) *Report of the Committee on Housing in Greater London*. London: HMSO, cmnd 2605.

Mishra, R. (1984) *The Welfare State in Crisis*. Brighton: Wheatsheaf.

Mortimore, G. W. (1968) An Ideal of Equality, *Mind* 77 (306): 222–42.

Mortimore, J. and Blackstone, T. (1982) *Disadvantage in Education*. London: Heinemann.

Nagel, T. (1977) Equal Treatment and Compensatory Discrimination. In M. Cohen, T. Nagel, and T. Scanlon (eds.) *Equality and Preferential Treatment*. Princeton: Princeton University Press.

—— (1979) *Mortal Questions*. Cambridge: Cambridge University Press.

Narveson, J. (1983) On Dworkinian Equality. *Social Philosophy and Policy* 1 (1): 1–23.

Newton, L. H. (1977) Reverse Discrimination as Unjustified. In B. R. Gross (ed.) *Reverse Discrimination* Buffalo: Prometheus.

Nickel, J. W. (1972) Discrimination and Morally Relevant Characteristics. *Analysis* 32 (4): 113–14.

—— (1973) Should Reparations Be to Individuals or to Groups? *Analysis* 34 (5): 154–60.

Nixon, J. (1983) Social Work in a Multi-Racial Society. *Social Policy and Administration* 17 (2): 142–57.

Nowell-Smith, P. (1954) *Ethics*. Harmondsworth: Penguin.

Nozick, R. (1974) *Anarchy, State and Utopia*. Oxford: Blackwell.

Nunn, W. A. (1973) Reverse Discrimination. *Analysis* 34 (5): 151–54.

O'Neil, R. M. (1975) *Discriminating Against Discrimination*. Bloomington: Indiana University Press.

Parker, J. (1975) *Social Policy and Citizenship*. London: Macmillan.

Perelman, C. (1963) *The Idea of Justice and the Problem of Argument*. New York: Humanities Press.

Phillips, D. L. (1977) The Equality Debate: What Does Justice Require? *Theory and Society* 4 (2): 247–71.

Phillips, D. Z. and Mounce, H. O. (1965) On Morality's Having a Point. *Philosophy* 40: 308–19.

Pilkington, A. (1984) *Race Relations in Britain*. Slough: University Tutorial Press.

Pinker, R. (1971) *Social Theory and Social Policy*. London: Heinemann.

—— (1985) Social Welfare and the Thatcher Administration. In P. Bean, J. Ferris, and D. Whynes (eds.) *In Defence of Welfare*. London: Tavistock.

Plant, R. (1980) Needs and Welfare. In N. Timms (ed.) *Social Welfare: Why and How?* London: Routledge & Kegan Paul.

Plant, R. Lesser, H., and Taylor-Gooby, P. (1980) *Political Philosophy and Social Welfare: Essays on the Normative Basis of Welfare Provision*. London: Routledge & Kegan Paul.

Plowden Report (1967) *Report of the Central Advisory Committee for Education: Children and their Primary Schools*. London: HMSO.

Pottinger, J. S. (1977) The Drive Towards Equality. In B. R. Gross (ed.) *Reverse Discrimination*. Buffalo: Prometheus.

Raphael, D. D. (1955) *Moral Judgement*. London: Allen & Unwin.

—— (1976) *Problems of Political Philosophy*. London: Macmillan.

Rawls, J. (1972) *A Theory of Justice*. Oxford: Oxford University Press.

Reddin, M. (1970) Universality versus Selectivity. In W. A. Robson and B. Crick (eds.) *The Future of the Social Services*. Harmondsworth: Pelican.

Rescher, N. (1966) *Distributive Justice*. Indianapolis: Bobbs-Merrill.

Resource Allocation Working Party (1976) *Sharing Resources for Health in England*. London: HMSO.

Rex, J. and Tomlinson, S. (1979) *Colonial Immigrants in a British City*. London: Routledge & Kegan Paul.

Robson, W. (1976) *Welfare State and Welfare Society*. London: Allen & Unwin.

Room, G. (1979) *The Sociology of Welfare*. Oxford: Martin Robertson.

Ross, A. (1974) *On Law and Justice*. London: Stevens.

Runciman, W. G. (1966) *Relative Deprivation and Social Justice*. London: Routledge & Kegan Paul.

Scanlon, T. M. (1975) Preference and Urgency. *Journal of Philosophy* 72 (19): 655–69.

Scarman Report (1981) *The Brixton Disorders, 10–12 April 1981*. London: HMSO, cmnd 8427.

Schuller, T. (1983) Learning and Democracy at the Workplace. In H. Glennerster (ed.) *The Future of the Welfare State*. London: Heinemann.

Seebohm Report (1968) *Report of the Committee on Local Authority and Allied Personal Social Services*. London: HMSO, cmnd 3703.

Sen, A. K. (1970) *Collective Choice and Social Welfare*. San Francisco: Holden Day.

Shiner, R. A. (1973) Individuals, Groups, and Inverse Discrimination. *Analysis* 33 (6): 185–87.

Sidgwick, H. (1930) *The Methods of Ethics* (7th edition). London: Macmillan.

Sidorsky, D. (1983) Contextualism, Pluralism, and Distributive Justice. *Social Philosophy and Policy* 1 (1): 172–95.

Silvestri, P. (1973) The Justification of Inverse Discrimination. *Analysis* 34 (1): 31.

Simon, R. (1977) Preferential Hiring: A Reply to Judith Jarvis Thomson. In M. Cohen, T. Nagel, and T. Scanlon (eds.) *Equality and Preferential Treatment*. Princeton: Princeton University Press.

Singer, P. (1978) Rights and the Market. In J. Arthur and W. H. Shaw (eds.) *Justice and Economic Distribution*. Englewood Cliffs: Prentice-Hall.

Smart, J. and Williams, B. (1973) *Utilitarianism: For and Against*. Cambridge: Cambridge University Press.

Smart, J. C. C. (1978) Distributive Justice and Utilitarianism. In J. Arthur and W. H. Shaw (eds.) *Justice and Economic Distribution*. Englewood Cliffs: Prentice-Hall.

Smith, B. (1976) *Policy Making in British Government: An Analysis of Power and Rationality*. London: Martin Robertson.

Smith, D. J. (1977) *Racial Disadvantage in Britain*. Harmondsworth: Penguin.

Smith, D. J. and Whalley, A. (1975) *Racial Minorities and Public Housing*. London: Political and Economic Planning.

Sowell, T. (1975) Affirmative Action Reconsidered: Was it Necessary in Academia? Americal Enterprise Institute: *Evaluative Studies* 27: 5–6.

—— (1977) Affirmative Action Reconsidered. In B. R. Gross (ed.) *Reverse Discrimination*. Buffalo: Prometheus.

Taylor, P. W. (1973) Reverse Discrimination and Compensatory Justice. *Analysis* 33 (6): 177–82.

Thalberg, I. (1973–74) Reverse Discrimination and the Future. *The Philosophical Forum* 5 (1 and 2): 294–308.

The Times (1982) Editorial. 30 March.

—— (1982) Editorial. 19 May.

—— (1982) Borough Excludes Whites in Training Scheme. 11 December.

—— (1983) Editorial. 30 March.

—— (1985) Firms with Too Few Blacks May Lose Deals. 14 October.

—— (1985) Ministers Clash on 'Jobs Quota for Blacks'. 15 October.

—— (1985) An Equal Workforce, Not Forced. 17 October.

Thurow, L. (1979) A Theory of Groups and Economic Redistribution. *Philosophy and Public Affairs* 9 (1): 25–41.

Timms, N. and Watson, D. (eds.) (1978) *Philosophy and Social Work*. London: Routledge & Kegan Paul.

Titmuss, R. (1968) *Commitment to Welfare*. London: Allen & Unwin.

Townsend, P. (1976) The Difficulties of Policies Based on the Concept of Area Deprivation. Barnett Shine Foundation Lecture, Queen Mary College, University of London.

Townsend, P. and Davidson, N. (1982) *Inequalities in Health: The Black Report*. Harmondsworth: Penguin.

Vlastos, G. (1962) Justice and Equality. In R. B. Brandt (ed.) *Social Justice*. Englewood Cliffs: Prentice-Hall.

Von Leyden, W. (1963) On Justifying Inequality. *Political Studies* 11 (1): 56–70.

Walton, R. (1969) Need: A Central Concept. *Social Services Quarterly* 3 (1): 13–17.

Ware, A. (1983) Justifying the Welfare State: The Problem of External Preferences and Democratic Theory. Paper presented to the SSRC Workshop on Political Theory and Social Policy, University of York: January.

Warnock, G. J. (1967) *Contemporary Moral Philosophy*. London: Macmillan.

Wasserstrom, R. (1976) The University and the Case for Preferential Treatment. *American Philosophical Quarterly* 13: 165–70.

Watson, D. (1980) *Caring For Strangers*. London: Routledge & Kegan Paul.

Weale, A. (1978) *Equality and Social Policy*. London: Routledge & Kegan Paul.

—— (1983) *Political Theory and Social Policy*. London: Macmillan.

Webb, A. (1980) The Personal Social Services. In N. Bosanquet and P. Townsend (eds.) *Labour and Equality: A Fabian Study of Labour in Power 1974–79*. London: Heinemann.

Williams, B. (1969) The Idea of Equality. In J. Feinberg (ed.) *Moral Concepts*. Oxford: Oxford University Press.

—— (1972) *Morality: An Introduction to Ethics*. Cambridge: Cambridge University Press.

Woozley, A. D. (1973) Injustice. In N. Rescher (ed.) *Studies in Ethics*. American Philosophical Quarterly Monograph Series No. 7. Oxford: Blackwell.

Young, K. and Connelly, N. (1981) *Policy and Practice in the Multi-Racial City*. London: Policy Studies Institute.

Name index

Subject index